The
Yogavasishtha
of
Valmiki

THE BOOK THAT BECAME
THE GITA FOR SRI RAMA

The
Yogavasishtha
of
Valmiki

KULDIP K DHIMAN, PhD

wisdom
tree

This edition first published in 2019

ISBN 978-81-8328-532-2

Published by
Wisdom Tree
4779/23, Ansari Road
Darya Ganj, New Delhi-110 002
Ph.: 011-23247966/67/68
wisdomtreebooks@gmail.com

Printed in India

With gratitude to

Dr Dharmanand Sharma
for showing the way

त्रिवर्गमात्रसिद्धयै यत्र मोक्षाय च तच्छ्रुतम्।
विपुलश्रुतचर्चासु तुच्छमश्रुतमेव तत्।।

The scripture which only shows how to achieve worldly gain,
not liberation from misery
Is considered by the wise to be inferior and not worth discussing.

CONTENTS

of choice, Rama begins to believe that destiny rules our lives, Vasishtha strongly debunks destiny and karma, Advocates action, hard work, relentless effort, Possibilities and limits of human action.

What is the subject matter of Vedanta? How is knowledge of the world gained? Means of phenomenal knowledge, Vedanta deals with knowledge of the self, Means of knowing according to Indian schools of logic, Can the self be known by the same means through which we know the phenomenal world?

Understanding the Vedantic teaching method, The use of language, grammar, logic, metaphors, analogies, Objectives of the Yogavasishtha, Who it is written for, What it deals with, The method of superimposition and negation, Why the statements in Indian texts are contradictory, Why there is excessive repetition.

For knowledge of the world we need a guru, but do we need a guru to know who we are? Problems of learning from a guru and scriptures, Importance of a guru, Qualities of a good disciple, How to find a guru.

Who created the world and why, Brahman's unlimited power of imagination, The problem of space, time and causality, The world of dreams, Multiple universes, Reality of the world.

Everything has a cause, Things do not happen just like that, The world must have a cause, If God created the world, who created God? If the world came into existence without a cause, the law of causation collapses, Indian theories of causation, The trouble with causation, Gaudapada and Vasishtha's critique of causation, Five ways things undergo change, Refutation of causation, Order in the cosmos, Causal relationship between the self and the world.

The ever-changing world, The unchanging reality behind the constant change, Brahman, the absolute behind the phenomenal, How we know about Brahman, Defining the indefinable, How things are defined and identified.

The individual and the universal self, Relationship between the two, Individuation and embodiment of the universal self, Glory of the body, Individual self and the individual body, Dimensions of the body, How the universal becomes the individual self, The cause of bondage, Kinds of ignorance and awareness, Strange worlds and strange creatures.

Definition of mind, Birth of the mind, Characteristics of the mind, The process of individuation, Understanding the mind.

The world gets created out of desire, Desire creates time, Why desires cannot be fulfilled, Each fulfilled desire creates thousands of new desires.

What is selfhood, It is natural to think that the body is the self, Who is the real self? Ego is the cause of suffering, Can we do without an ego? How the ego works.

Two methods have been advocated to attain final liberation: the path of self-knowledge and the path of yoga, The path of self-knowledge is easier,

How the mind is quietened, The four guardians of liberation, The self has no second, Giving up desires and ego, The seven bases of knowledge, Three seeds of bondage.

Yoga is also a valid means to liberation, though more difficult than self-knowledge, Relationship between the body and the mind, Internal organs and life force, How life force is regulated through breath control.

The path of action, What we mean by human action, Voluntary and involuntary actions, Action, inaction, non-action, Good and bad actions, Desirable actions, undesirable actions, ignorable actions, A liberated person does not give up actions but only the claim to be the author of actions, Sense of detachment, We must perform actions according to our inherent dispositions.

What is karma? Every action is necessarily followed by some result, The unpredictability of the result, Good and bad results of actions, Only the actions done with a sense of being their author are credited to our account.

Life after self-knowledge dawns and liberation is gained, Different kinds of liberated persons, A liberated person does not have to become a recluse, The yogi must come back to normal life and become a super-mendicant, super-doer and super-enjoyer.

ACKNOWLEDGEMENTS

There is a vast literature that helped me understand the finer points of Vedanta. Commentaries by Gaudapadacharya, Adi Shankaracharya and other ancient commentators were invaluable, as were the books by Swami Ram, Swami Chinmayananda, Swami Bhoomananda Tirtha, Swami Dayananda (Coimbatore), Swami Gambhirananda, Swami Ramsukh Das, Swami Tejomayananda, Swami Maheshananda Giri, Swami Haridas Tyagi, Swami Prakhar Pragyananda Saraswati, Paramahansa Yogananda, Bhagwan Shri Rajneesh Osho, S Radhakrishnan, PT Raju, TMP Mahadevan, JN Mohanty, Chandradhar Sharma, and M Hiriyanna.

I thank Swami Brahmeshananda, Pt Diwakar Mishra, KB Chhabra, Vikas Chhabra, Mukul Bansal, Gautam Kalotra, Jitendra Kumar, DS Kapoor and Harman Kapoor for being very helpful. Rajini Seetharam gifted me several of her valuable books and encouraged me in every possible way. Belated thanks to Kamlesh Gupta, one of the finest teachers I ever had. From him, I learned the art of making even the most difficult concept easy to comprehend.

Special thanks to Linda Bahnan, writer and lecturer in academic writing and examiner for Oxford, Cambridge and London universities, who not only edited this book to a high degree of professionalism but also pointed out areas that required further clarification.

And I appreciate the efforts of Shobit Arya in extending all cooperation in the publication of this book.

INTRODUCTION

THE QUEST OF ALL QUESTS

As the Yogavasishtha opens, we are introduced to King Arishtanemi, who has become disenchanted with the world because, no matter how much wealth he has accumulated, how many comforts he has, how many battles he wins, deep down he is always unhappy. All the wealth and power cannot fill the void within. What is the use of such wealth? Having realised the futility of finding happiness in worldly possessions, he hands over his kingdom to his son, performs severe penance, and as a result receives a boon to go to heaven (*svarga*) from Indra, the king of heaven.

Before accepting the boon, Arishtanemi asks what heaven means. He is told that according to the scale of one's good deeds (karmas), one enjoys pleasures in heaven.

'Is the stay in heaven permanent?' asks the king. 'No,' he is told. 'Once the stock of good deeds is expended, the individual returns to earth.'[1]

This is because heaven is a *bhoga yoni* (a place of enjoyment), not a *karma yoni*. One can expend one's karmas there, but one cannot earn fresh good or bad karmas. It is like some prosperous foreign land where you can spend your hard-earned money, but not earn more money. It is a place where you can never achieve permanent citizenship.

Arishtanemi says that he would not wish to go to such a heaven. What would be the use, if he would only have to come back and get into the same vicious cycle of birth–death–misery again? He would rather have lasting bliss if that were possible. Indra tells him that only knowledge of the self (*tattva gyana, atma gyana*) can free a person from the miseries of life. For that, Indra advises him to go to Valmiki.

The king then goes to Valmiki, author of the Yogavasishtha, who tells Arishtanemi the story of Rama's dialogue with Vasishtha, after which Rama becomes free of the miseries of the world.

The book that narrates this dialogue is called the Yogavasishtha. It is said that one can become free of worldly miseries merely by reading the Yogavasishtha.

The title 'Yogavasishtha' is a compound noun made up of the words yoga and *vasishtha*.[2] In popular conception, the word 'yoga' conjures up images of postures and exercises to keep the body and mind healthy. However, the word has a much broader and more significant connotation. To limit the scope of yoga to physical exercises would be a gross misinterpretation.

The word 'yoga' comes from the Sanskrit root *yuj*, and has several meanings. One is to unite or join. Unite what? It means to unite the individual self with ultimate reality, so that the feeling of misery, the feeling of being insignificant is gone, and supreme bliss is attained. Other meanings of the word yoga are: solution (*upaya*), logic and reason (*yukti*), penance (*tapa*), meditation (*dhyana*), dispassion (*vairagya*), connection and relevance.

PHILOSOPHICAL BACKGROUND

After Valmiki wrote the epic Ramayana, called in full, Poorva Ramayana, he was approached by Brahma, the creator of the world, to write a book that would free humans of worldly misery and make them eternally blissful. Thus, was born the scripture known variously as Uttara Ramayana, Maharamayana, Arsharamayana, Gyanavasishtha, Vasishtharamayana, more popularly called the Yogavasishtha.

The two most important questions we can ask concern how to live a good life and how to attain supreme bliss. One is about 'ought' and the other about knowing the 'self'. In the Ramayana, Valmiki showed how one ought to live a good life, how a king ought to rule and how a husband, a wife, a brother and friends ought to be.

By learning the 'oughts' of life, we can lead a good life, but this does not make us free of suffering. Even a so-called 'good' person may be plagued with troubles such as anger, envy, jealousy, disease and old age and, ultimately, death. Being a good person is not enough; something more is required. It is to teach this 'something more' that Valmiki wrote the Yogavasishtha. In fact, one can properly understand the popular Ramayana only by reading the Yogavasishtha.

A WAYLAYER TURNS POET

One day Valmiki was standing on the banks of the river Tamsa. He sees two cranes engaged in love play. Suddenly the male bird is struck by an arrow and dies. The female begins to move around her dead mate in utter grief. Valmiki turns around and notices that a hunter had shot the arrow. Seeing the sorrow of the heartbroken she-crane, these words (in Sanskrit) came effortlessly out of Valmiki's mouth:

May you never find mental peace, O hunter!
For you have killed an innocent bird in love.

Valmiki then felt that, although the hunter had killed the bird, he too had not done right by putting a curse on the hunter. The hunter merely did what his profession demanded. However, Valmiki was surprised by the words that had come out of his mouth. He had unwittingly uttered words in metrical form, although he was not a poet.

He was actually uneducated. What he uttered unknowingly is considered to be the first verse in Sanskrit literature. This is why Valmiki is known as *adikavi*, the first poet. Later, Brahma, the creator of the world, heard these words and urged Valmiki to write the Ramayana.

Valmiki was a waylayer before he became a sage. His name was Ratnakar, and he was raised by hunters, after he was separated from his Brahmin parents. It is said that once the celestial singer Narada was passing through a forest, and Ratnakar waylaid him. Narada asked, 'Why do you rob people?'

'To feed my family,' replied Ratnakar.

'You know robbing people is a sin. Ask your family if they would share the consequences of your sins.'

Thinking he might be tricked, Ratnakar tied Narada to a tree and went home and asked his family if they would share the consequences of his sins. They all said they would not. To feed them was his duty, but how could they share the outcome of his sins? He would have to pay for his deeds himself, as this was the law of Karma. Hearing this, Ratnakar went back and surrendered himself to Narada. There followed a total transformation of his character and he became a great sage.

Self-knowledge, freedom from bondage, metaphysics, ethics and philosophy of the mind are the main concerns of this text. The author's aim is to show how one can eliminate the conflicts of the mind, attain freedom from worldly bondage and still lead a normal active life. It is claimed that studying the Yogavasishtha leads seekers to *moksha* (total freedom from misery) without having to renounce the world, and it is for this reason that the book is also called Mokshopaya Samhita.

The Yogavasishtha was written for someone who has begun to realise that worldly objects cannot fill the void within. It is for people who wish to attain supreme bliss. It was written for people who are neither intellectually mature nor immature. The intellectually mature do not need to read works such as the Yogavasishtha, as they can attain liberation without the help of a book or guru. Those who are uninformed or not mature enough cannot benefit from this book as they do not have the capacity to understand the issues discussed in it. The Yogavasishtha was written for people between these two extremes.

Regarding the greatness of the Yogavasishtha, Valmiki, its author, is quite eloquent himself. At several places in the text, he says that, as far as self-knowledge is concerned, there is no scripture better than the Yogavasishtha.[3]

Although this book has inspired great scholars and thinkers, such as Shankaracharya, Madhvacharya and Narayana Bhatta, it has not yet achieved the popularity of the Bhagavad Gita and the Upanishads.

The complete text of the Yogavasishtha can be found in *Srimad Valmikimaharshipranitah Yogavasishthah*, by Vasudeva Laxmana Sharma Pansikar. There is a shorter version of the Yogavasishtha, called *Laghu Yogavasishtha*, compiled by Abhinanda, a scholar from Kashmir. This work was translated into English by KN Subramanian.

In the 1930s, BL Atreya earned his doctorate on the Yogavasishtha, and later published it as *Yogavasishtha aur Uske Siddhant* in Hindi. In this book, he makes a thorough categorisation of the ideas discussed in the Yogavasishtha. This book is out of print now. He also wrote *Yogavasishtha and Its Philosophy*, *Yogavasishtha and Modern Thought* and *Vasishthadarshanam*.

A good Hindi translation along with commentary is available in five volumes titled *Yogavasishtha Maharamayanam*. It was written by Krishnapant Shastri, and published by Achyutgranthmala Karyalaya, Kashi. Thakurprasad Dwivedi's *Yogavasishtha-Maharamayanam* is a two-volume Hindi translation published by Chaukhamba Sanskrit Pratishthan. Another translation by Pandit Shriram Acharya was published by Sanskrti Sansthan, Bareilly in 1979.

Swami Bhoomananda Tirtha wrote a short but insightful book, *The Quietitude of the Mind* (1975), which is based on the Upashama Prakaranam of the Yogavasishtha. Another book, titled *The Supreme Yoga: A New Translation of the Yogavasishtha,* was published the same year. It was written by Swami Venkatesananda, and published by The Chiltern Yoga Trust, South Africa. *Sri Yogavasishtam (Maharamayanam),* written by PN Murthy, was published by Bharatiya Vidya Bhavan in 2001. In 2009, Chaukhamba Prakashan published *Yogavasishtha Saar,* by Swami Prakhar Pragyananda Saraswati. This short book explains the fundamental concepts of the Yogavasishtha in simple Hindi.

Devadu Narasimha Sastri wrote a Kannada translation of the Yogavasishtha, under the patronage of His Highness Maharaja Sri Sir Jaya Chamarajendra Wodeyar Bahadur of Mysore. This was published by Hemant Sahitya, Bangalore, in 1946. There are various translations and commentaries available in Marathi, Bengali, Telugu and other languages.

The sheer volume of the Yogavasishtha is enough to deter most readers. It is stated in the Yogavasishtha that it consists of 32,000 verses divided into six books (Prakaranams), namely: the Vairagya Prakaranam, the Mumukshuvyavahara Prakaranam, the Utpatti Prakaranam, the Sthiti Prakaranam, the Upashama Prakaranam, the Nirvana Prakaranam (Poorvardha) and the Nirvana Prakaranam (Uttarardha). The number of verses is, in fact, much less. In the introduction to *Srimad Valmikimaharshipranitah Yogavasishthah,* GV Tagare puts the number at 23,734 verses.[4]

The first book, the Vairagya Prakaranam, describes Rama's disillusionment with the world. The issue discussed here is whether *gyana* (knowledge of the self) or *karma* (work, effort) is more important in attaining liberation from the misery of the world. The answer is that both are equally important, just as a bird needs both its wings to fly.

The Mumukshuvyavahara Prakaranam is about the qualities of true seekers of liberation and their mental attitude. How the world was created and how it evolved is discussed in the Utpatti Prakaranam. The Sthiti Prakaranam talks about the preservation of the universe. The world appears to be real, but with the realisation of Brahman, the mind is silenced and the world appears as nothing but Brahman. The Upashama Prakaranam is about quieting the mind through proper understanding; the Nirvana Prakaranam, as the name suggests, is about ultimate freedom. It suggests that knowledge of the self is the best way to break free from the miseries of the world.

It has to be pointed out that the structure of the Yogavasishtha is very loose, and apart from the first Prakaranam, almost all the major themes are discussed and repeated throughout this mammoth text. As for the division of chapters within each Prakaranam, there seems to be no order. Some chapters have as few as six verses, while others run into hundreds. Often a chapter ends abruptly, and the discussion is continued in the next chapter and the next. Often, while one concept is being discussed, there is a sudden digression and another topic begins. Later, the speaker returns to the previous conversation. The Nirvana Prakaranam is as large as the first five combined. For some reason, it is divided into two huge sections: the *Poorvardha* and the *Uttarardha*.

Interlaced with the dialogue are approximately fifty-five allegorical stories and stories within stories to illustrate the philosophical matters discussed. Here again, certain stories are told in about ten verses, while others, such as that of Chudala, stretch over several chapters.

All these stories and subplots make it difficult for the modern reader to keep track of who is speaking to whom. For instance, the Yogavasishtha begins with a Brahmin named Suteekshna, who goes to the sage Agasti and asks about ways to get out of the misery of the world. To answer his question, Agasti tells him the story of Karunya, a very learned man, well-versed in the scriptures, who has lost interest in life. Noticing this, his father tells him the story of King Arishtanemi, who is sent to Valmiki for the resolution of his sorrows. Valmiki then tells Arishtanemi the story of Rama's dialogue with Vasishtha.

The reader need not get overwhelmed by these plots and subplots. It does not matter if it is difficult to keep track of who is saying what. It does not matter who is asking questions and who is answering them. All that matters is that a disciple is asking the questions and a guru is answering them. The questions and answers themselves are important, rather than who is asking or answering.

The idea of using subplots is a technique peculiar to ancient Indian scriptures, possibly to drive home the point that such questions arise in sensitive people in every age. In our age, who would not get disturbed by what is going on around them? Who would not ask fundamental questions? In every age, discerning people approach learned seers to dispel their anxieties and doubts. Ages change, customs change, but the questions remain the same.

It is generally accepted that over the centuries several thinkers have added new verses to the original Yogavasishtha making it a mega tome. There is no agreement about the time of its composition, but as the name of Valmiki is associated with the Yogavasishtha, many believe it to be at least as old as the epic Ramayana (3,000 BC). Most scholars, however, think it was composed in its present form between the sixth and fourteenth centuries AD.

Encyclopaedic in its scope, the Yogavasishtha deals with ontology, epistemology, metaphysics, ethics and psychology. The underlying philosophy of the Yogavasishtha is predominantly of Advaita Vedanta. There are several verses of the Yogavasishtha which are also found in many Upanishads and the Bhagavad Gita. BL Atreya made an exhaustive comparative chart, and believed that being a voluminous scripture, the Yogavasishtha may not have been freely available in the days when books were written by hand.

Anthologists must have picked up some useful verses from it and used them to create new Upanishads.[5]

CORE PHILOSOPHY

Although the Yogavasishtha is voluminous, its central message can be expressed in a few statements: Nothing exists except absolute consciousness (also called universal consciousness or Brahman), and the world is the imagination of this universal consciousness. The universal consciousness is absolute and perfect. All change happens in the phenomenal world (which has no independent existence, as it is just an imagination of absolute consciousness). All the beings of the world are no different from the universal consciousness, as they emerged out of it. All the misery that is experienced by individual beings happens because they mistakenly identify themselves with their body and forget that they are essentially the same as the universal consciousness, Brahman. Since misery arises out of ignorance of the self, it ends with knowledge of the self.

These statements need to be elaborated and explained, otherwise they create misunderstanding and confusion.

'Absolute', for instance, does not mean that the universal consciousness is static. Absolute means it is all-encompassing. It, therefore, includes perfection as well as imperfection, good as well as evil, whole as well as part, subtle as well as gross, supreme bliss as well as misery, supreme knowledge as well as ignorance, freedom as well as bondage, truth as well as untruth. Truth or reality is that which does not go out of existence in the three periods of time, that is, past, present and future. An untruth, unreality or illusion (*mithya*), on the other hand, is that which exists only fleetingly.[6]

That which does not exist before the beginning and after the end
(of the universe),
If it is seen in the present for a while, take its existence to be an illusion.[7]

WHAT IS VEDANTA?

The Vedas primarily consist of two portions: Karmakanda and Gyanakanda. Karmakanda is also called Poorvameemamsa, and as the name suggests, deals with actions, duties, rituals, sacrifices and other practical acts. The author of this section of the Vedas is Jaimini. The goal of this section of the Vedas is to help us achieve what we do not have, such as wealth and pleasures, and to help us deal with any obstacles that arise in life.

The second portion, called Gyanakanda, is also known as Uttarameemamsa or Vedanta, and deals mainly with self-knowledge. Its author is Vyasa, who was the guru of Jaimini. The goal of Uttarameemamsa is final freedom, moksha, *kaivalya* or nirvana. It holds that the individual and the universal self are one, and bondage arises because of ignorance of the self. Since ignorance can be killed by knowledge alone, no physical effort or method is required.

Vedanta is a very old system of thought which over time became divided into three major streams: Advaita Vedanta, Dvaita Vedanta, and Vishishta Vedanta.

Advaita Vedanta is the core philosophy of the Yogavasishtha, and its aim is to show that there is no difference between ultimate reality and the individual. The difference is experienced because of ignorance of truth. With the knowledge of the self, this ignorance is removed and the individual unites with the absolute. With this, ends all misery.

The phenomenal world that we see is an untruth, unreal, as it came into being at a certain time in the past, which means it was not there before it, and it will end one day, which means it will not be there in the future: therefore, this world is unreal or illusory, according to Vedanta. But there is one underlying reality behind the three periods of time, and that is Brahman, which is absolute, unchanging, ever-existing, conscious and blissful (sachchidananda, sat+chit+ananda).

Another definition of untruth is that it does not have an

independent existence. A wave, for instance, cannot exist without an ocean, while an ocean can exist without a wave. The ocean is *satya* (truth) and the wave is mithya (illusion). The word 'mithya' is generally translated as 'illusion', and this is misleading. When Vedanta says that the world is mithya, it does not mean it is illusory like a mirage. 'Mithya' means something that does not have an independent existence. Following this, it is to be shown that Brahman is satya and the world is mithya. In fact, it is mithya that proves there is something 'real' behind it. An imaginary or illusory horse, for instance, proves that there are real horses otherwise how can we imagine a horse?

Brahman incorporates all dualities, and never changes at the core. The change that we see is only on the surface, just as the sea is quiet at the bottom but has waves on the top. In fact, as we shall see later in the book, all change is illusory. The Yogavasishtha stresses that the phenomenal world grows out of the imagination of Brahman, and hence it is like a dream, which means it is not real. Yet it appears to be real because of our ignorance, just as dreams are unreal but in sleep they appear to be real.

Imagination itself is the mind, and it is no different from the imagination;
Just as water is no different from liquidity, and motion no different from wind.[8]

We come to know the existence of the wind only when it moves, that is the reason when the characteristics of the five elements are enumerated, the characteristic of wind is given as touch. We come to know of it only when it touches our skin.

It is further said that, since the entire cosmos emerged out of pure consciousness, everything in the cosmos has to be fundamentally pure because whatever emerges from the pure and absolute has to be pure and absolute. This is why our fundamental nature is pure consciousness, and by this logic every creature and thing in this world is nothing but pure consciousness or Brahman.

Hence, the famous assertion, *Aham Brahmasmi*, I am Brahman. Our misery arises because we have forgotten that we are nothing but Brahman. However, even in this state of forgetfulness, we never lose our absolute blissful nature. A king who has lost his memory and lives like a pauper is a king no matter what he thinks he is. This means that nothing actually needs to be done except to get out of forgetfulness and realise we are nothing but bliss. There is no point in running away from the world, as there is no place to go; everything is nothing but Brahman.

Absolute consciousness is known by different names, such as Brahman, Shiva, chit, chidakasha, Paramatman (or *atman* for short). The phenomenal world that emerges out of the imagination of Brahman is generally called samsara.

The Yogavasishtha sometimes calls the phenomenal world the imagination (*kalpana*), sometimes the will (*sankalpa*), forgetfulness (*vismarana*), feigned ignorance (*avidya*) and sometimes the pulsation (spanda) of the supreme consciousness (*Brahman*). These words are used synonymously; one need not be concerned about their usage. No matter what term is used in a particular context, as far as the Yogavasishtha is concerned, the phenomenal world has no independent reality or existence of its own, as it is just a projection or an illusion created by ignorance.

Having stated the core philosophy, it must be added that, according to the Yogavasishtha, a belief in God as a super human figure running the affairs of the world is not necessary. The most important thing is to attain supreme bliss, *ananda*, and this can only be done by quieting the mind. Some might find it easier to attain ananda by positing faith in God or a deity, while others might achieve the goal without this. It all depends upon the disposition of the seeker.

Some people are more emotionally inclined, and since their path is that of love, they need an object for their love, so they need

The Yogavasishtha of Valmiki

a deity. Others are governed more by intellect and reason; such people do not necessarily need faith in a deity. The former is called the *asti* (assertive) method, and the latter the *nasti* (negative) method. Asti says 'yes' to supreme reality, ultimate truth and existence, and the nasti uses the negative or eliminative approach to realising the ultimate truth to attain bliss. Both approaches are equally valid and useful depending upon the kind of person we are, but they are both in the domain of the mind. They are like two boats that help us cross a river. It does not matter which boat we take; in the end whichever one we take, has to be abandoned, as the ultimate goal is beyond both asti and nasti.

Whether one is an atheist or a believer, the consciousness that one possesses is neither atheist nor believer. It just is; it is sachchidananda — truth, consciousness and bliss. It is the one thing that can never be negated. Our search for the ultimate truth ends here, as we cannot go beyond it. It is the universal witness (*sakshi*) that observes everything, but cannot itself be observed as it is absolute subjectivity.

As a word of caution, it must be mentioned that it is easy to confuse the teachings of Vedanta with nihilism (nothing exists), hedonism (seeking only pleasure) and solipsism (only I exist). On the surface, these appear to say the same thing, but Vedanta is in total opposition to all of them. The Latin word 'nihilism' means 'nothing'. It is a philosophical doctrine that negates all meaningful aspects of life, and argues that life is without objective meaning, purpose or intrinsic value. It holds that knowledge is not possible, or that reality does not exist; therefore, life has no meaning.

A hedonist believes there is nothing beyond the physical self and matter, so one should indulge oneself as much as possible; there is nothing called 'virtue' or 'sin'.

In contrast to this, Yogavasishtha says that since the world is just a creation of the mind, from the phenomenal standpoint it exists, but from the absolute standpoint it does not. It is neither real nor unreal. It is indescribable, as no assertive or negative statement can be made about it.

It is not 'nothingness' because it affects us. When we mistake a rope for a snake in the dark, this misapprehension has an effect on us; it makes us afraid. We cannot say the snake is unreal, and we cannot say it is real; it is just a misapprehension.

No doubt there are verses in the Yogavasishtha which say that the world does not exist. It has to be noted that in such cases the word 'exist' is being used in a technical sense. We have already stated that in Advaita philosophy only that which exists in the past, present and future can be said to 'exist'. All other things are phenomenal, as they come into existence only for a short time. Even one hundred billion years is a short time from the absolute perspective.

The word 'exist' here stands for 'eternal'. It is in this sense that the Yogavasishtha says the world does not exist.

Further, when the Yogavasishtha says there is nothing other than supreme consciousness, that this world is unreal as it was never created, does this lead to solipsism? What about other beings? What about the objects of the phenomenal world? We might ask, if the world is unreal, who are sages such as Vasishtha trying to teach?

The Yogavasishtha does not say nothing exists; it says we are not seeing things properly. Solipsism says only 'I' exist, and Vedanta says everything that exists is nothing but 'I'. There is a great difference between the two assertions. The first is centred on the self, while the second says since everything is the self, all differences are meaningless. The individual and the rest of the world are one.

The world may be an illusion, but an illusion cannot arise on its own; it arises out of wrong cognition of something. That something is Brahman, and once we realise this, we realise that each individual is nothing but Brahman. In other words, everything is nothing but Brahman, and there is no plurality. Other individuals exist, but they are manifestations of the same absolute self as we are. This is not solipsism.

The idea that the world does not exist in reality is called *Ajativada*, the doctrine of no-origination, and it has been attributed to Gaudapadacharya, who was the guru of Shankaracharya's guru, Govindacharya. It is also claimed that Gaudapada was inspired by the Yogavasishtha. The reason for this is that the authorship of the Yogavasishtha is attributed to Valmiki, who predates Gaudapada by several centuries. While there might be a large number of interpolations and additions to the original text, Ajativada is the foundation of the Yogavasishtha and it does not waver on this.

It is also claimed that Gaudapada was not only influenced by the Yogavasishtha but also by Nagarjuna, the Buddhist propounder of no-origination. The following verse from Gaudapada Karika is quoted by the supporters of this view.

My obeisance to the 'enlightened one', the supreme among men, who has known
That which is space-like and is not different from the object of knowledge.[9]

Many scholars argue that the word *sambuddha* in the original verse actually means any enlightened person and not Gautama Buddha specifically, as his real name was Siddhartha. After enlightenment, he came to be known as the Buddha. They argue that the word 'sambuddha', which means 'the enlightened one', is used as an adjective here and not as a noun.

There is a third view. In his commentary on Gaudapada Karika, Shankaracharya says that in this verse, Gaudapada is giving his obeisance to Acharya Shrinarayana, his guru of the Badri Ashrama. In fact, the word 'buddha' is used in several verses in the Yogavasishtha and other literature to mean 'learned', 'knowledgeable' and 'enlightened'.

It is difficult to ascertain the real truth of who originally came up with the idea of no-origination, and it should not matter, as the idea of no-origination existed in Indian thought long before Gaudapada, Nagarjuna or even the Buddha. What matters is how no-origination can be useful in reducing the doubts and dilemmas of life.

Ajativada means that the world was never created (*aja*) as it is imaginary or illusory. What can we say about the origin of a thing that is imaginary? It was there always as imagination of absolute Brahman, hence we cannot ask the question when it was born. Only Brahman truly exists, and Brahman or the absolute is non-dual.

REAL AND UNREAL, TRUE AND FALSE

Often, words used in one language do not mean the same in another language and in another culture. This is a major problem when texts are translated, especially from Indian languages to Western languages. A word is not just a word; it often comes with heavy cultural and emotional baggage.

In Indian literature, and especially in the Yogavasishtha, we often come across the words 'real', 'unreal', 'truth', 'untruth/falsehood' and 'exist'. The word 'real' usually implies something that exists physically, and 'true' is used to talk about a statement. In Vedantic literature, the word 'real' is used in a special sense. You may be sitting on a chair, so for you the chair is real, it is solid, but in the Vedantic sense the chair is not real, as its existence is temporary.

The reason for this is that the world can be experienced and spoken about from different levels:

Truth is one, but it is expressed by the learned from different levels.

A thing may be real in one dimension and unreal in another, just as when awake, the dream we had is considered to be unreal, but while we were dreaming, it was as real as the waking state.

Mundaka Upanishad (I:2-5) talks about two kinds of knowledge: *aparagyana* (pragmatic, worldly knowledge) and *paragyana* (transcendental, other-worldly knowledge). All practical knowledge of any kind comes under 'apara', and the knowledge through which we come to know about our true self and attain liberation is called 'para' or transcendental knowledge.

The word 'real', for instance, has a different meaning on these two levels. When used on the pragmatic level, it means something that has physical appearance, but on the transcendental level, it has a different meaning. 'Real' on the transcendental level means something that has always existed. It further means something that was never born and will never perish because a thing that is born means it did not exist earlier and it is going to go out of existence. Anything that comes into existence temporarily (even if it is a hundred billion years) cannot be said to 'exist' in the Vedantic sense. It is in this sense it is said that the world does not exist, or is false, untrue or illusory. In fact, no positive or negative statement about the existence of the world can be made. Its status is said to be beyond words, *anirvachaneeya* (indescribable).

The Yogavasishtha says that it is mentioned in the Upanishads that there is absolute Brahman and, opposed to it, there is the phenomenal world (samsara) and illusion (maya). The Upanishads say this because this is the only way to express absolute and indescribable reality so that people understand. For example, when we teach language to children we start with 'a' for 'apple'. In fact, 'a' does not stand for 'apple'; it is just an initial aid to teach language.

When the Yogavasishtha says that the world does not exist, it means that the visible world is a creation of the mind. It is only real on the condition that it is perceived through the mind. The moment you transcend the mind, it becomes unreal. This does not mean that everything ends in nothingness. What happens when a dream ends? Do we end in nothingness? We just return to the waking state, relatively speaking.

The Yogavasishtha repeats endlessly that consciousness or Brahman is the only eternal reality. When the world dissolves after an apocalypse, Brahman alone remains. Brahman alone existed before the creation of the world and it alone will remain after the end of the universe. The cycle of creation and annihilation of the world is endless.

The phenomenal world, its objects and beings exist only as long as ignorance exists. All talk of knowledge, mind, ego and liberation makes sense only while we are in a state of forgetfulness or ignorance. Regarding the argument for no-origination of the world, Gaudapada says:

This thesis is for instruction alone; after self-knowledge, duality is not seen.[10]

The scriptures are words of the enlightened to awaken those who are taking their dream to be real. Once we wake from the dream, we realise that nothing has to be gained because nothing was ever lost. No one has to be liberated because there was no bondage in the first place as the absolute can never be bound.

Ultimately, there is neither bondage nor liberation for the self;
Illusion alone keeps all trapped in the vicious cycle of the world.[11]

All that ends after knowledge dawns is the illusory world, not the eternally blissful self. Liberation and bliss are our intrinsic nature (*svabhava*), and svabhava means that which can never be taken away from us. The truth, therefore, is that the mind has no existence other than in the imagination of the absolute. That absolute is not nothingness; it is complete and encompasses all, and whatever emerges from it is also absolute.

From the whole emerges the whole, and the whole is situated in the whole;
Thus, whatever is there in the whole exists in its wholeness.[12]

MAIN QUESTIONS

Ever since humans began to think and wonder, they have asked many questions. If we examine all these questions, we realise there are ultimately no more than a dozen fundamental questions. Such questions would arise in any thinking person anywhere in the world in any age. They are perennial questions, and throughout the Yogavasishtha, these questions have been asked several times by Rama or some other disciple: What is this ever-changing world?

Why is it there? Who created this world and why? What was there before the creation of the world, and what will remain after it is destroyed? Why do we see so much misery around us? What is man? Where do all beings come from and where do they go? What is mind, and how is it quietened? How is illusion (maya) created, and how does one break this illusion and see the absolute truth? How does ignorance arise in pure consciousness?[13]

Most of these questions, however, have no answers as they are beyond the scope of the intellect. When we try to answer these questions, we only get into further mess, and that is why the wise have called them ultimate questions, *atiprshnas*. One must, therefore, not waste time trying to solve these eternal questions, but find ways of quietening the mind and becoming blissful.

Nearly at the end of the Yogavasishtha, Vasishtha tells Rama about a dialogue between him and King Pragyapti.[14] The king puts twenty questions to Vasishtha, and the latter answers them in five chapters. If we read just this section properly, we would understand everything that is discussed in the Yogavasishtha.

Throughout the Yogavasishtha, Vasishtha answers Rama's questions so thoroughly and repeatedly that at the end of it even a stone would get liberated. He says many things, and gives many proofs and arguments, but ultimately all these boil down to just one thing: how to quieten the mind and realise our intrinsic blissful nature.

WHAT YOU CANNOT ASK

It is natural for us to ask questions, but there are certain questions that cannot be answered at all; hence they ought not to be asked as we would only be wasting our time. Such questions are called 'atiprshna' (*ati* is ultimate, extreme, or impossible, and *prshana* is question). The word 'atiprshna' is for the first time seen in the dialogue between Yagyavalkya and Gargi in the Brihadaranyaka Upanishad. 'Atiprshna' is a question which cannot be answered by any reason or logic.

Gargi, daughter of Vachknu, asks what the world is pervaded by and she is told 'by water'. She then asks if the world is pervaded by water, what is water pervaded by? Yagyavalkya tells her that water is pervaded by air. She then asks what was air pervaded by, he replies it was pervaded by sky. When she asks what the sky is pervaded by, the reply is by the world of Gandharvas (celestial beings). What is the world of Gandharvas pervaded by? By the world of sun. What is the world of sun pervaded by? By the world of the moon. What is the moon pervaded by? The stars. What are the stars pervaded by? By the world of gods. What is the world of gods pervaded by? By the world of Indra. What is the world of Indra pervaded by? By the world of Brahma. And what is the world of Brahma pervaded by? By Brahmaloka. Gargi then asks, and what the world of Brahmaloka is pervaded by? At this point Yagyavalkya says, 'Gargi, do not ask atiprshna, else you shall lose your head!'(III:6:1) He says this metaphorically, as head is the locus of all thoughts and curiosity.

Some have interpreted this warning by Yagyavalkya as a means to shut Gargi up as she was a woman, by threatening to behead her if she pursues the matter too far. This is not the case, as Yagyavalkya would have said the same to anyone who asked such questions because if you question the very fundamentals, inquiry becomes impossible as there can be no satisfactory answer to them. Such questions shall be forever beyond our knowledge, and if you persisted, you would only go insane in the process.

In the Prashna Upanishad, too, Kaushalya asks the Sage Pipplada, 'Where does life force come from? How does it enter the body? How does it distribute itself over the body? How does it support external objects? Before answering these questions, the Sage says, 'You are asking an atiprshna'(III:2).

If we asked a scientist where the earth exists, we would be told in the solar system. Where does the solar system exist? We would be told in the galaxy. If we persisted, the scientist would probably ask us to shut up in the same way as Yagyavalkya did. There is no end to the 'why' question. In the present age, we have been trained to question everything, and this has become a kind of disease, and most of us seem to have 'lost our heads' in the process.

The Yogavasishtha of Valmiki

We might wonder, if our true nature is blissful, and if our misery is just an illusion created out of ignorance, why can we not realise this simply by being told the fact. What is the need for so much discussion and logical analysis? The answer is that it is as simple as opening our eyes and seeing the truth that is staring us right in the face, but our conditioning is so deep that before opening our eyes, we ask a million questions. Especially in the modern age of rationality, we have been taught not to accept anything without questioning it thoroughly. That is a good thing if it does not convert into a new kind of disease. Earlier, people believed any nonsense they were told, and now they go on asking questions even if the truth is right in front of them. It is for this reason that a simple matter has to be explained using various techniques. That is why Vasishtha goes on answering questions one after another, until Rama's rational and logical mind is satisfied.

Vasishtha relies solely on reason. He does not advocate any kind of blind faith, worship or rituals. It is for this reason the Yogavasishtha could have a tremendous appeal to any modern thinking person, provided they have the patience to listen to the full argument. No other Indian text analyses the human condition as thoroughly as the Yogavasishtha does. Vasishtha himself says:

What is in it is nowhere else, what is not in it is not elsewhere;
Hence the learned have called it a repository of scriptures.[15]

People normally think that those who seek self-liberation ought to withdraw from active life and lead the life of a hermit—praying, meditating and performing rituals. Vedanta does not advocate this type of life. It says that you ought to go on doing whatever you are supposed to, but remember all the time that you are not the doer. Do everything with a sense of detachment and be unaffected by whatever is happening around you, just as a lotus grows in a pond without getting wet.

The Yogavasishtha does not advocate worship of any kind, rituals, neither ablutions nor prayer to a deity, not even meditative techniques. It, however, seriously discourages escapism and laziness, and strongly advocates human effort.

Through effort and maturity alone is the self known, Rama,
Not through penance, holy bath and other such actions.[16]

In stressing self-knowledge, the Yogavasishtha is very close to Ashtavakra Gita, another obscure text which is a dialogue between the sage Ashtavakra and King Janaka.

Pure, intelligent, blissful, absolute, unmeshed and free from sorrow;
The self cannot be known by those who try to know it through method.[17]

It is worth noting that Janaka continued to rule his kingdom even after gaining liberation. This shows that one does not have to become a mendicant or perform severe penance for liberation. After liberation, one ought to share one's bliss with others and make their lives free of misery. That is why self-knowledge was initially given to the rulers, and so it was called *rajavidya*, knowledge for the kings.

LIBERATION FOR ALL
One striking feature of the Yogavasishtha is that its vision is secular. Furthermore, it does not believe in gender, race or caste discrimination. All that is required on the part of a seeker is to be a sincere and determined disciple. In fact, the main character of one of its longest stories is a queen named Chudala. She not only acquires self-knowledge but also teaches her husband the means of acquiring it. The Yogavasishtha goes even further by showing that one need not be of high birth to attain self-knowledge: anyone can have it. It names people from lower castes and wild tribes, and gives instances where animals, too, become liberated. Even Sheshanaga, the deadly snake, is liberated, as is Kakabhushunda, the crow. This might sound far-fetched, but the point being made here is that anyone can become blissful if they really wish to.

The Yogavasishtha of Valmiki

That is because if a king is himself not free of misery, how can he make his subjects happy?

In the following chapters, we shall see how well Vasishtha answers Rama's questions and dispels his anxieties forever so he could rule as a wise ruler, as a true philosopher king, and not as a selfish despot or politician.

ENDNOTES

1. I:1:32-39; Just as worldly gain obtained through effort (karma) diminishes here, the same way the rewards of heaven also diminish. (Chandogya Upanishad VIII:1:6); The immature consider the means to attain worldly pleasures described in the Vedas as supreme. As a result after exhausting the rewards of their good deeds in heaven, they return to lower life forms here on earth. (Mundaka Upanishad, I:2:10)

2. Vasishtha was the son of Brahma, and guru of the Ikshwaku dynasty to which Rama belonged.

3. III:8:11-17; VIB:103; VIB:163

4. Pansikar, Vasudeva Laxmana Sharma (Ed.), *Srimad Valmikimaharshipranitah Yogavasishthah*, Vol I, Motilal Banarsidass, Delhi, p VII

5. Atreya BL, *Yogavasishtha aur Uske Sidhdhant*, Shri Krishna Janamsthan Seva Sansthan, Mathura 1986, p 4; for comparative charts see pages 45-59, 67-69 of the same book.

6. V:5:9-10. The Bhagavad Gita also says: The untruth (unreal) has no existence at all, and the truth (real) can never be non-existent; their true nature is understood by the those who know the reality. (II:16)

7. V:93:72

8. III:4:43

9. Gaudapada Karika, IV:1

10. Gaudapada Karika I:18

11. V:18:27

12. VIB:53:20

13. V:2:13-16

14. VIB:206-210

15. III:8:12

16. III:6:9

17. The Ashtavakra Gita, 18:35

CHAPTER I

THE MEANING OF LIFE

In the opening chapters of the Yogavasishtha, we find the sixteen-year-old prince Rama[1] in a contemplative frame of mind. After a round of pilgrim centres all over India with his brothers, he suddenly loses interest in life and begins to 'dry up like a pond in the winter season'.[2] He is between childhood and youth, an age when one usually goes through tremendous stress owing to physical and mental changes.

Rama begins to keep to himself, and is always worrying about something. His father, King Dasharatha, sends his guards to find the cause of his son's lack of interest in life. They come back and report that when asked about his problems, all that the young prince says is, 'It is nothing, it is nothing', and then goes back into his shell. His brothers, too, are behaving like him. The guards tell the king that Rama is totally disillusioned with life and its attractions. They are alarmed as he has started asking questions such as: What is the point in acquiring worldly possessions? What is the purpose of life? What will I gain from kingdom? What will I gain from the pleasures of the world? Who made this world and why? Why do we see so much misery around?[3]

The guards tell the king that the young prince seems to have lost faith and hope in everything. He is not an immature person to behave like this, but he is also not an enlightened person, so this cannot be dispassion towards the world.[4]

Later, King Dasharatha sends Vishvamitra, the guru who trained Rama and his brothers in warfare and other worldly skills, to speak to Rama and get him out of the negative frame of mind. Vishvamitra meets Rama and asks him the cause of his worries and dispassion towards life. The pensive prince asks his guru if one could ever be happy in this ever-changing world where creatures are born only to die one day.

Alas! How can one be happy in this ever-changing world
Where people are born to die, and die to be born again?[5]

Like fools we keep running after ephemeral things and suffer just as
Deluded deer fruitlessly runs towards distant forests for waters of the mirage.[6]

When we realise the fact that we cannot get happiness from ephemeral objects of the world, most of us usually lose interest in life. We wonder why we should bother getting things that are not going to last. Why make any effort to pursue a mirage?

As the eldest son, Rama is going to be king one day, but he wonders why he should bother about the throne as death is going to catch up with him sooner or later.

Why should I care for the kingdom and pleasures? Who am I? Why am I here?
If everything is illusion, let it be so; why should I bother about it?[7]

Rama is bothered about the fundamental questions regarding self-identity, purpose of life, death, disease and old age, and rightly so because, even after becoming king, he is not going to be impervious to disease, old age and death. He is right in thinking that life is extremely uncertain and death cruel; youth is also momentary, and so is childhood.[8]

Death is the most important issue here. It is said that if there were no death, no one would ask philosophical questions. But death is very much there. In fact, it appears to be the only certain thing.

All these concerns have plunged Rama into the depths of despair. However, he does not show his grief openly, as it would demoralise his brothers and others in the kingdom.

Seeing the sorrows of the world, my heart has become an impermeable stone;
But I do not shed tears as I am afraid of public ridicule.[9]

We see so much misery around us that most of us become insensitive to it. However, not everyone can remain unaffected by the trials and tribulations of life. The more sensitive we are, the more it hurts us, and the situation can make us pessimistic. It is necessary to help thoughtful people like Rama get out of this negative state of mind because:

If a thoughtful person does not find mental bliss,
Why would he suffer the tribulations of the world?[10]

Contemplative people need peace of mind more than those who are not sensitive. Rama cannot bear the torment any longer and he says if his mind does not find peace soon, he might do something drastic.

It is significant that Rama is asking these questions at a tender age. It is generally believed that these questions should be asked at a later stage in life. It is in the advanced years that one should seek answers to such concerns, but Yogavasishtha says that people must be given self-knowledge at a young age so that they can live the rest of their lives peacefully.[11] What is the point of learning the secrets of lasting bliss when you are in your eighties or nineties? It would be like looking for a doctor after suffering an entire life in ill-health.

Listening to Rama's concerns, Vishvamitra begins to wonder

if he can help him. Vishvamitra was a supreme teacher as far as warfare was concerned, but he wonders if he could help his disciple in fighting the battles of the mind.

He goes back to Dasharatha, and advises him to seek the help of the great sage Vasishtha, who is also the king's family guru.

After Vasishtha arrives, Rama is sent for. As Rama enters the court, he sees his father flanked by Vishvamitra and Vasishtha.

Even before Vasishtha begins his teaching, there is a symbolic suggestion here. Vishvamitra symbolises physical power, whereas Vasishtha is the epitome of wisdom. By placing Dasharatha between Vishvamitra and Vasishtha, Valmiki is giving the message that a good person ought to have power, as well as wisdom on his side. Power in the hands of a fool can only bring misery, and wisdom without power is of no use. Therefore, only a person who is wise and powerful is worthy of sitting on the throne. Rama has acquired the methods of wielding power from Vishvamitra. Now he must acquire wisdom from Vasishtha so that he can become a powerful and wise king.

After speaking to Rama, Vasishtha tells Dasharatha not to worry as Rama's lack of interest in life is a good sign because people like Rama do not normally get disturbed by the minor ups and downs of life. Therefore, this situation is going to bring about beneficial results.

According to Vasishtha, the state Rama is in is just right for achieving ultimate freedom. He is neither too immature to be insensitive nor does he have self-knowledge yet to be unaffected by the ordeals of life. Such persons, who are in-between, are ready to benefit from a guru's teachings.

Both the immature and the enlightened go about the world unaffected by what is happening around them because they are free of problems, but there is a great difference. The enlightened are calm and quiet in this world because they have solved all their problems, and for the immature, the problems have not even begun as they are not sensitive enough to realise they have a problem.

In contrast to the immature and the enlightened, the ones who are in between are miserable as they are not certain about things. They see that all is not well around them but they do not have the answers. They are in doubt and it is doubt that kills us, not ignorance. This is a good sign, and the reason why the wise in the court who hear Rama's words exclaim:

O! It is a propitious sign that the prince has uttered
Words of wisdom and dispassion that bring good.[12]

KINDS OF DESPONDENCY

Disenchantment with the world has several explanations. When we become uninterested in life, it is called *rajasic vairagya*, which is nothing but an inversion of our desires. Earlier, we ran after wealth and power; now we have become hermits but continue to indulge in activities with the same mad fury. Nothing has changed; only our direction has changed.

Then there is *tamasic vairagya*, as a result of which a person withdraws from the world to justify his escapism and laziness.

Sattvic vairagya or *viveka vairagya* happens when a person truly realises the worthlessness of the world.[13]

Who would not become uninterested by seeing the detestable;
But supreme disinterestedness is born out of maturity (viveka).[14]

Those who become disinterested without any personal reason;
They are truly mature, and their mind becomes free of blemishes.[15]

Rama's lack of interest in life is natural. It has arisen out of his own contemplation on the world around him. All he needs is a slight push from a guru to attain supreme bliss.[16]

When individuals ask such philosophical questions, they are usually quietened by being forced to accept the authority of religion, threatened with hell or even killed. But a thinking person cannot be silenced. You cannot expect him to bow down to authority and accept things blindly. Vedanta does not ask you to accept the authority of anyone, not even God, guru or scriptures. It might quote the scriptures but ultimately you have to decide whether or not to follow what they say. Vedanta pulls down everything that you try to cling to. It stresses on examining the problem to the core and encourages you to ask questions until a satisfactory answer is found.

The kind of questions that have engulfed Rama would trouble anyone who cares to contemplate what is going on around them. It is a natural tendency to look for the meaning of life. What is the purpose behind this huge universe? Why should there be billions of planets without life? Why are we born, why do we suffer, and why do we die? What if nothing existed at all?

When we do not find answers to such mindboggling questions, disenchantment, dissolution and dejection are sure to follow. The young become disturbed when they do not find any meaning in life.

We try to look for meaning in life, but if we observe life carefully, we find it has no meaning at all. What is the meaning in being born if we are going to die any moment? Why is the rose red? Why is ice cool? Why does fire burn? Why do planets go around the Sun? Why is there anything at all?

What answer do we have for such questions? No matter how well they are answered, we always ask 'why' in the end, because things could have been otherwise. That is why such questions have been called ultimate questions (*atiprshna*).

Since our intellect cannot accept the fact that we do not know the meaning of life, we impose meaning upon life. We are totally free in thinking what is meaningful in life and what is not. This is why there are so many religions and philosophies in the world. It all depends upon how we view life.

We might, for instance, conclude that we are nothing but a physical body which is full of filth and which is going to perish one day. Contrary to this, we can marvel at the beauty and complexity of the body and try to make the best of it. We can also say we are not just a corporeal body but much more than that. We are a conscious self. We can say that the self is pure and blissful, and it does not end with the death of the body.

All these viewpoints are right, for matter and the conscious self are connected and we are free to adopt any one of them. However, our lives are affected by what we choose to call 'meaningful'. If we choose to attach meaning to matter, we feel we are limited and perishable and we deprive ourselves of the subtler experiences of life.

Although we are free to choose any point of view, it is always better to give significance to subtler things than grosser ones if we wish to give meaning to life.

The fact is that life itself has no extrinsic meaning. All we can do is flow with life and be free of suffering, or struggle with life to find meaning in it.

Wise persons would not bother to find meaning in life because it is beyond intellectual capacities. They would rather look at the entire mindboggling complexity with a sense of wonder and participate in it because life is a game, *krida*. We can play the game well or badly, but we cannot look for meaning in the game.

For example, we may love the game of chess, cricket or football, but if we look deeply, what meaning do these games have? Just a few pawns made of wood, placed on a board of black and white squares. Regarding cricket, George Bernard Shaw said, 'Cricket is a game played by eleven fools and watched by eleven thousand fools.' His opinion could apply to any game. All games look nonsensical to many, but those who participate, love them.

It is the same with life. If we try to look for meaning in it, we find it absurd, but if we participate in it, it can be a wonderful experience. There is nothing to be too serious about, as it is just a game. Play it to the best of your ability and have fun.

However, if we took life too seriously, we would only burden ourselves with insurmountable problems. Let alone life, we are so foolish that we even take games seriously. Quite often we hear of two teams getting violent, and hooliganism during matches is common. We take everything so seriously that all joy in life has disappeared.

The young are too impatient to understand the complexities of life. When they see misery and injustice around them, they are bound to be angry and feel compelled to do something about it. They try to find solutions to the problems of life but when they cannot, they think that by pulling down the existing structure they will solve the problem. Most revolutions have come about through anger and bloodshed, but whatever comes out of anger cannot bring happiness. Anger only gives birth to more anger.

Why do we get angry? Why are we unhappy? What is the cause of our misery? Is there any way out of it?

Although we may not know the answer, we intuitively know that we can get out of this misery and be happy. That is why we continue to live.

Until we find the final answer, we give meaning to life in family, money, fame, job, religion, literature, charity and philosophy. But these are merely interim measures; they can never give us lasting bliss.

THE ULTIMATE PURSUIT

We may not know what true happiness is and how to get it, but our entire quest, be it for wealth, health, love, sex, religion or the good life, is actually for ultimate happiness.

Hinduism talks of four pursuits of life (*purusharthas*): *dharma, artha, kama* and *moksha*. Dharma is rightful living, artha is worldly resources we need to survive, kama is the pleasure that we try to derive from life and moksha is ultimate freedom from the misery of the world.

If we examine them deeply, the first three pursuits are essentially for final liberation, although we may not be aware of this fact.

Why do we seek resources? Why do we seek pleasure? Why do we try to lead a rightful life?

We run after money not for the sake of money but for the security it provides. If money did not provide security, we would not bother to earn it. All the money on a deserted island would be worthless.

Why do we try to lead a rightful life? We do so to avoid trouble. Why do we seek pleasure? We believe it leads to happiness. All the wealth in the world might give us pleasure but not happiness. We see unhappy people even in palaces, and we also come across people who are happy despite having nothing.

Most of us think that we are miserable but others are better off, until we hear their stories. Our misery, however, is not total; it is not unbearable, otherwise we would do something to get out of it or commit suicide. We go on living, nevertheless, as amid misery there are moments of joy as well.

But why is there misery at all? What did we do to deserve it? Why are some born in luxury and others in penury? Why are some born with a good physique and others with disease or handicap?

If we are told that nature is like that, we wonder why, and we feel it is unfair. If we are told it is because of past life karmas, again it sounds unfair. Why should we suffer for something we did in our past lives, especially when we do not even remember what we did?

With the rapid growth of science and improvement in general living conditions, it was hoped that people would be happy. The comforts the poor enjoy today were not available even to emperors in the past. But are we in any way better off than the cave man?

To end suffering, all sorts of religious doctrines and governments have been tried, all sorts of systems have been tested, but nothing has worked. Each new system gives some relief in the beginning, but sooner or later it becomes ineffective because a new system ends the old type of exploitation, but generates a new kind.

There was a time when illiteracy was considered the root cause of human suffering. With the rapid spread of education and science, far from finding meaning in life, many serious modern thinkers realised the sheer meaninglessness of life, and as a result they got thoroughly disenchanted with it. Some of them went insane, while others committed suicide.

The question is why are we so miserable in spite of all the progress we have made, especially in the past 300 years?

We are miserable because, no matter what we achieve in life, most of us feel we are limited beings. From birth, we have a fear within us about our survival. We realise that we are limited to a physical body, and most of the time we are not happy with it. This body is subject to disease and old age, and it is also limited by time, as death is going to consume it sooner or later. We are limited by the resources we have, and there is fierce competition for them as there are other people around to thwart our attempts to achieve what we wish to.

We try to overcome this sense of insecurity by acquiring more and more resources, wealth and power. But at some stage in life, we realise that no matter how much wealth and power we acquire, the sense of insecurity remains. In fact, a paradoxical result is obtained. The more we acquire, the more insecure we become. To acquire more, we not only have to put in more hard work, but we also have to protect what we have managed to acquire. We realise that this is not possible, as whatever is acquired does not last.

A strange realisation dawns. First of all, we cannot acquire all the things that we wish for. Then we do not like most of what we have managed to acquire and whatever little we like out of it does not stay long. This is the main cause of our misery.

The paradox of life is that we wish to free ourselves of the sense of insecurity and inferiority through things which are themselves limited and ever-changing. It is like a drowning person trying to cling to the waves. All that we try to hold on to is itself impermanent, and therefore, the sense of security that we get from them is also impermanent.

In such a state of affairs, we normally turn to religion or philosophy, and we may be told that we must accept that we are limited beings; and that there is God up there. We are mere insignificant beings who can only hope for salvation through worship, ethical life and compassion towards others.

All this might comfort us for a while, but the problem persists. If we accept the fact that we are insignificant beings in the hands of an all-powerful God, it means we are condemned to being insignificant. As far as God's grace or salvation is concerned, it happens only after death, so there is no way to confirm whether it really happens or not.

Regarding ethical life, most of us cannot agree about what is good and bad. About helping others, we cannot be sure if what we are doing for them is helping or harming them.

By giving alms, we may think we have helped a beggar, but it could be argued that we have created a beggar by giving alms. Even if we accept the fact that we are limited beings, that God will accept us one day, that ethical life is good and that we ought to do charity work, the sense of despair that we are limited in space and time remains.

Vedanta says our misery is due to the fact we are seeing things wrongly and our idea about ourselves as limited and hopeless beings is fundamentally flawed. If we are limited, there is no possibility of eternal freedom because how can a limited being become unlimited?

Vedanta says we are not limited. We are already unlimited, absolute and free. It says that the feeling that we are limited and bound is incorrect.

This is exactly the state Rama is in. He seems to have accepted the fact that he is a limited being, helpless at the hands of time and destiny. He says in despair:

Time is tough, cruel, harsh and mean;
There is nothing that time has not swallowed.[17]

Other than this time, there is another time which is the crown jewel of evil;
Known as destiny, it is the one that creates and annihilates the world.[18]

The cycle of pleasure and misery that we experience is nothing but
A dance floor of time on which it dances to its heart's content.[19]

It may be interesting to note here that in the Bhagavad Gita, Arjuna is also in a similar condition. There is, however, a significant difference between Arjuna and Rama. Arjuna is facing an emergent crisis. He is on a battlefield where the opposing side consists of his cousins. As he belongs to the warrior class, fighting a war is the least of his problems, but he is in a moral dilemma: Should he kill his relatives or not? He asks Krishna for advice, and Krishna gives him more than he asked for. Krishna gives him knowledge of the self instead, as we face some kind of battle every moment of our lives.

Rama, on the other hand, is not facing any immediate crisis. In fact, most of us would think he is in a very fortunate situation. He seems to have everything going for him. He is young, handsome, brave, born in riches, and will be king one day. Yet, he is in despair because he is not insensitive to the facts of life. He may be fortunate, but fortune brings its own miseries. Besides, he is not blind to the sufferings of others.

It also shows that you may have everything in this world, but you can still be miserable. Rama's dispassion, *vairagya*, has arisen in spite of his favourable situation, and this is a sign of his maturity. This is why, while the Bhagavad Gita was set in a battlefield, the Yogavasishtha was delivered amidst a king's court. In a battlefield, it is not unusual for people to become dispassionate, but it takes real maturity to become dispassionate amid wealth and prosperity.

Rama's dispassion towards the world is not mere idle curiosity or a passing fancy. He says he will end his life if his mind is not quietened. It is this kind of urgency that becomes a stepping stone to liberation.

The desire for liberation should not be one among other desires. We may have so many desires at the same time. Right now we may be hungry, but we may not eat immediately as the desire to do many other things might also be present simultaneously. But once hunger becomes intense, we give up everything else and eat.

In the same way, the desire for moksha has to be so urgent that it becomes priority number one, and also it should be lasting, not mere passing fancy.

In fact, the desire for liberation is not a desire, but if you call it desire, it should be a 'burning desire'. If the house is on fire, do we wait for the advice of a guru? We try to put the fire out or jump out of the window.

Rama is ready to pay any price to find answers to the questions that torment him, and as a good teacher, Vasishtha knows exactly where to begin. Rama is feeling hopeless, and has accepted the fact that he is helpless at the hands of destiny. He has begun to believe that humans have no free will.

Having heard Rama's words, Vasishtha decides to get him out of this hopeless state of mind first. He has to give Rama 'mental first aid' for immediate relief. Higher knowledge can follow later. In order to get him out of despondency, Vasishtha begins by stressing human effort and free will because Rama has become a victim of hopelessness and fatalism.

ENDNOTES

1. Also referred to as Sri Ramachandra or Raghava
2. I:5:4
3. I:12:6-14
4. I:10:45, The guards do not seem to understand that Rama's dispassion is not of the ordinary kind, like the one most of us have when things go against us in life. His dispassion has grown out of maturity and understanding of life (viveka vairagya). The guards also fail to make a distinction between 'faith' and 'hope'. What we do not have, we hope (asha) for; but what we have already, we cannot hope for it—we have faith (astha) or trust in it.
5. I:12:7, most Indic religions believe in life after death.
6. I:12:11
7. I:12:15
8. I:26:9
9. I:12:22
10. II:12:8
11. VIB:198:6
12. I:33:29
13. The Jyotirbindu Upanishad also talks about three kinds of vairagya: manda (mild), tivra (intense), and tivratrara (very intense), Mantra 4.
14. II:11:23
15. II:11:24
16. Those who consider Rama as a reincarnation of Vishnu, might wonder how is it that he is suffering like a common man. It must be pointed out that Rama's ignorance is a feigned one. He is a reincarnation of Vishnu, who had a curse on him that would make him ignorant in a future birth to suffer like a common man. (I:1:55-62). Gurus tell us that even our ignorance is a feigned one.
17. I:23:9
18. I:25:1
19. I:25:4

CHAPTER II

NO PLACE FOR DESTINY

When we are in the depths of despair, when all our efforts to achieve what we desire fail, we begin to wonder whether we are the masters of our destiny or if everything is governed by some unseen force.

It is true that to achieve anything in our lives, we have to make some effort: nothing is achieved by merely wishing. As the saying goes:

By hard work alone are jobs done, not by wishful thinking;
Do deer themselves ever enter the mouth of a sleeping lion?

Similarly, if we wish to go somewhere, we do not get there by merely thinking; we have to make some effort. If we wish to pass exams, we have to study hard and if we wish to rise in our career, we have to work hard. Even to steal something, effort is required. It is, thus, natural for us to conclude that whatever we achieve is brought about through our actions; there is no unseen hand conducting our affairs.

Yet, we see that what we have control over is minimal compared with what we do not. All the heavenly bodies in the cosmos keep on moving without regard for us. Weather changes all the time, tides come and go, earthquakes happen, and we can do nothing about these natural phenomena. We had no choice in the matter of our birth, the kind of parents we were born to, the country we were born in, the kind of body we have and, most importantly, we have no control over how long we are going to live. We wonder, if we have no control over our birth and death, how can we have any control over a life which is such a short span between birth and death?

It is true that, with effort, we often achieve what we set out to, and without any effort we do not, but we also see that sometimes we succeed even without trying and at other times we fail to achieve our goals in spite of leaving no stone unturned.

The matter becomes more complicated when the results of our actions are the opposite of what we intended. Most of the time, we cannot repeat success because the formula that worked in the past will not necessarily work again. This leads many to believe that it is part effort and part destiny that is responsible for success or failure. This leads to a greater confusion, for who decides what was caused by our efforts and what by destiny?

Generally, when we succeed, we say that it was due to hard work, and when we fail, we blame destiny or God. This is rather unfair. Whichever view we hold, we should stick to it. We should either take the responsibility upon our own shoulders or attribute everything to some higher force. If we hold both views, we will end up confused all our lives.

It is important to know that whichever view we hold will have a tremendous impact on our lives, although, in the final analysis, the view we hold is of no consequence. The world goes on, irrespective of the view we hold.

In the present age, the general belief among those educated according to philosophies such as Scientism, Materialism, Existentialism and Marxism is that we are the makers of our own destiny, and that a belief in chance or fate is rooted in blind faith.

Around the time these philosophies were gaining ground, Sigmund Freud suggested that most of our decisions were motivated by the unconscious mind. This had tremendous implications, as it meant our choices were not under our control and hence not rational. Rationality is considered the quality that distinguishes human beings from animals. Freud's theory also threw a spanner in the works of the principle of causation. If our actions are motivated by the hidden unconscious mind, how can we know what motivates our choices?

Predictably, there was fierce opposition to what Freud asserted, as it implied that our actions are determined by some mysterious hidden force. Freud, it was alleged, was taking us back to the dark ages, and that is why many declared that he was no scientist at all. Ironically, the latest research in neuroscience suggests that more than 95 per cent of human actions are guided by forces that we are not conscious of. Freud's claim that the unconscious mind constitutes two-thirds of the mind is modest in comparison.

Vedic thinkers have laid great emphasis on free will; in fact, they go to the extent of asserting that the fundamental nature of the self is absolute freedom and bliss. One might ask, if that is so, why are humans miserable rather than blissful?

Before going further, we have to first understand the concept of freedom. True freedom means the liberty to rise and fall, to be happy or miserable, and to live according to our own choices. As Ashtavakra says in the Ashtavakra Gita:

If you think you are liberated, you will become liberated,
if you think you are in bondage, you will become bound;
There is truth in the old saying that what we think, so we become.[1]

It is the glory of humans to be able to choose. The world functions on duality or plurality (*dvandva*).[2] Without darkness, light has no meaning; without sorrow, there can be no happiness; and without bondage, freedom is meaningless. If we had no option but to be free, what kind of freedom would that be? We ought to have a choice; only then does 'free will' make sense. Animals do not seem to have free will as they are governed by instinct. That is why, when an animal is hungry it will eat and when it is not hungry it will not, but humans might choose not to eat even though hungry, and to eat when not hungry.

As animals are guided by instinct, they have no conflict. They never seem to be confused or in a dilemma. Humans are always in conflict because they have free will, and the options are not simple or binary. To be able to choose is a wonderful thing, but it is choice that creates all our problems as choices are complex. Take the simple example of food. Animals eat a certain kind of food so they are never in conflict about what to eat. A cow, for instance, has no mental conflict about eating meat or not. It knows its own diet by instinct so it does not even look at meat. Humans, on the other hand, try all sorts of food, often eating things that are not good for them.

Although the fundamental nature of the self is absolute freedom and bliss (sachchidananda), it is up to us to realise our freedom or remain in the bondage of misery.

Let us now look at what the Yogavasishtha has to say on the closely related issues of human will and predestination. If we are free to act, can we act mindlessly? Do we not have duties?

We have seen that Rama, who has just come of age, becomes dejected with what he sees in the world, and because of this, he loses interest in all activities. The great seer Vasishtha is entrusted with the task of taking Rama out of despondency so that the young prince can take up the responsibilities of the kingdom of Ayodhya. Giving up action and running away from his duties at this stage is not going to get him anywhere. That is why Vasishtha argues strongly in favour of human effort and self-determination.

Furthermore, as a prince, Rama has to lead by example because what he does will be emulated by others. If he gives up his duties, the kingdom will be ruined.

There is a similar situation in the Bhagavad Gita, when Arjuna asks Krishna why he is urging him to fight the war and not allowing him to leave the battlefield and become a hermit. Krishna replies that although there is nothing in the universe for him to achieve as he is the lord of the universe, he continues to work incessantly because if he did not, people would follow his example, neglect their worldly duties and become lazy and lethargic.[3]

Incessant action is the inviolable law of the world. Wherever we look, all living beings, as well as non-living things, are in constant flux. A king, or any important citizen, has to lead by example, and act in a way that others get inspired.

HUMAN WILL AND ACTION, NOT DESTINY

Sensing that Rama is becoming lethargic, Vasishtha strongly advocates the glory of human effort (purushartha), and criticises people who blame their failures on destiny.

All work is done through effort alone, not otherwise;
Destiny does nothing, as it is an imagination of fools.[4]

But we have to put all our energies into our pursuits. Most of the time, we do not succeed, either because we only make a half-hearted effort or because we lose interest in what we seek.

Whatever one wishes to have, one works to achieve it accordingly;
And it is certainly attained if effort is not abandoned half way through.[5]

Purushartha means any kind of work or effort that is done to achieve something. The word 'purushartha' is made up of two words: *'purusha'*, which means 'man', and 'artha', which means 'aim' or 'goal'. Here, 'man' means 'human being'. 'Purushartha' thus means 'what is sought by humans'.

Purushartha is an end which is sought through our free will. Unintentional or involuntary actions cannot be termed purushartha.

If we say our actions are intentional, there is the natural law that every action will have an effect, and depending upon the effect our actions have, we term them good or bad.

The word '*purushakara*', generally, is used interchangeably with purushartha. 'Purusha', as mentioned earlier, means 'man' and '*kara*' means work. Together, the meaning is 'work done by man'. We shall stick to the word 'purushartha', as this is the word most commonly used in the Yogavasishtha.

The Yogavasishtha defines purushartha as:

When the individual seeks things in the outward world
It is known as purushartha, and it is also called karma.[6]

Vasishtha defines human effort as the determination to work towards our intended goals, whatever they might be. Whatever we pursue becomes the most important goal for us and our life is shaped accordingly. Among the four pursuits — dharma, artha, kama and moksha — whichever one we think is beneficial to us, takes precedence over the rest.[7]

It must be noted that, although freedom (moksha) is included in the four purusharthas, it cannot truly be considered purushartha. Purushartha means making an effort to achieve something we do not have. According to Vedanta, freedom is our fundamental nature; that is, we already have it. Bondage and misery arise because we have forgotten our true nature.

If we accept for a moment that we are free already, do we have to work for it? No. We can only strive for something that we do not have. This is why many do not include moksha among the purusharthas. Some early Hindu scriptures talk of three purusharthas, which has led some scholars to conclude that Hindus included the idea of moksha much later. We shall leave this point for later discussion and accept the four purusharthas for the moment.

Of the four purusharthas, most of us are engaged in seeking those that help us find pleasure and avoid pain. Pleasure is a natural thing to seek: there is no creature in the world that does not seek pleasure of some kind. We pursue wealth, only because we think it is a means to achieving things that give us pleasure. It is also natural for all creatures to avoid things that are painful and destructive.

Following this natural tendency, it has been argued that whatever we do in life, knowingly or unknowingly, we do it for liberation from misery alone. We seek moksha because it is the ultimate good, *summum bonum*. Our problem is that we confuse comfort and pleasure with moksha.

There are things in the world that can give us comfort. An air conditioner gives us comfort in the summer, a comfortable home makes us feel warm and secure, a car helps us go from one place to another without inconvenience, but these are just comforts that might lead to pleasure. The pleasures that we seek make us feel good for a while, but they cannot give us lasting bliss because they are just a means to further happiness; they do not by themselves give us happiness. True bliss, on the other hand, is an end in itself.

We must, therefore, be careful about what we pursue. We must think rationally and apply our energies towards what we wish to achieve. Since it is possible that we could be misguided in our pursuit, it would be prudent to be guided by scriptures and wise men.

Vasishtha says human effort is of two kinds: one sanctioned by the scriptures and wise men, and the other not. The former leads us to supreme bliss and the latter results in utter misery.[8] One must consult the scriptures in order to negate accumulated past karmas of this life as well as previous lives.

These karmas, says Vasishtha, are termed 'destiny' by the uninformed. Certainly, the past affects the present, but the effect of the past can be undone, as the present is always more powerful than the past, hence the present karmas can easily negate those of the past.

Like two rams of unequal strength, past and present actions fight;
The weaker among the two gets overpowered in the struggle.[9]

What the fatalists call destiny is nothing but human effort (purushartha) of the past,[10] and what is human effort today will be called destiny in the future. Ultimately, it is only human effort and not destiny that shapes our lives. Just as an adult can overpower a child easily, our present actions can negate the karmas of our past because the present is always more powerful than the past as it is nearer.

However, if we believe in destiny, destiny becomes powerful, and if we believe in human effort, it becomes powerful. The choice is ours alone.

We should perform our duties with unwavering determination in order to attain our goals. When we fail, in spite of our sincere hard work, we should know that it is because of wrong or insufficient application of our actions. In such a case we must examine our past actions and press harder.

It is true that we may not always succeed but we must not despair. If we fail in one place and time, we must try again later in some other place and time, but we must never give up trying.[11]

Cautioning Rama, Vasishtha says that the idea of destiny is often used by the lazy to justify their inactivity and lack of zeal, but even ordinary goals, leave alone ultimate bliss, cannot be attained by being idle and waiting for things to happen. If there were no lazy people in this world, everyone would be successful and prosperous.

Vasishtha says that because sometimes the results of our actions become apparent after a long period of time, people are unable to connect the two and erroneously call it destiny.[12]

People believe in destiny because of the fact that unequal results are obtained by similar actions done by different people. For instance, there are many who work hard, but only a few are recognised as achievers, whereas many dull-headed people attain high office without much effort. This leads people to believe in destiny.

Refuting the belief in destiny, he says if it had been predicted by fortune tellers that a certain person was going to live a long life, and this person continued to live even after being beheaded, then destiny could be considered supreme. If astrologers predicted that a person was going to become a great pundit, and he became one without studying, we would consider destiny to be everything.[13] Vasishtha gives the example of the great sage Vishvamitra, Rama's guru. Vishvamitra belonged to the warrior class, but became a Brahmin by dint of relentless effort and nothing else.[14]

Our success or failure depends upon the acts we perform: like actions bring like rewards. Destiny is nothing but the sum of our past deeds in this and previous births. But we need not feel helpless, as the effects of our past deeds can be changed with determination and hard work.

Just as the past evil deeds can be annulled by the present good deeds;
Likewise, we must always be industrious and do good deeds.[15]

Children as well as adults know that like efforts bring like results;
Nowhere is destiny seen; everything is achieved by human effort alone.[16]

One must work with a strong will until the effects of past deeds are annulled. The false belief in destiny should be given up by quietening the mind (*shama*), controlling senses (*dama*), listening to the wise and reading scriptures (*shravana*), and above all through contemplation (*manana*).[17]

Hearing this, Rama asks, if his present deeds can annul his previous actions, why is he helpless to change his past?[18] To this, Vasishtha says that he is possibly not trying hard enough. It is only through sheer determination to overcome past misdeeds that we rise above them.[19]

Rama is not fully convinced, and asks how self-determination can help in negating the evil effects of our past deeds. The answer to this point will be discussed later in the book, but for now it is enough to know that each individual is a conscious being. This consciousness is self-luminous like the Sun. There is nothing beyond this conscious self, for if there were another conscious entity behind this consciousness, it would mean there is another conscious entity behind that consciousness, and this would lead to infinite regression.

You are the supreme consciousness, not the corporal body,
You are illuminated by your own consciousness, no one else's.[20]

If some other consciousness illumines you, who illuminates that one?
This leads to infinite regress, and nothing is proved by it.[21]

This is why Vasishtha tells Rama that he alone is that all-powerful conscious self, and only he can create good desires in him and overcome past misdeeds. Rama need not depend on anyone else to redeem his past.

Vasishtha says, if in the past we have made bad desires strong, in the present we can cultivate good desires to counteract this. If in the past lives, we cultivated good desires, we can further cultivate good desires and find liberation quickly. In both cases, cultivating good desires is the answer.[22]

In any event, we must still cultivate good desires because if our desired result is not obtained, we lose nothing, but if we attain the desired result, then an atheist would get a befitting reply.[23]

The upshot of Vasishtha's argument is that to achieve anything in life, not just final liberation, it is our determination, zeal and untiring hard work that are the main causes of our success, not destiny or anything supernatural. Therefore, in order to succeed we must use our rational faculties rather than relying on divine intervention or chance.

Contemplation (manana) is important because Vasishtha says it is fine to be a frog in the mud, a worm in the filth or a snake in a dark cave, but it is no good for a human to be devoid of contemplation.[24]

THE LIMITS OF HUMAN ACTION

Although everything can be obtained by human will and effort, we must not try to achieve that which is undesirable and that which would bring about misery and disaster.[25] We must be careful in choosing our goals, as human actions are lawful or unlawful. The former leading to success and joy and the latter to failure and misery.

THE HOLY DIP

A farmer decides to go on a pilgrimage to Haridwar. It is not unusual for people in India to consult a pundit before embarking upon a pilgrimage. The pundit asks him why he wishes to go to Haridwar. The farmer says he wishes to bathe in the Ganges. Hindus believe that bathing in the Ganges is very auspicious as the Ganges washes away sins. Hearing this, the pundit advises him to abandon the journey.

'Why,' asks the farmer.

'Because your stars say you will never bathe in the Ganges.'

'You mean, never? You mean I don't have free will?'

'I don't know, but according to your chart you will never bathe in the Ganges.'

'Nonsense! Let me see who can stop me,' said the farmer and left in a huff. He went over to the railway station, bought a ticket and left for Haridwar. After reaching there, the next day he woke up early and went to the banks of the Ganges. The weather was rather chilly, but he decided to take the holy dip anyway. Before doing so, he said aloud:

'Listen friends, I was told by a pundit that I was not destined to bathe in the Ganges. He told me I did not have free will. Look, I have reached Haridwar. The Ganges is right in front of me. Now can any power in the world stop me from taking the holy dip? Who can stop me? Nobody can. But I will not bathe, as I don't feel like bathing. I have the free will to bathe or not to.' Saying this, he put his clothes on and went back to his village of his own free will.

Besides this, we must consider the amount of time and effort that would be required to achieve our desired goals, as we have a limited lifespan. There is no upper limit to the amount of effort we can invest in a job, so we ought to be practical and do only as much work as is necessary. We must also estimate the worth of our goals and not waste time pursuing those that may be useless or harmful.

Further, our goals must be realistic, because even with great endeavour, we cannot turn a stone into a gem.[26] A desire for the undesirable is a characteristic of madmen, nothing good comes of such effort.[27] One must try only for those things that can be obtained through hard work, through the advice of a guru and scriptures.[28]

Most importantly, whatever we aim for must bring prosperity and well-being to society. We must not desire that which brings misery because of our own selfishness. At times, we must give up our own pursuit if we see it is going to bring overall misery. We have to be careful what we aspire to achieve because:

The way desire arises in the self, pulsation is created in the mind likewise;
The body acts accordingly, and the fruits of actions are gained likewise.[29]

Our efforts are fashioned after our desires, and in accordance with them, we perform physical, mental and vocal deeds.[30] Vasishtha says one must cultivate them under the guidance of a guru until knowledge of the self is gained.[31]

STRIVING FOR WHAT WE HAVE

Talking about the knowledge of the self, here comes the paradox which was mentioned briefly at the beginning of this chapter. So far we have argued strongly that we must work hard to attain what we want, what we desire for, or what we dream about. But do we have to work to achieve what we already have?

If I am away from home, I have to do something to get back, but if I am already at home, do I have to do anything to get back? If I already have two eyes, do I have to do something in order to attain two eyes? This means that if we are not aware of what we have, no action is required to achieve it; all that is required is the knowledge of it.

This is the whole argument of Vedanta, and we shall examine it and try to understand it as we progress. This is important, because Rama's questions are not about attaining name, fame and worldly possessions. He wishes to know how he can get out of worldly misery and yet continue to lead a normal life.

However, there is a time for everything. At the time of this dialogue between Rama and Vasishtha, the kingdom of Ayodhya was tormented by demons, and the people were terrified of them. Being a young prince, Rama's first duty was towards them. It is for this reason that, after imparting self-knowledge to Rama, at the end of Yogavasishtha, Vasishtha says:

O! Strong-armed Rama, O! Great conscious one;
This is not the time to relax; be the saviour of the people.[32]

Until people are given what is rightfully their due,
It does not behove a yogi to sit in meditation.[33]

Towards the end of the initial discourse, Vasishtha successfully gets Rama out of despondency and languor. Rama is ready for the next stage now. We would have to see if Vasishtha succeeds in making Rama free of worldly misery too.

To understand how Vasishtha goes about imparting self-knowledge to Rama, we first have to understand the Vedantic teaching method, otherwise we will not be able to understand the teachings properly. The first question is this: Just as we know other things in the world, is it possible to know the knower (the self)? More simply put, is it possible for the eye to see itself?

ENDNOTES

1. The Ashtavakra Gita, I:11
2. The correct word for 'dvandva' in English is 'duality', but since this can lead us to think that the world is binary, 'plurality' is appropriate to talk about the diversity of the world.
3. O Partha! In the three worlds, I am not duty-bound
   To do anything to achieve, yet I continue to do work. (The Bhagavad Gita, III:22)
4. II:4:10
5. II:4:12
6. III:67:70
7. VIA:55:32
8. II:4:11
9. II:5:5
10. (The actions of past life are called destiny)
11. II:6:23
12. II:7:21
13. II:8:18,19
14. II:8:20
15. II:8:4
16. II:7:6
17. II:5:13
18. II:9:23
19. II:9:24
20. II:9:28
21. II:9:29
22. II:9:34
23. II:9:38
24. II:14:46; As John Stuart Mill says in *Utilitarianism*: 'It is better to be a human being dissatisfied than a pig satisfied; better to be Socrates dissatisfied than a fool satisfied. And if the fool or the pig are of a different opinion, it is because they only know their own side of the question.'
25. II:7:26
26. II:5:23
27. II:7:26
28. II:7:27
29. II:7:5
30. I:9:13
31. II:9:41
32. VIA:128:96
33. VIA:128:97

CHAPTER III

KNOWING THE KNOWER

The subject matter of Vedanta is called *adhyatmavidya, Brahmavidya, paravidya* and *arshavidya*. The word *vidya* means 'knowledge'. Adhyatmavidya means knowledge of the self; Brahmavidya is knowledge of Brahman; paravidya is transcendental knowledge, and arshavidya means knowledge handed down by the seers.

When we talk about knowledge (vidya), it means there must be something that is to be known (object), and there must be a method or means of knowing it. More importantly there must be a knower (subject), without whom the question of knowledge will not come up at all.

Physics, for instance, is about matter and energy; History about past events, and Biology about living organisms. The question naturally arises, what is Vedanta about?

The central teaching of the Yogavasishtha and Vedanta can be stated in four ultimate propositions or assertions. The first one is 'Pragyanam Brahman',[1] which means, consciousness is Brahman. This is called *lakshana vakya* — a statement that defines the property of what is being defined. In this case, it is Brahman, the absolute reality behind the phenomenal world. The statement says: Brahman is knowledge (*pragya*).

The second ultimate proposition is, *tat tvam asi*[2] — you are that. This is called *upadesha vakya*, or a proposition used by a teacher to instruct.

When disciples contemplate this deeply, the teacher leads them to conclude *aham Brahmasmi*[3] — I am Brahman. This is called *anusandhana vakya* — introspective proposition.

When disciples are convinced that the self itself is Brahman, they conclude: *ayam atman Brahman*[4] — this very self is Brahman. This is known as *anubhava vakya*, a proposition that comes out of personal experience.

These propositions may sound different, but they have just one message to convey — the relation of identity between the individual self and the universal self. The individual self is not limited by space, time, old age, disease and death but it is as blissful and eternal as the universal self. Only because of self-ignorance the individual self begins to feel limited and miserable.

The entire Vedantic literature can be easily understood if the meaning of even one of the above mentioned four assertions is grasped.

For the sake of simplicity, we might begin with 'aham Brahmasmi' — 'I am Brahman'.

This proposition is one of the most difficult to understand, and easy to misinterpret. When heard out of context, it sounds blasphemous, as it equates the individual with absolute. It is difficult to understand because we try to understand it the way we understand other propositions, such as, 'I am human'; 'I am tall' or 'I am sad'. In these statements, 'human' refers to species, 'tall' refers to height, and 'sad' indicates state of mind.

In case of the super statement, *mahavakya*, 'I am Brahman', we know what 'I' stands for, but we have no idea what 'Brahman' means. We have only heard about it from others, or read it in the scriptures.

The sole aim of Vedantic literature is to explain what 'I' stands for, and what 'Brahman' is, and to prove that 'I' and 'Brahman' are one.[5]

Just as geography deals with the Earth, History deals with the record of past events and physics with matter, energy and natural laws, Vedanta is about the knowledge of the self. This is because Vedanta promises that only by knowing the self can we free ourselves of the miseries of life and attain everlasting bliss. In other words, you may know about everything in the world, but if you do not know your own self, all your knowledge becomes useless. That is why Vasishtha says:

The scripture which only shows how to achieve worldly gain,
not liberation from misery
Is considered inferior and not worth discussing by the wise.[6]

Although we may not know much about what Vedanta professes, this much is obvious, that statements such as, 'I am Brahman' indicate the equivalence between 'I' and 'Brahman'. Now it is up to the guru to prove it to us that the seeming difference between the two arises out of ignorance. This means, proper knowledge of at least the first half of the statement can give us an understanding of the other and lead to liberation.

We may have no clear idea of the meaning of 'Brahman', but all of us have some idea of 'I'.

One might ask, if this is the case, why is moksha or final liberation eluding us? Why are we miserable?

Vedanta says, you think you know who you are, but whatever you have so far considered yourself to be is erroneous, and this wrong thinking is the main cause of your misery. Once the true nature of the 'self' is known, all misery will disappear like a bad dream. This is why Vedanta constantly stresses the knowledge of the self.

The question is this: can we know the self the same way we learn about matter, energy, land masses and other things in the world?

HOW WE GAIN KNOWLEDGE

All knowledge is gained by a subject; that is, the person who wishes to know, and an object, gross or abstract, that is to be known or inquired into. In the pursuit of knowledge, the inquirer uses the senses and the intellect. The intellect functions with the help of language and logic in order to experience and express the knowledge that has been gained.

According to Indian philosophy, knowledge (*prama*) is gained through the association of *pramata* (inquirer), *prameya* (object of inquiry), and *pramana* (means of inquiry).

Without an object of cognition (prameya), we cannot begin an inquiry. We cannot inquire about 'nothing'. To inquire, we also need the sense organs of inquiry. For example, we cannot know colour without eyes, which are the means of seeing.

Pramata stands for the conscious person who is inquiring into something. Knowledge is not possible without a conscious being.

Even if there is a conscious knower or inquirer, and even if there is an object, knowledge will not take place if the right sense organs are not employed. Conscious persons who are deaf cannot enjoy music as they do not have the capacity of to hear.

Let us say there is a flower in front of you. You are seeing the flower; in this case, you are the subject of cognition, pramata. The flower is the object of cognition, prameya, and the organ of cognition in this case is your eyes because you cannot know the colour of the flower through your ears or nose. The knowledge you gain by this three-fold association of the knower, the object to be known and the organs of knowing is called prama.

It is interesting to note that sometimes we will not know or perceive a thing even if all means of knowledge are present. When we are thinking about something, our eyes and ears might be open, but we may not see what is happening around us or hear the sounds around us. This is because our mind is preoccupied. Contrary to this, the mind can create things, sounds and smells for us even if nothing is present. Hence the mind is a very important part in knowing things, and it is called the internal organ (*antahkarana*).

Pramana, the 'means of knowledge', can also be translated as 'proof'. According to the Nyaya system of Indian philosophy, there are four pramanas through which we gain knowledge, although other systems do not agree on this number. We shall concentrate on the Nyaya system, as Vedanta is largely in agreement with it.

The four means of knowledge, according to Gautama, the founder of the Nyaya system, are: *pratyaksha* (direct sense cognition), *anumana* (inference), *upmana* (comparison, analogy, simile) and *shabda* (word, verbal testimony of trusted experts or scriptures).

In addition to these four means, Vedanta accepts two others: *arthapatti* and *anupalabdhi* (also called *abhava* by some scholars). Arthapatti is generally translated as 'presumption'. For instance, when we see that all the city roads are wet, we presume it must have rained. This kind of knowledge is called *a priori*. 'Deduction' is a better word for 'arthapatti'.

'Anupalabdhi' (or abhava) is usually translated as 'non-existence' or 'non-apprehension'. It means to know or realise the absence of something. Through non-apprehension we come to know about the absence (abhava) of something, such as discovering that there is no food on the table.

It is important to understand the term 'non-existence', as Vasishtha often declares, 'This world does not exist'. What kind of non-existence is he talking about?

Non-existence or absence is of broadly two kinds: Mutual Non-existence (*anyonya-abhava*) and Co-relational Non-existence (*samsarga-abhava*), which is of three kinds.

1. Mutual Non-existence (anyonya-abhava): This 'non-existence'

has the sense of being different. For instance, a pot is different from a chair. Their qualities are different. They are mutually absent in each other — the pot is not in the chair and *vice versa*.

2. Co-relational Non-existence (samsarga-abhava): This type of non-existence is inherent within the object itself. There are three types of such 'co-relational non-existence', differentiated by the time at which the non-existence occurs.

• Prior Non-existence (*prag-abhava*): Before any object comes into existence, it is non-existent. Prior non-existence is important because if an object was not initially non-existent, there would be no question of 'creating' it. If there is no non-existence, it means that the object already exists. For example, before a pot comes into existence, its non-existence prevails without any beginning. This non-existence is called prag-abhava. However, when the pot is produced, its non-existence ends. An important point to note is that prior non-existence has an end, but no beginning.

Prior Non-existence is important from the Vedantic point of view. People often ask, how and when did ignorance emerge in the atman? The guru says, 'Ignorance is beginningless.' It must be remembered that gurus also say that atman is beginningless; in other words, it is eternal.

We have earlier argued that a thing that has no beginning cannot have an end. Now, the disciple asks, if ignorance also has no beginning, it implies it would have no end just like the atman. In such an event, how can one talk of final liberation that happens after the end of ignorance? The guru replies, ignorance is a case of prior non-existence; that is, ignorance has no beginning, but it has an end. No one can say when ignorance emerged in the self, but it certainly ends with the knowledge of the self.

- Subsequent Non-existence (*pradhvamsa-abhava*): When a pot, for instance, is destroyed totally, never again will the same pot come back into existence. It is to be noted that while prior non-existence has an end but no beginning, subsequent non-existence has a beginning but no end. We can add here that once ignorance ends, it ends forever. After self-knowledge dawns, it has subsequent non-existence like the broken pot.
- Eternal Non-existence (*atyanta-abhava*): This applies to things that never existed in the past and will never exist in the future, for example, a four-sided triangle.

We shall illustrate the above-mentioned means of knowledge through examples. Let us say a panther has strayed into our neighbourhood. We can know about it in four ways. If we see the panther ourselves, this would be direct sense cognition (pratyaksha pramana).

If we do not actually see the panther but we hear a roaring sound, we infer that it must the roar of the panther that has strayed in. This is inference (anumana pramana).

We may never have seen a panther before, but we have heard that it looks like a tiger. Now if we spot an animal that looks like a tiger in the neighbourhood, we immediately conclude that it must be the panther that people are talking about. This is called knowledge by comparison, analogy or similitude (upmana pramana).

Finally, if a few trusted friends tell us that there is a panther in the neighbourhood, we take them at their word because we trust them. This is called verbal testimony (shabda pramana).

This is how we gain knowledge of the phenomenal world. Now the question arises, could the 'self' or the 'conscious knower' be known through these four means of knowledge?

Let us take the first means of knowledge, direct cognition. To recognise the objects of the world, we need the five senses, but to know if we exist or not, do we rely on the senses? With our eyes closed, our ears and nose blocked, even with total sense deprivation we 'know' that we exist. Hence, direct cognition is not necessary in knowing the self.

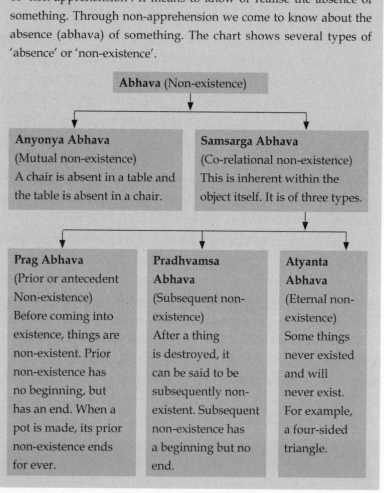

NON-EXISTENCE

Anupalabdhi (or abhava) is generally translated as 'non-existence' or 'non-apprehension'. It means to know or realise the absence of something. Through non-apprehension we come to know about the absence (abhava) of something. The chart shows several types of 'absence' or 'non-existence'.

Abhava (Non-existence)

Anyonya Abhava
(Mutual non-existence)
A chair is absent in a table and the table is absent in a chair.

Samsarga Abhava
(Co-relational non-existence)
This is inherent within the object itself. It is of three types.

Prag Abhava
(Prior or antecedent Non-existence)
Before coming into existence, things are non-existent. Prior non-existence has no beginning, but has an end. When a pot is made, its prior non-existence ends for ever.

Pradhvamsa Abhava
(Subsequent non-existence)
After a thing is destroyed, it can be said to be subsequently non-existent. Subsequent non-existence has a beginning but no end.

Atyanta Abhava
(Eternal non-existence)
Some things never existed and will never exist. For example, a four-sided triangle.

The Yogavasishtha of Valmiki

One important thing to remember is that direct cognition (pratyaksha pramana) is the king of all means of knowledge. Other proofs are based on it. If its usefulness is dismissed in knowing the self, inference and simile, deduction and non-apprehension collapse. However, we will also examine the other means of knowing.

Inference will not work in knowing the self because inference depends upon direct cognition. Comparison will not work because the self is like no other thing; deduction also will fail, as will non-apprehension, as they all depend upon perception. We cannot say, 'I do not perceive myself'. If we did, someone would ask who was making this statement.

We also do not need the verbal testimony of a knowledgeable person to know that we exist. We just know because the fact that we are a self and that we exist is self-evident (*svatah siddhah*). We do not need any proof for it, so none of the means of knowledge is useful in knowledge of the self.

Some might assert that the self was not there before our birth and will not be there after death. This point is valid, but it can never be proved. Vedanta stresses personal direct experience. It does accept inferential knowledge, but considers it to be indirect.

CAN THE UNKNOWN BE KNOWN?

We have seen that in the statement, 'I am Brahman', we do not know what 'Brahman' stands for, but we do know what 'I' refers to. It refers to our own self, although what we take to be the self might be erroneous.

All we have to discover now is what the term 'Brahman' refers to.

Brahman stands for the unchanging reality behind the ever-changing universe. Change can take place only against something that is stationary. A wheel can move only on a stationary axle. If the axle also moved, movement would not be possible. According to

Hinduism, Brahman is that eternal and unchanging ground against which all change takes place.

Almost all cultures believe in the individual person, as well as a supreme power behind all creation. The individual is limited, and suffers from old age, disease and death, while the supreme power is all-powerful, all-pervading and ever-existent. This much is common. Vedanta takes an intuitive leap and concludes that you, the individual, and that supreme power are one. It is this part that is hard to accept. All Upanishads and other Vedantic texts were written in order to explain this counter-intuitive idea.

How can the limited individual and the supreme power be one and the same? The universal or supreme self is omnipotent, omnipresent, omniscient, and we the individuals are limited by space, time, power and resources. How can the two be one?

Even if they are, how did we acquire the knowledge that the universal self and the individual self are one?

Certainly not by direct sense cognition, inference or similitude. We got this knowledge through verbal testimony (shabda pramana) of liberated individuals.

Why should we trust them? The answer is the same as that given for why we trust a dictionary, an encyclopaedia and books written by scientists.

We believe scientists when they say that the Earth goes around the Sun, although we have not seen it go around the Sun. When we buy a product, we often have no choice but to trust the word of the company that made it.

If we felt the need to keep checking everything through direct sense perception, life would become impossible. We would not be able to drink even a glass of water. So, in the majority of cases, we accept the word of authoritative persons unless we have good reason to doubt their word. This is called *shraddha* (conviction). The word 'conviction' is being used here, as there is no better English word for shraddha. Most translators use the word 'faith'. In this connection, 'faith' does not mean blind faith, but a suspended belief in a wise guru or scripture.

Patanjali, the author of Yogasootram, says for the union of the individual self and the universal self the following are required:

Conviction, vigour, memory, one-pointedness and wisdom.[7]

Let us say, we have heard about a certain remote village from travellers who have been there. We have seen maps and pictures of the place. We reach the place following a map. Upon reaching it, how do we know it is the same place? If the description matches what we read about it, we become satisfied that we have reached the right destination; if not, we conclude that either what we read about the place was inaccurate, or we have reached the wrong place.

So, shabda pramana, verbal testimony is useful but if it fails to be accurate to what it claims, either the testimony is misleading or we are incapable of understanding it.

Shabda pramana, we must remember, is indirect knowledge. In the case of the above example of the remote village, we can verify whether it exists or not by going there. Until the village is verified, its knowledge is 'indirect' (*apratyaksha* or *paroksha*). After we verify it, the knowledge about it becomes 'direct' or 'immediate' (pratyaksha or *aparoksha*).

It has to be noted that not all verbal testimony is verifiable. Scriptures, for instance, talk about heaven and hell too. There is no way we can verify their existence as long as we are alive, and after death we do not come back to tell whether they exist or not. Even if someone comes back and tells us about hell or heaven, the knowledge for us is still indirect. This kind of knowledge is called 'forever mediate' or 'forever indirect' (*nitya-paroksha*), as it can never be verified.

We have seen that the self can neither be known through sense perception, as it is not an object, nor through inference, simile or verbal testimony. We need none of these means of knowledge because the 'self' is known to us independently of these means. It is self-evident (svatah siddhah). Hence, knowledge about it is 'forever immediate' (nitya-aparoksha).

In the first part of the statement, 'I am Brahman', the pronoun 'I' is self-evident. The thing that is left to be known is the second part of the statement — Brahman — which stands for the ultimate reality behind the phenomenal world. More importantly, we have to see if the self is identical with Brahman.

The only way of proving the veracity of this statement is to examine it and see if it is true. How do we verify it?

We are told that Brahman is eternal and blissful. If, at the end of our inquiry, we become free of bondage and misery, we should accept the super statement; if not, we should reject it. Thus, ultimately, it is our own experience that counts, no matter what the guru and the scriptures say.

As Shankaracharya says in his commentary on the Bhagavad Gita:

Even if a hundred scriptures say that fire is cold and does not emit light, what they say should not be counted as proof.[8]

He further adds that if the scriptures say something that does not match with experience, there is a possibility that we have not understood them properly.

Let us come back to the question of the self. We keep using the word 'self' or 'I', but if someone asks us what we mean by the 'self', we are normally at a loss. Most of us think that either the body is the self or the mind is the self. But Vedanta dismisses such claims and says that we have the wrong idea about the self and, until it is corrected, we will be miserable. How can we correct our wrong notion?

Suppose there is a bird, twittering on a pole. We see it with our eyes and hear the twittering sound with our ears. The question is whether the one who is seeing and the one who is hearing are two persons or one? If it is two, how is the knowledge of seeing and hearing possible at the same time, as the eyes cannot hear and the ears cannot see? Our experience tells us that the same person is experiencing the phenomena of seeing and hearing. Now the question arises of who this person is. Is the knowing person the body and the senses, the mind, or the intellect?

Charvakas, the Indian materialists, hold that it is the body that knows. In other words, the self (atman) is the body, and consciousness is just a property of the body (*bhutebhyashchaitanyam*). Just as molasses, in combination with certain grains, form an intoxicating brew, the combination of various elements of the body gives rise to consciousness. In other words, consciousness is one of the epiphenomena, by-products of physical processes. This is also the view of most modern materialist philosophers, scientists and psychologists.

Vedanta and Nyaya schools object to this contention. Some of the objections are stated here briefly. If the body is the conscious self, why is consciousness not found in a dead body? If consciousness is attributed to the body, which is material, we would also have to attribute it to other gross objects, such as pots, rocks and wood. If the entire body is conscious, its parts should also possess that property. But this is not the case. For example, a severed limb does not appear to be conscious.

If we accepted that all the parts of the body possessed consciousness, it would mean there was not one conscious self but several. In this event, knowledge would become impossible, as there would be several knowers. Further, the body changes in size and quality from childhood to old age. This would result in a change of conscious knower. It would imply that there was no continuity in what we learnt at different stages in our lives. But this is patently not the case.

There are those who hold that the senses themselves are the conscious knower. If this were the case, people who lost their eyesight would not remember anything they had seen earlier. But those who become blind do remember what they had seen earlier in life.

Further, if the senses are the conscious knowers, who synthesises the different inputs provided by the senses? It follows that the knower has to be different from the senses. To know this knower, do we need senses? Do we need intellect?

Vedanta holds that the coordinator of all sense data is the witnessing consciousness (*chaitanya drishta*). The sense of selfhood is with us all the time—it is self-evident. In fact, the self is the only thing in the world that is self-evident, and that is why it is said to be beyond intellect, language and logic.

Yet, Vasishtha uses rigorous logic because it is one of the best means we have to speak about that which is beyond language and reasoning. This is because, in Indian systems, logic should also serve the ultimate goal of our life—knowledge of the self and freedom from misery.

BL Atreya, a leading academician, who wrote several books on the Yogavasishtha and Indian logic says, 'Logic has rarely been studied in India as an independent subject, as it has been in Western countries. The problems dealt with in Indian logic are more psychological, epistemological and metaphysical than purely logical.'[9]

Logic is used because how else can we communicate in language? Vasishtha says that nothing can be as convincing as a logical argument.

With reason alone can the individual be given the knowledge of the self; Through reason alone can be explained that which cannot be explained though a hundred other means.[10]

What the wise prove by knowledge should not be ignored;
Those who believe in the illogical are seen as fools by the learned.[11]

It is interesting that the first verse of *Tarkabhasha*, a Sanskrit treatise on logic, also claims that moksha can be gained by using the proofs of logic.[12] This implies that logic should be used to gain knowledge of the self.

Vasishtha, however, cautions Rama several times that the use of reason and logic should not end up as sophistry. In Indian philosophy, logic is often considered an immature means of gaining knowledge, as the invocatory verse of the treatise *Tarkasangrha* suggests:

Tarkasangrha was composed so beginners can comprehend (the truth) easily.

Logic is not required to know the self because the self is self-evident, but logic can be used to correct our wrong idea about the self and to show that the self and Brahman are one.

We might ask why we should bother to know the self at all. Why should we want to know about ultimate reality? The answer is that if all is well with our lives, there is no need to inquire into our true self. But how many of us can sincerely claim that all is well with us?

Vasishtha says that inquiring about the real self is desirable because:

If the self (Brahman) does not exist, what do you lose by contemplating it? If it exists, you cross the ocean of the world by contemplating it.[13]

ENDNOTES

1. The Aitareya Upanishad, III.3
2. The Chandogya Upanishad, 6.8.7
3. The Brihadaranyaka Upanishad, 1.4.10
4. The Mandookya Upanishad, 1.2
5. Vedanta is propounded to show the identity between the atman and the individual—Shankaracharya, Adhyasabhashya, Brahmasootra.
6. VIB:197:31
7. Patanjali Yogasootram, I:20

8.   Bhagvadgitabhashya,18:66
9.   Atreya, BL, Elements of Indian Logic, Hindu University, Benares, 1934, p 1
10. VIA:49:19
11. III:7:45
12. Shukla, Badrinarayan, Tarkabhasha, Motilal Banarasidass, 2010, p 4
13. II:13:35

CHAPTER IV

THE METHOD OF THE YOGAVASISHTHA

Having set the background to the Yogavasishtha in the previous chapters, it is appropriate to understand the Vedantic teaching method because Vedanta has its own peculiar teaching methodology. It is paramount that we become familiar with it otherwise what is being taught can never be understood properly. In fact, it would lead to gross misunderstanding.

Most modern readers are baffled by contradictory statements, esoteric expressions and excessive repetition in Indian scriptures. This is because modern readers do not understand the teaching method being employed. Since most of the scriptures begin with invocatory verses, modern readers think they are an integral part of religious literature.

In every age, people possess the intellectual understanding peculiar to that age, which can appear strange or meaningless in another age. The way people are currently dressing looks fashionable to us, but a thousand years from now, it might be laughable.

Like fashion, methodology also undergoes many changes over centuries. To be fair to the writers of scriptures and commentaries, we must first understand their method.

Traditionally, scriptures were read under the guidance of a guru, who resolved the doubts of the disciples in person. With the advent of the printing press and mass media, scriptures became easily available in print and electronic versions. Although gurus can still be found, most seekers read the scriptures without the guidance of one. Unless the reader is familiar with traditional teaching methods, language, grammar, logic and philosophical concepts, there will only be confusion and misunderstanding on reading the scriptures.

It is thus necessary that we try to understand the method Valmiki employs in the Yogavasishtha before we take up the main text. It is a traditional method used by ancient seers to impart knowledge to their disciples.

Like most Indian scriptures, Valmiki uses dialogue in the Yogavasishtha, which is an interaction between Rama, the disciple, and Vasishtha, the guru. The main aim of Vasishtha is to relieve Rama of worldly suffering through Vedanta, Advaita (non-dual) Vedanta, to be precise.

Hinduism has four ancient texts called the Vedas. The knowledge that they contain is of two kinds. A large portion of the Vedas is about practical, worldly knowledge, and is called *Karmakanda*. The other portion that deals with alleviation from worldly misery is called *Gyanakanda*.

Since the second portion is generally placed at the end (*anta*) of the Vedas, it is called Vedanta (Veda+anta=Vedanta), 'that which is at the end of the Vedas'. There are hundreds of texts that propound Vedanta, but the Upanishads, the Brahmasootra, and the Bhagavad Gita are considered to be the three essential entry texts (*prasthanatraya*) for the study of Vedanta.[1] Although the

The Yogavasishtha of Valmiki

Yogavasishtha is not a part of this trio, it is a quintessential Advaita Vedantic text.

Every treatise is written with specific objectives. Indian texts are written with the four-fold objective called *anubandha-chatushtaya*, and tradition says that the four objectives must be stated at the very beginning by the author. 'Anubandha' means 'limit', 'connection', 'relation' or 'order', and 'chatushtaya' means 'four-fold'. Here it could mean a four-fold connection or relation with the prospective reader. We could also understand 'anubandha' in the sense of 'limitation'. Writers ought to limit their discourse to a certain subject and reader; otherwise they might go on writing about irrelevant issues.

The first of the four-fold objectives is to specify the eligible reader or seeker (*adhikari*) for whom the treatise is written. For example, a book on higher mathematics expects readers to be proficient enough in the subject to understand it; otherwise it would make no sense to them.

The second objective that must be stated is the subject matter (*vishaya*), so that only those who are interested in it take the trouble of reading it.

Sambandha, the third objective, is the relationship or relevance between the text and the subject matter, the manner in which the work is related to the individual who takes it up for study, and the manner in which the method is adopted to expound the central theme. The author also has to state how the theme is connected with the ultimate goal of the treatise.

Finally, the text ought to state the objective (*prayojanam*) with which it was written. In other words, what the writer hopes to attain by presenting the thesis.

Regarding the qualified or eligible seeker (adhikari), Valmiki says that the Yogavasishtha was written for someone who has come to realise that they are bound and miserable in this world, and that they need to free themselves from misery and bondage. It was written for someone who is neither too immature nor too mature mentally, because those who are too immature will not understand it, and those who are wise will not need it as they already know what is in it.[2]

Having said this, it must also be stated that the Yogavasishtha is a text that is considered to be convoluted, and difficult to understand, so most teachers do not recommend it to beginners.

As Swami Krishnananda says, 'The Yogavasistha is not a book to be read by the beginner. It is regarded as a text meant for the perfected ones or *siddhas* and not for the seekers or *sadhakas*. The method of teaching employed in the Yogavasistha is in answer to the needs of the human mind. Generally, the doctrine is stated at the beginning, and is illustrated by a story which effectively instils the philosophy into the mind. The author of the book is confident that in the presentation of philosophical and mystical truths the work is incomparable and it exhausts every question of metaphysics, psychology and ethics.'[3]

Coming back to the worthiness of the seeker, the Yogavasishtha says that knowledge should not be imparted to unworthy persons as they are more likely to bring harm to themselves and the world by misinterpreting it. Those who teach the undeserving disciple eternal truth such as, 'I am Brahman', push them into hell, and they themselves deserve eternal hell.[4]

For example, if someone who is ambitious and wants to make a fortune in business goes to a guru for guidance, it would be improper if the guru told him that all worldly possessions are nothing but *maya*. This person is not seeking liberation but something else; it would be wrong to teach him Vedanta. He is not ready yet. Vedanta is the last thing he should know.

Vasishtha says that if you tell a person who is engrossed in the pleasures of the world that this world is unreal and only Brahman is real, he will only ridicule you.[5] When the learned seer tells the uninformed that whatever we see is Brahman, it is like sharing one's sorrow with the stem of a tree.[6]

Vedanta believes that we ought not to disturb a person's equilibrium. Only those who have a refined intellect, who have overcome self-indulgence, and who are sincere are worthy of Vedantic discourse.[7]

Further, Vedanta does not believe in imparting knowledge forcibly. As the Bhagavad Gita says, this knowledge should not be given to those who are unwilling listeners.[8] It should also not be given to those who are merely interested in pedantic debate and intellectual quibbling.

'Unworthy' (anadhikari) does not mean someone of low position or rank. It means someone who is not mature enough for the knowledge of the self. For example, it would not be right to give self-knowledge to a child, as he is not intellectually mature, or to someone who eagerly seeks worldly success. Anyone who is really interested in breaking free from the misery of the world is a worthy subject irrespective of is age, gender or social standing. It is also true that the idea of 'unworthiness' was later misused to keep the masses in ignorance.

The Yogavasishtha has a very secular vision, and it does not limit its discourse to the privileged classes. Women are equally worthy of moksha. In two of the longest and most important stories of the Yogavasishtha, women not only attain moksha, they also teach others how to acquire it. Not just humans, but serpents and crows can become liberated, as the story of Kakabhushunda illustrates.

Vasishtha says that only those who have controlled their senses and mind are worthy of benefitting from the teachings of a guru. The fools who have no control over their senses and mind can never attain liberation, just as it is impossible to extract oil from sand.[9] 'How can one teach those who have not conquered the dumb and blind serpent called the mind?' asks Vasishtha.[10]

WHO IS A GOOD DISCIPLE

A worthy disciple ought to have four-fold qualifications called *sadhana-chatushtaya*.[11] First, he or she should clearly understand the difference between the absolute and the ephemeral (*nityanitya vastu viveka*). Vairagya, the second qualification, means disinterestedness in worldly pleasures. 'Disinterested' here does not mean 'uninterested', which means to lose interest in life or to be dejected with it. To be 'disinterested' means 'not to get affected by the presence or absence of worldly objects'. It implies enjoying all the pleasures if they come your way, but not craving them. The third qualification is *shamadi sadhanashad sampatti* (six treasures of inner calm) These are shama, dama, *uparati, titiksha*, shraddha and *samadhana*. Shama means control of the mind; dama is the control of the senses; uparati means to perform one's duties according to one's natural disposition and station in life; and titiksha means forbearance in times of difficulty as well as happiness. We are normally asked to treat difficulties with forbearance. The fact is, however, that most people manage to survive extreme sorrow, but many are unable to handle extreme happiness.

Shraddha is faith, but faith here does not mean blind faith. We cannot learn from a guru and scripture if we do not have faith in them. Without some interim faith (*shrddhaya satyamapyate*), no progress can be made. When we consult a dictionary, an encyclopaedia, or a text book, we do so in good faith unless we have a good reason to be sceptical about them. Samadhana is a state in which the mind becomes free of distractions, and focuses itself on one thing alone. Finally, *mumukshutva* means the desire for liberation or moksha.[12]

Mumukshutva is translated as 'desire' but this is not the exact word. It is used for want of a more suitable one. The 'desire' for liberation should be intense and not idle curiosity. Suppose the room you are in catches fire. You immediately try to put out the fire or run out of the room, not because a desire arose in you to run out of the room. You try to extinguish the fire or rush out of the room because that is the only way to save your life.

Strictly speaking, this action cannot be called desire: it is exigency and expediency. Thus, mumukshutva means the urgency to get out of worldly misery because all our efforts to find happiness have failed. Until this exigency and urgency is felt, we cannot be said to have a real 'desire' for liberation.

Most people are not interested in final liberation; they just want to find happiness without changing the status quo. The Yogavasishtha says that people are born, they live a miserable life and then die like mosquitoes in a dirty pond, but they do not do anything to get free from their misery.[13] Such people are not worthy of Vedantic teaching.

Further, merely listening to the guru is not enough; one has to put the teaching into practice.

Not just the disciple, even the guru ought to be worthy, for it is foolish to seek knowledge from someone who does not know.[14] If you are interested in finding out about literature, there is no point in going to a logician.

In the person of sage Vasishtha and the disciple, Rama, we have the ideal combination of a good teacher and an able disciple. Vasishtha is the best of teachers, and Rama is a prince, who has had the best of education. He is intelligent and brave. He is thus ready to know the higher truth. But even with him, as we shall see, Vasishtha is in no hurry. He imparts the absolute truth to Rama step by step, gradually going along with his disciple's level of maturity.

Regarding maturity, it must be said that age has nothing to do with it. An older person is not necessarily more capable intellectually. The Yogavasishtha believes that self-knowledge must be imparted to people in the prime of their youth so that they can lead the rest of their lives in a more balanced way. What is the use of knowing the ultimate truth on the deathbed?

Rama is barely sixteen, and his brothers are even younger. If they are given the knowledge of the self now, they will be able to perform their duties more wisely, without causing mental conflict to themselves or others. Self-knowledge makes one level-headed in joy and sorrow; in life and death. The Yogavasishtha says that the bliss which arises out of perfect balance cannot be had, even by acquiring kingdoms or other pleasures of life.[15]

Coming to the core subject of the Yogavasishtha, it is the unity between the individual self and the supreme self (*jeeva-brahman-aikyam*), and the assertion that Brahman is real, whereas the world is illusory (*Brahman satyam, jagat mithya*). We shall be discussing this at length in the forthcoming chapters, as this is the sole message of the Yogavasishtha and Vedanta.

To show the sambandha or the relevance between the text and the subject matter and method, the Yogavasishtha laces rigorous logic with poetic language, such as similes, examples, analogies, metaphors and allegorical stories, so that difficult philosophical concepts are understood easily.

As for the prayojanam or goal of Yogavasishtha, we can say that it is freedom from misery and bondage. And Valmiki is confident that the Yogavasishtha is the best scripture for this purpose.

Among the great scriptures that teach self-knowledge;
The Maharamayanam (Yogavasishtha) is the greatest.[16]

THE METHOD OF SUPERIMPOSITION AND NEGATION

Contradictory statements and repetition are two of the characteristics of Indian scriptures that befuddle modern readers. At times, Rama himself complains to Vasishtha about the contradictory nature of his discourse. Vasishtha defends himself:

All my statements are true and none of them is devoid of reason;
Not one of them is unrelated to absolute truth, nor are they contradictory.[17]

Vasishtha says that all discourse is there to drive home a particular point, but the discourse itself is not the ultimate truth. We have already explained the problem of talking about the non-dual reality in language. This being the case, although what is being taught is false from the ultimate standpoint, it is not meaningless because it serves the purpose of showing the way.[18]

Vedantic discourse is like teaching the born-blind about light. The born-blind have no concept of light. If we speak the truth and tell them about brilliance and luminance it makes no sense to them. On the other hand, if we try to give them some hints about light through the concepts familiar to them, whatever we say will be false and contradictory, although it might give them some idea about light and encourage them to have their eyes cured. If their vision is restored, they are not going to complain that we said false things about light.

Vasishtha tells Rama that he will give up all words, meanings and methods once he manages to impart self-knowledge to him.[19]

Indian texts seem to make contradictory statements because the modern reader is not familiar with the methodology of imparting self-knowledge. For example, Hinduism says there is only one supreme reality, yet there are thousands of gods and goddesses; it says the supreme reality has no form, yet we see idols everywhere.

Indian sages believe that society is not homogenous; people are not only physically and economically different, their mental development is also not the same (*buddhi bheda*). To give just one kind of teaching to all would be unfair.

Further, the teacher should consider the mental level and emotional disposition of the disciple, and teach accordingly. We write sentences with relative ease now, but as children we had to be taught the alphabet through the use of pictures. We were told 'A' is for 'apple'; 'B' is for 'ball' etc. As we mastered the language, we were encouraged to give up the pictorial method because we had graduated to a higher level. If we still use the pictorial method to write sentences, it means we have not matured. Similarly, an advanced student of mathematics can multiply or divide numbers mentally, but as a child the same student was taught to do sums using pebbles or an abacus. It would be unfair if everyone were forced to use pebbles or an abacus to calculate.

When Hinduism says that there is only one reality, which is formless, this statement is for the advanced disciple. Although ultimately true, the statement might not help someone who is not mature enough to grasp it. Since such persons are not capable of understanding the ultimate reality which is without attributes, the guru gives a name to the one who is without any name. Any name would do, as a name is just a label.

I am without a beginning and end but the uninformed use the words
Such as Brahman, atman, Paramatman and other labels to name me.[20]

The guru might also make use of idols or symbols in order to teach a student who is at the beginner level.[21] In the story 'Arjunopakhyana' from the Yogavasishtha, Arjuna asks Krishna if he should worship him as a deity with a form or as formless entity. Krishna says:

Until you attain the knowledge of the self;
Worship me as a four-armed deity.[22]

As you attain self-knowledge, you will know my formless nature;
Knowing which you will become free, and will never be born again.[23]

Once disciples have graduated to experiencing abstract reality, they do not accuse the teacher of making contradictory statements. The blind need a stick to walk around, but once the vision is restored, the stick is no longer required, though it has served its purpose well.

Until we know the higher truth, the teacher has to give us a provisional or interim knowledge, only to be discarded later. This is why, in response to Rama's sceptical questions, Vasishtha tells him to suspend his enquiry. He urges, 'For the sake of learning, accept my words as true for the moment, and listen to my discourse.'[24]

This method of teaching is called *adhyaropa apavada*, the method of superimposition and negation. Employing this method, first something is superimposed or propounded, and later negated. In our example of language learning methods, the word 'apple' was superimposed on the letter 'A', and later negated. This is because the learner is now at a higher level.

We must keep in mind the level from which the guru is speaking. If we mix the levels, the statement is bound to appear contradictory or inconsistent.

In the Yogavasishtha, for example, we come across passages stating that there is one supreme, absolute Brahman and nothing else and there is a phenomenal world that grows out of it. This gives us the impression that there is a causal relationship between Brahman and the world. This seeming contradiction can be resolved by understanding the principle of superimposition and negation.

For example, suppose we have a pot made of clay in front of us. From our viewpoint, the pot is real, but the teacher wants to correct our understanding by showing that a pot is just an incidental transformation of the clay, because not just the pot, a cup or a jar could also be made out of clay. It is clay that has reality because the pot cannot come into existence without the clay, but clay can exist without the pot. The guru makes us realise this truth in four stages.

He begins with what we believe, so he says that the pot is an effect of the clay. He then takes us to the next stage by asking us what the cause (material cause) of the pot is. We say it is clay. So far he seems to be saying what we already know, but then in the third stage he asks us to investigate if there is any way the pot could exist without the clay; that is, whether an effect (pot) could exist without a cause (clay). We are forced to conclude that it is not possible, so the guru says in that event we would have to accept that the clay and the pot are not different—the cause and effect are not different.

Now the guru proceeds to the fourth stage and points out that if the effect is no different from the cause, it would not be wrong to say that only the cause exists. If we have come so far, we are bound to accept this conclusion. In that case, we can abandon the idea of a cause altogether because without effect, the word 'cause' has no meaning. We have transcended the cause–effect duality.

In this example, the guru first superimposes the pot on the clay, and in the last he negates it, taking us to the real non-dual relationship between them.

All the passages that talk about the creation of the universe in the Yogavasishtha belong to the first three stages, *adhyaropa*. In these, Brahman, also called atman or *chit*, is first established as the cause of the universe. This is because, the beginner cannot think beyond cause and effect. For the convenience of the student, the teacher might say God is the cause of the universe, and we could get out of misery by worshiping Him. In the final stage (*apavada*), however, the non-dualistic nature of the world is taught, that the world and Brahman are one, and you are that one—tat tvam asi. There is no need of God at this stage.

The teacher imparts education step by step, making us discard our previous knowledge and concepts until our mind is free of all concepts.

Disciples are often too impatient, and wish to know the ultimate truth at the first stage. In the Sthiti Prakaranam, for instance, Rama shows the same impatience to know the ultimate truth. We hear him say, 'Tell me right now' and 'Free me of doubt immediately', but Vasishtha tells him his question is not relevant at the moment; he will give the answer later because then Rama will be mature enough to understand it.[25]

At first, Vasishtha uses language and logic to impart his teachings because Rama is not mature enough to understand without the aid of language and logic. Rama himself insists that he be taught through logic:

Through what logic can the self be known? How can it be proved?
If proved by logic, how will nothing be left to be known?[26]

Vasishtha knows that he has to use logic to teach Rama, but he gives an indication that ultimately he will have to abandon logic and reason.

The uninformed learn through reason, the mature through direct knowledge;
Without the use of reason and logic, the uninformed can never be taught.[27]

Later, when Rama graduates to a higher level of understanding, Vasishtha teaches by taking Rama beyond the domain of the intellect.

So far I have taught you through reason, as you were a beginner;
Now that you are an advanced learner, I shall teach you through better means.[28]

Regarding contradictory statements, it must be said that once again that the level from which they were made must be kept in mind. For instance, at one place Vasishtha says everything arises out of Brahman, and at another he says duality or plurality of the world is not there at all as everything is non-different from Brahman.

Rama objects to this contradiction and says that in such a case, meaningful discourse is not possible at all.[29] Further, if the world is unreal, whom is the discourse meant for? Vasishtha meets the objection by saying that statements such as, everything arises from Brahman, are made only to teach those who lack self-knowledge. It would be improper to make such statements to a person who has acquired self-knowledge.[30]

At this point, it would be appropriate to discuss the problem of using language to describe the state that is achieved after acquiring self-knowledge.

Most Indian systems make a distinction between worldly knowledge (*aparagyana*), and transcendental knowledge (*paragyana*), and we must realise that the means used for acquiring them are not the same.

Worldly knowledge is known through the mind and intellect, whereas the latter is known when the mind and intellect are transcended. In the former, language and logic are the means of communication, and in the latter they are not necessary. At the transcendental level, one can communicate in silence.

The spoken word, shabda, however, has had great significance for all major Indian schools. They believed that as sound (*dhvani*), and word (shabda) are the non-material source of material manifestation, they could be the key to our liberation, as they are the link between the material and the transcendental.

Dandin, the sixth-century writer and aesthetician, declared that the three worlds would have become engulfed in darkness had there not been the light of word (shabda). In the Vedantic tradition, they go so far as to call it Shabdabrahman or Parabrahman—equating 'word' with Brahman, the ultimate reality.[31] These theorists speculated about the origin of the 'word' in the mind and body of the speaker, how it is articulated, how it is communicated, and how it is understood by the listener. It is necessary to know the nature of the 'word' because, although the 'word' can liberate us, it can also bind us.

THE MEANING OF 'MEANING'

We generally think that we can understand meaning by analysing sentences, words and the roots of words. While this seems right, many linguistic philosophers have realised the limitations of such an approach. Bhartrihari (fifth century AD), for instance, objected to this approach and rejected 'word' as an autonomous unit. He argued that a word is meaningful only in a particular context. He held that language cannot be analysed in terms of phonetics, syntax and grammar.

He came up with the concept of *sphota*. In his seminal work, *Vakyapadiya*, he argues that it is sphota that makes communication between the speaker and the hearer possible. The Sanskrit word 'sphota' is etymologically derived from the root, *sphut*, which means 'to burst, explode, flash, or bring insight'. It literally means the feeling or emotion that is experienced after hearing a word. Bhartrihari held that it is the capability of using language that makes humans able to experience ultimate reality, which is why it is also called shabdabrahman (the word is Brahman).

The concept of sphota had been developed long before Bhartrihari by grammarians such as Patanjali, but Bhartrihari developed it further and expanded it to three levels: *varna* sphota (the syllable level); *pada* sphota (the word level), and *vakya* sphota (the sentence level).

Bhartrihari makes a distinction between sphota, which is whole and indivisible, and nada, the sound, which is sequenced and therefore divisible. Sphota is thus the intention behind an utterance. Bhartrihari does not limit the concept to the speaker alone, for sphota is also experienced by the listener. Uttering the nada induces the same mental state or sphota in the listener. Bhartrihari held that it comes as a whole, in an intuitive flash (*pratibha*).

For Bhartrihari, sphota is a potential state in the linguistic form just as a pea-hen's egg contains all the colours of a fully-grown peacock in its potential state. Bhartrihari's concept of potentiality of meaning was later extended by Anandavardhana in his work *Dhvanyaloka*, in the latter half of the ninth century. He speaks of suggested meaning (*vyanjana*), along with the primary (*abhidha*) and secondary (*lakshana*) meaning of words. He stresses this third sense because of its capacity to suggest a meaning other than its metaphorical and literal sense.

Language, no doubt, is a powerful tool, but its importance is often overemphasised. One might ask why language is incapable of expressing subtle truths.

Leaving lofty philosophical concepts aside, even to describe the taste of something as common as sugar convincingly to someone who has never tasted anything sweet is beyond the scope of language.

There is no way to know the taste of sugar other than by tasting it;
The nature of the self, too, cannot be known without experiencing it.[32]

Language is a product of the mind and the mind is a complex device. It is perhaps the most complex entity in the universe. One of its essential features is that it cannot function without the help of the sense organs. Because of this, all the information that it receives is broken up into dualities or polarities or what is called dvandva in Sanskrit. Eyes for instance, give us visual input alone, leaving out other information, and ears give us only audio input.

The mind cannot work if the input is not broken up. For example, we can see things only if there is a combination of light and shade. When there is only light or only darkness, we cannot see things because the mind fails in such an event.

Since language is a product of the mind, it too can express only those entities or concepts that are dual. Anything that is not dual cannot be handled by language.

Absolute reality is larger than the mind and by implication language and logic, because it incorporates all dualities or polarities, otherwise it cannot be called absolute.

Absolute reality, as proposed by many schools of Indian philosophy, is non-dual in nature. What one experiences in moksha or nirvana is non-dual, and this non-dual cannot be expressed in language, as language can only express concepts in terms of dualities. This is the main problem: the ultimate truth is non-dual; it is beyond the scope of the mind, the sense organs and language.

FOUR LEVELS OF LANGUAGE

As most of us depend on language to acquire and communicate knowledge, the process of expression must be understood. We might begin with what classical Indian grammarians and *Tantra* theorists had to say about it.

When we wish to express a thought aloud, certain parts of our body are activated. As a result, thought is manifested through dhvani (sound). It is also called shabda, the spoken word. Just as a thought passes through several stages before it becomes clear, shabda also passes through various stages before it is understood by the listener.

These stages are *para, pashyanti, madhyama* and *vaikhari*. Although the manifestation of shabda starts from para, it moves down to pashyanti, madhyama, and finally to vaikhari. In order to understand them better, we shall take them up in reverse order.

Vaikhari is uttered speech. It is the grossest level of speech. This is the stage in which nature shows the power of action (*kriya shakti*). Madhyama is the intermediate and unexpressed state of sound, and its centre is the heart. Although it is not expressed, it is speech at the mental level, and we use it to think. At the vaikhari and madhyama stage, there is a clear distinction between the sound and the object. Nature's power of knowledge (*gyana shakti*), manifests itself here.

Pashyanti, in Sanskrit, means that which can be seen or articulated. Here, the sound possesses qualities such as colour and form. The navel is the centre of Pashyanti. Here the distinction between languages disappears, and intuition becomes dominant. Nature's willpower (*ichha shakti*) is strong here. Experienced yogis are said to communicate with each other at this level.

Para is the highest level of speech, where the sound is transcendental because the senses are not involved in producing it. There is no distinction between the sound and the object in para. As this level is experienced when one goes beyond the mind and the intellect, only enlightened people can make use of para to communicate.

As the mind can see only dualities, the phenomenal world, samsara, is created. Wherever there is duality or dvandva, there is samsara, and wherever there is samsara there is conflict and misery. In non-duality alone there is no conflict as there are no divisions.

The ultimate reality might be non-dual, but we live in a world that is dual. Since mind is a tool that we use to survive in the world, it has to think all the time, which it cannot do without language. The mind has to think in terms of what is useful, what is harmful, who is an enemy, who is a friend, what is good, what is bad, what is desirable and what is undesirable and so on. As we are evaluating things, persons and situations all the time, we store this information in our minds, and use it in life.

Language is not possible without dualities, and we cannot describe anything without dualities, that is, without referring to other things. A thing or a concept cannot be described by referring it to itself. In order to describe a horse, we cannot say 'a horse is a horse'. This would be tautology. To describe or define something; we have to put it in contrast with what it is not. This method serves our purpose, but only if we know what is being described and what it is being contrasted with.

If someone asks us what darkness is, we might say it is the absence of light, and if someone asks us what light is, we say it is the absence of darkness. Such definitions are circular. They say nothing about light or darkness, but as we are familiar with light as well as darkness, we understand what is being said. But if someone had no idea of either light or darkness, they would not understand what was being said.

We normally think that those who are born blind have no idea of light, but they must have an idea of darkness. This view is false. To have an idea of darkness, one must know what light is. For that one ought to have the capacity to see. Those who are born blind have no capacity to see, so what they experience can never be said.

We can only say that their world cannot be dark as they have no idea of light.

Since the self is pure subjectivity and totally different from the world of objects we know, would this method of describing something through comparison and contrast work in knowing the absolute self?

Limitations of language notwithstanding, the situation is not impossible. Language can certainly give us hints about that which is beyond its scope by arousing curiosity in us. The self is me. Do I need to be told about my own self in any language? The guru may not be able to talk about supreme bliss, but he can make us experience it.

NAILING THE POINT HOME

Repetition is common in all Indian scriptures and more so in Vedantic literature. There are several reasons for this. One reason is that the fundamental message of Vedanta is to show the oneness between the individual self and the supreme self, and to show that the seeming difference between the two occurs because of lack of self-knowledge. This has been stated in three or four super statements (mahavakyas) such as, 'You are that', 'I am Brahman', 'Brahman is real and the world is unreal'.

Since these simple sounding statements are not comprehensible to the common sense view, and as they give rise to hundreds of questions, the guru has to state the same truth again and again to drive the point home. This method is called *sthanu khanin nyaya*. 'Sthanu' means 'nail' 'pillar' or 'peg', and 'khanin' means 'to dig'. Just as while erecting a pole, we dig the ground deeper and deeper, in order to make the pole stand firmly, the guru hammers the same point till it is firmly understood.

But, owing to youthful over-confidence, disciples often declare that they have understood everything. At one point, Rama declares that all his doubts have been resolved, and that he has found eternal peace,[33] but Vasishtha knows that the declaration is premature so he ignores the claim and asks him to listen to the discourse again.[34]

If Vasishtha is a severe taskmaster, Rama, too, is a determined seeker. He does not hesitate to ask the same question repeatedly.

In the Yogavasishtha, Valmiki has perhaps tried to show that forgetfulness is part of human nature, and our minds have been conditioned so much that the simple truth is forgotten again and again. In order to stick it firmly in the memory, the point has to be repeated until self-knowledge dawns. This is because it is very difficult to make people unlearn what has been fed into their heads since childhood. Vedanta is all about unlearning because the truth is with us already.

Regarding repetition, Vasishtha says that when a thing is repeated, it gets understood even by the dim-witted.[35] Further, even after self-knowledge is gained, the student has to practise it until the desired goal of the teaching is attained.

Vasishtha is a very patient guru. He listens to Rama's questions and praises him for his intelligent queries. At times, he politely chides Rama by saying he has answered the question already.[36] When Rama frames a question wrongly or asks an irrelevant question, Vasishtha tells him that his question is not valid.[37] In order to make sure Rama is paying attention, he asks, 'Do you remember what I said earlier?'[38]

When Rama does not understand a point, Vasishtha explains it all over again without getting annoyed, but at times he does lose his temper, as Rama goes on asking a question that has been answered several times: 'I am screaming and telling you that, without firm resolve, liberation is not possible.'[39] In response, Rama implores him not to be upset, as he is asking playfully for the sake of others so that they can also be enlightened.[40]

Sometimes, asking questions becomes a kind of disease for

the disciple. When Rama seems to have exhausted his questions, the desire to ask more questions is still in him. Almost at the end of the Yogavasishtha, having seemingly run out of questions, he exclaims, 'What should I ask now?'[41]

Vasishtha hammers knowledge home so rigorously that towards the end Rama asks questions and then answers them himself.[42] Vasishtha is happy, but to be fully sure, he reverses the roles and tests Rama by asking him questions as a disciple would.[43]

Rama asks dozens of questions in the Yogavasishtha, but they are fundamentally about causation: Who created this world and how? If the world was created, there must be some purpose, for nothing is created without a purpose. Rama wants to know, if Brahman is supreme bliss, why is the world that came out of it full of misery? Most importantly, is there a way out of this misery? In order to get out of misery, do we have to perform actions or is self-knowledge enough? Further, do we have free will or are we puppets in the hands of destiny?

He also asks several technical questions regarding ontology, epistemology, logic and grammar.

We shall see in the following chapters how Vasishtha answers these questions, and how he leads Rama to ultimate freedom.

ENDNOTES

1. The Upanishads are called shruti prasthana (one that is heard), because they usually consist of a dialogue between a guru and disciple, husband and wife, or father and son; the Bhagavad Gita is called smriti prasthana (one that is remembered), as it is a dialogue between Krishna and Arjuna recalled by Sanjaya; the Brahmasootra is called tarka (logic) prasthana, as it gives knowledge through the rigorous use of logic.
2. I:2:2, VIB:172:31-33
3. Krishnananda, Swami, *A Short History of Religious and Philosophic Thought in India*, The Divine Life Society, 1973, p 104
4. IV:39:21-26
5. IV:31:21, 24
6. VIA:49:20
7. IV:39:25

8. Do not impart this supreme knowledge to the one without forbearance and devotion; Nor to the unwilling listener, nor to one who speaks ill of me. (The Bhagavad Gita, XVIII:67)
9. VIB:5:1,2
10. V:14:7
11. The concept of the qualifications of a good disciple is called adhikarivyavastha.
12. Tattavabodha by Shankaracharya begins with a discussion of these four-fold qualifications.
13. VIB:6:5
14. II:11:45
15. VIB:198:10
16. III:8:8
17. IV:41: 4
18. IV:41: 6
19. IV:41:7
20. VIA:53:37
21. VIA:30:5
22. VIA:53:38
23. VIA:53:39
24. VIB:52:6
25. IV:21:6-7
26. III:8:1
27. VIA:49:21
28. VIA:49:22
29. III:84:18
30. III:95:3, 4
31. Compare the following verses from The New Testament: In the beginning was the Word, and the Word was with God, and the Word was God (John:I:1). He was with God in the beginning (John:I:2), All things were created through Him, and apart from Him not one thing was created that has been created (John:I:3).
32. V:64:53
33. VIA:5:1
34. VIA:6:1
35. VIB:198:1
36. IV:44: 2
37. VIA:33:13
38. V:4: 15
39. VIB:I:11
40. VIA:50:3
41. VIB:190:32
42. VIB:192; VIB:201
43. VIB:195:10-11

The Yogavasishtha of Valmiki

CHAPTER V

THE ROLE OF GURU

We discussed in Chapter III that the self (atman) does not require
any proof of its existence as it is self-evident. We are the self. That
being the case, do we need anyone else to tell us who we are? This is
why many seers say that even scriptures and gurus are not required
to know the self.

The question arises, if scriptures and gurus are not required, why
are so many scriptures written about the knowledge of the self, and
why is the guru given so much importance?[1] That is why Rama asks:

Are guru and scriptures necessary in knowing the self or not?[2]

The answer to this question is tricky, like the answers to all
fundamental questions of life — it is both, 'yes' and 'no'.

The universal self, by Vedantic definition, is beyond the senses
and intellect. This means it is beyond the scope of language, as it is
inexpressible. The words of a guru and the scriptures, however, are
expressed in language, otherwise discourse would be impossible.
We have already argued that language cannot deal with that which
is beyond the capacities of intellect.

Regarding the necessity of scriptures and guru, at one place Vasishtha says that other than the teachings of a guru there never was nor will there ever be a way to attain moksha.[3] At another place he says that a guru and scriptures are not necessary.[4] As the learned seers experience moksha after ignorance is annihilated, it is not a matter for discourse.[5] Contrary to this, at another point Vasishtha says that those who ignore the teachings of the scriptures are like worms.[6] He later adds that the supreme self can neither be known through scriptures nor guru. One knows it when one's mind becomes free of the ego. It may be asked how one becomes free of the ego?

Here the guru and scriptures could be of help.

However, we also see that many people spend their entire life in the company of a guru but they seem to be as miserable as the rest of us. On the other hand, we also see people who are uneducated and have never had a guru, leading a blissful life. This is because most of us interpret the message of the guru and scriptures according to our own limited understanding. It is our own mental maturity that finally matters.

The cause of self-knowledge is the disciple's purified intellect, Raghava.[7]

It is true that the self is self-evident, and we do not need anyone to tell us about it. The matter, however, is not that simple. In fact, we complicate it ourselves through our own ignorance. Our problems arise because we take the body and the mind to be the self. This is a natural tendency, and all that is required to gain ultimate bliss and freedom is to correct this false identification. This is why it is said that any genuine seeker can know about it through contemplation and practice alone.

Vasishtha says that, just as a child who is rubbing two pieces of coal together soils his hands, but after the pieces are no longer there, the child's hands can become clean on their own. In the same way,

The Yogavasishtha of Valmiki

one can clear the dark stains of ignorance through contemplation and constant effort.[8]

A guru merely reminds us about our true nature, which we have forgotten or have wrongly taken for something else.[9] This 'reminding of the self' is called self-knowledge (*atma gyana*).

Vasishtha says that we can be searching for our necklace all over the place until someone reminds us that we are wearing it.[10] Once we realise that the necklace is around our neck, all our anxiety about its loss disappears. Did we do anything to regain the necklace? The knowledge that reminded us that it is around our neck was enough to relieve us of our anxiety because we had never lost the necklace in the first place.

This is the reason the importance of self-knowledge is stressed so much. Vasishtha defines self-knowledge as:

That which frees us from the cycle of birth and death alone can be called knowledge;
All other knowledge that helps us acquire the basic needs is mere professional craftsmanship.[11]

We might ask what we would lose by not knowing our true self and what we would gain by knowing it. The fact is, without self-knowledge, nobody is going to perish. Having it is not going to get us a job, a life partner or any other attraction of life. In fact, if we are happy with the way things are, we need not bother about self-knowledge because worldly things can be pursued without knowledge of the self. We can conduct the affairs of our lives quite well without it. Animals too, survive quite well without knowing the self. To get along in life, self-knowledge is not necessary. All we need is self-identity.

The problem with us is that we wish to go on living the way we are but we do not want to be miserable. This is like someone who wants to be slim without giving up fatty food. The Yogavasishtha says people are born, and they die living their miserable lives but, like mosquitoes in a lotus, they do not care about ultimate liberation.[12]

If, in spite of all comforts and achievements, we feel emptiness within us, and realise that all our accomplishments are meaningless, we might begin to look for the knowledge that frees us from sorrow. Intuitively, we know that there must be some way out of this misery. Who would continue living if there were no way out of suffering?

Vedanta says that there is a way out of it, and that is by the knowledge of our true self, because by knowing the self we come to know of everything else. Just as by examining a lump of clay, we learn about all the clay in the world.[13]

THE PROBLEM OF LEARNING FROM A GURU

This brings us back to the question: are scriptures and a guru necessary in order to know the self?

We can begin with the role of scriptures regarding self-knowledge. The scriptures were written by people who, after they had first-hand experience of supreme bliss, decided to write about it for the benefit of others. These people were themselves great teachers. What greater teacher can one think of than Valmiki, Vasishtha, Vyasa and others? It is only because of the scriptures written by such wise gurus that that the knowledge of the self was handed down to us.

However, there are certain problems that accompany learning from gurus and scriptures.

What the guru says is grasped through the senses, while Brahman is beyond the senses.[14]

This is a major problem, for what is beyond the senses and the intellect is also beyond the scope of language. Scriptures are written in some language or the other. In the text, words make up sentences, and sentences run into chapters. The message of a scripture is understood by reading the whole, just as a painting can only be appreciated by looking at it in its entirety. A painting would make no sense to us if we looked at it through a lens inch by inch.

With a painting, as it is visual art, it is possible to see the whole thing. All we have to do is stand at a reasonable distance from it. This method does not work with scriptures. In order to understand the whole text, we have to read every word and sentence. The problem is, by reading the scripture part by part first, how can we understand the whole? Each word makes sense only in relation to the sentence, and each sentence makes sense only in relation to the paragraph, and each paragraph makes sense only in the context of the entire text.

We are caught in a bind: without knowing the whole we cannot know what each word and sentence conveys, and without going through the parts, we cannot know the whole. Words and sentences mislead us if we do not grasp the whole. The solution is to read the scriptures several times. When you read it first, you may understand it faintly, but if you read it again, your understanding might be a little better. Good commentaries and guru can be of great value in understanding the scriptures.

There is one more problem. When we read, we often do so with preconceived notions. We interpret the message according to our own limited understanding and prejudices.

It is for this reason that a guru is required. The guru cleanses our mind of conditioning and the clutter of preconceived notions. After this cleansing, self-knowledge dawns on its own, just as the Sun appears in its brilliance when the sky is clear of clouds.

It might be asked from whom the guru acquired self-knowledge. We may be told that he learnt it from his guru. From where did his guru get it? Again the answer would be—he got it from his guru and so on.

This chain ought to end somewhere. In other words, someone, far back in time, must have got it without a guru. How did they get it? We are told that they got it by sheer contemplation. The point then is, if they managed to get it without a guru, a guru is not actually necessary.

This is true, but only a rare individual gains ultimate freedom without a guru. Most of us need the help of scriptures and gurus. It is a tricky situation, and varies from person to person.

Most of us do not attain self-knowledge because we do not seek hard enough. Some rare individuals who wish to seek it do not know how. Regarding the teaching and learning of self-knowledge, the Katha Upanishad says:

Many do not even get to hear about it, and even if they hear, many do not understand it;
The one who can teach it is extraordinary indeed, and extraordinary indeed is the one who understands it.[15]

We do not know the true nature of the self because we do not contemplate properly, which is why we are ignorant and miserable. We also ought to be determined enough to know the ultimate truth. In rare moments, all of us become contemplative and ask eternal questions but we soon forget them. The enquiry into the self should not be idle curiosity. One has to try really hard, as this ignorance has become dense because of conditioning over the years. Vasishtha tells Rama:

The disease of ignorance is age old and perennial;
Its name is world, and it cannot be cured without knowledge.[16]

I shall teach you through stories and parables;
Listening to them you will certainly become liberated.[17]

However if you become impatient and leave midway;
You will gain nothing, just as animals are incapable of learning.[18]

In Kiratopakhyana, one of the stories from the Yogavasishtha, a village miser loses a cowrie (a common seashell that was used as currency in ancient times) in the forest. Dismayed at his loss, he looks for it all over the forest, but even after three days of rigorous search he does not find the cowrie. He, however, finds a wish-fulfilling gem (*chintamani*) in the process.

Vasishtha says, without making an effort to go to a guru and listen to his teachings, the self cannot be known, just as without searching for a cowrie, the miser would have not found the wish-fulfilling gem. Vasishtha elaborates the point:

Brahman is beyond the senses, and scriptures are heard through the senses;
Hence, it cannot be known through discourse and scriptures.[19]

Even so the self cannot be known without guru's teachings;
Without searching for a cowrie, who has ever found a wish-fulfilling gem?[20]

Since Brahman is beyond the scope of the senses, and since a guru's teachings are heard through the senses, at most his words can cleanse the intellect of the obstructions that are not allowing the disciple to see the truth. Thus, the guru is a cause of self-knowledge without being a direct cause.

It is for this reason that the Yogavasishtha sometimes asserts that the self is known with the efforts of the disciple, message of the scriptures and the guidance of a guru.[21] Guru and scriptures can create a sincere thirst for self-knowledge. They can guide us in the right direction and caution us against the pitfalls. This is why discourse is necessary, and to give meaningful discourse, language and logic are indispensible. Through them the guru makes the disciple ready for self-knowledge.

Once the disciple becomes capable through the teachings of the guru;
Knowledge of the self dawns on its own with or without the help of a guru.[22]

We must, however, remember that the main purpose of Vedanta teaching is to release us from worldly misery, not to keep us involved in endless debates and philosophical hair-splitting. Vasishtha tells

Rama that language — sentence construction and word meaning — are all actually false and misleading, but they can be helpful in understanding the ultimate truth.

What is propounded in the scriptures is for instruction alone;
Do not be infatuated with the falsehood of word meaning and construction.[23]

Once we realise the ultimate truth, we will understand that all language and discourse are actually false. Their usefulness over, we give them up. We then realise that the maze of words and logic is created only to teach those who are ignorant of the ultimate truth.

After Rama becomes enlightened, Vasishtha tells him, that although language has its limits, and can mislead, it is only because of his discourse that Rama has attained bliss.[24]

Vasishtha, however, cautions Rama against indulging in pedantry. He encourages him to become enlightened, not a pedant or hair-splitter (gyanabandhu). One who merely accumulates worldly information and uses it for endless argumentation or professional gain is called a gyanabandhu.

O Rama! One should become wise, not a hair-splitter;
I'd prefer an uninformed person to a pedant.[25]

An uninformed person is better than a pedant because he has a greater possibility of learning than a pedant who thinks he knows everything. Cautioning Rama against scholasticism, Vasishtha asks if he has correctly understood the web of words woven by him, because the intricate web of language, logic and philosophy can be alluring.[26] One must be careful not to get lost in this web by losing sight of our ultimate goal — freedom from misery. Otherwise, instead of having our disease cured, we end up contracting a more deadly disease called pedantry.

Though Vasishtha uses language and logic with rigour, at times he goes silent. When Rama asks how a person would perform worldly activities after the fall of the ego—in other words, after self-knowledge dawns—Vasishtha does not answer. He says, 'Now that you are enlightened (*gyani*), I shall answer as an enlightened person. That is, in silence, as all language is misleading.[27]

This is because there comes a stage in the guru-disciple relationship when words are no longer required. This communication is direct and free of distortion, as language is not used to communicate. Once this stage is reached, there is no further need of scriptures or guru. At this stage we must give them up, just as we give up medication after regaining health. If we kept taking medicine after getting well, we would only harm our health. A boat is necessary to cross a river, but once the river is crossed, one has to get off the boat. It would be foolish to carry the boat on the head and walk about just because the boat was useful in crossing the river.

At this point, a question might arise: How does one find a good guru? The world is full of fake gurus; how would we know who is our real guru?

It may be asked whether a disciple has the capability to judge who is a good guru and who is not. This capability comes only after you become mature. As a disciple, all you can do is become a good disciple, cultivate the six-fold qualities of disciplehood,[28] and the guru will come looking for you. He will be eager to answer the questions that have dogged you since you began wondering what the cause of the world and your purpose in it were.

ENDNOTES

1. VIB:196:8
2. VIB:196:9
3. VIB:175:68
4. VIA:118:4
5. VIB:31:37
6. VIA:4:7
7. VIA:83:13
8. VIA:41:4-10
9. *Atsmin Tadbudhhi*, (Brahmasootra, Adhyasabhashya)

10. VIA:41:13
11. VIB:22:4
12. VIB:6:5
13. The Chandogya Upanishad, VI:4
14. VIA:41:12
15. The Katha Upanishad, I:2:7
16. III:8:2
17. III:8:3
18. III:8:4
19. VIA:83:25
20. VIA:83:26
21. VIA:41:16
22. VIA:41:14
23. IV:41:6
24. V:29:61
25. VIB:21:1
26. VIA:1:23
27. VIB:29:27-32
28. The six-fold qualities are: shama (control of the mind), dama (control of the senses), uparati (performing one's duties), titiksha (forbearance), shraddha (faith), and samadhana (making the mind free of distractions).

CHAPTER VI

THE COSMOS: A FIGMENT OF THE IMAGINATION

It is natural for us to wonder, 'Who created this world? Who made the immense sky and the innumerable stars?'

Regarding the creation of the universe, some believe that God, who is all-powerful, created it. This is because they believe everything in the world has a cause. Things do not come into existence without a reason. If there is a universe, there must be a maker of it, and that maker has to be all powerful, all knowing, and all pervading.[1]

Atheists counter this argument by saying that if everything necessarily has a cause, God too must have a cause, and if He has a cause, that cause should have another cause and so on. This leads to infinite regress, and this is why they hold that there is no God — the world came into existence on its own. It has no cause.

By asserting this, atheists dig their own graves. They cannot explain how the world came into existence without a cause. And if the world came into existence without a cause, anything can come into existence without a cause. Why look for the cause of other events and phenomena? This makes the theory of causality, on which the scientific edifice rests, collapse like a pack of cards. The problem of causation will be discussed more technically in the next chapter; here, we simply lay the groundwork.

The Yogavasishtha rejects all theories of causality because whatever view we take leads to absurdity. The intellect is incapable of finding a solution to the problem of causality.

Those who claim that God created the world could be asked why God should wish to create anything if He is absolute and blissful. Further, if the world was created out of His will, it would mean He, too, has desires. In that case, how is He different from us? On the other hand, if there is no creator, how the world came into existence has to be explained.

No satisfactory answer can be given regarding the cause of the creation of the world, because no matter what answer we give, in the end one can always say, 'Why'? All explanations are provisional. The answer that satisfies us says more about ourselves than the truth about creation. This is why the Rig Veda is bold enough to concede:

Who knows and who can say how and why this world came to be.
Since the gods were born after the creation, how can they know its cause?[2]

How the world originated, who created it or did not create it;
Its organiser in the sky knows, perhaps he too does not know.[3]

The Yogavasishtha, too, accepts that there is no answer to the question of creation. Since the absolute is beyond space and time, whatever we say about it in language will be misleading.

Having stated this, the Yogavasishtha gives an explanation of how the world came into existence. There is an entire section comprising 122 chapters called Utpatti Prakaranam, which deals with the creation of the universe.

It is important to explain the process of creation because, without knowing the cause of things and events, we become insecure and uncomfortable. However, Vasishtha repeatedly reminds Rama that all explanations are provisional, and are just indications because the ultimate truth will always be beyond comprehension.

At this point, it would be apt to note that the Sanskrit word 'srishti' is generally translated as 'creation'. The word 'creation' is not wrong, but it gives the impression that the world is created the way a potter creates a pot with the help of materials such as clay, water and potter's wheel. This means the potter (the creator) is different from the pot (creation). It means the creator of the world is different from the world he created. In the Vedantic sense, this is not a right metaphor for creation of the world. A better metaphor is that of a dancer. The dance cannot happen without the dancer. It is to be noted that the dancer can exist without the dance, because the dancer does not dance all the time. The dance, however, cannot exist without the dancer. Another metaphor which conveys the idea fairly well is that of the wave and ocean. Waves are formed in the ocean, but they cannot be formed independently of the ocean. They appear out of the ocean and disappear in it. The same way the world comes out of the Brahman and dissolves in it.

Further, to ask when the world came into being is like asking when the waves came into being in the ocean. If the ocean is there, the waves will always be there. They are co-existent. It is the very nature of the ocean to have waves.

Vasishtha says that creative power or imaginative power (*viranchi bhava*) is the very nature of the absolute Brahman or Paramatman.[4] The world simply emanates from it like fragrance from flowers. It emerges from the mind like a dream. In a dream, for instance, we see people and objects. Everything looks real. What reason can we give for the world of dreams?

The phenomenal world is known by various terms such as, 'the will of Brahman', 'prakriti', 'samsara' and 'maya'. Regarding its creation (srishti), the Yogavasishtha says that when Brahman or universal atman imagines or wills, the world gets created.

It is the real nature of the all-pervading consciousness that
Whatever it imagines becomes manifested there and then.[5]

THE SEEDS OF THE WORLD

According to the Yogavasishtha, there are four 'seeds' that create the world: *samvedanam, bhavanam, vasana* and *kalana*. That which is enjoyed through the senses is called samvedanam. To go on thinking about sense objects when they are not available is called bhavanam. Fixation that arises after constantly thinking about objects is called vasana. To crave for the body even at deathbed is called kalana. This is because we would like the body to survive longer as no matter how long we may have lived, life is never long enough to fulfil our desires. This last-minute desire to live more is the cause for life after death.[6] These four seeds create a vicious cycle of birth and death in which the individual self becomes bound.

It is this mind that creates the world. The Brihadaranyaka Upanishad declares, 'As far as the mind extends, so far extends the heavens, and so far does the sun (fire).'[7] The Amritabindu Upanishad says that mind alone is the cause of human bondage, as well as freedom. When the mind attaches itself to sense objects it becomes the cause of bondage, and when it does not, it becomes free.[8] The Jyotirbindu Upanishad says the same, and adds that mind tainted by *rajas* and *tamas gunas*, leads to bondage. Once purified by *sattva guna*, it leads to liberation.[9] With desires the world comes into being, and without them, it ends.

WHAT DOES EXISTENCE MEAN

It was mentioned in the Introduction that the idea of reality is quite different in Hinduism. 'Reality', 'existence', and 'truth' are used interchangeably in Vedanta. They stand for something that exists eternally. Anything that comes into existence is bound to end one day. Such a thing would not be called real in Vedanta. When Vasishtha says that the world is not real, it does not exist, or it is untrue, he only means that it is not eternal. Its reality is only as authentic as the reality of a dream. It is just an illusion.

The Shiva Gyanamrita Upanishad says that the world of names and forms is mere appearance. It has no independent existence apart from Brahman. Just as in the dark we may mistakenly take a rope for a snake, the world and body are superimposed upon Brahman through ignorance. (Mantra 1)

The Yogavasishtha says that the world is a creation of the mind, and is thus ephemeral. It is real only if it is perceived by the mind. The moment we transcend the mind, it becomes unreal. This means that the existence of the phenomenal world depends upon the mind. The Jyotirbindu Upanishad, for example, says that the world ceases to be a separate entity when the mind is annihilated (Mantra 12).*

But this does not mean everything ends in nothingness. The Yogavasishtha repeats endlessly that consciousness or Brahman is the only reality. When the world dissolves altogether, Brahman remains.

It must be noted that the word 'real' in general conversation means physical reality. When talking about things in the world in day-to-day life, even a diehard Vedantin would not say that the world and the things in it are illusory. We must always be clear about the level from which a statement is being made. By mixing levels, we create confusion and misunderstanding.

See also Tripura Rahasya, Chapters XI-XIV

The Yogavasishtha agrees, and carries the argument further:

Mind alone is the creator, and it is the one that wills,
Expands itself and creates the phenomenal world.[10]

That the world is a creation of the mind is the fundamental argument of the Yogavasishtha. Without a conscious mind, we cannot even begin talking about the world (this matter will be discussed in detail in Chapter X). The mind, however, is not the absolute reality (Brahman). It is the imaginative power or willpower of Brahman that creates the mind, and later the cosmos with its laws.

The conscious and absolute Brahman is the cause of everything;
It becomes the cause of creation and then establishes the law of karma.[11]

It then creates the first Prajapati (Brahma, the creator), and later;
The way the creator imagines, the world gets created accordingly.[12]

An important point is to be noted at this stage. Brahman is not the creator of the world, in the sense as a potter is the creator of the pot. Brahman is absolute, so no change in it is possible.

Vedanta says, when absolute Brahman wills,[13] it 'seemingly' creates the phenomenal world. This world is 'seemingly' created like the world we create in our dreams. The things that we see in our dreams are not there, yet we see them, and are affected by them. So the dream world exists in one sense and does not exist in another. In the same way, the world we live in exists in one sense and does not exist in another. How do we explain this paradox?

It is a matter of levels of experience. From the absolute level, the world cannot be, as the absolute would not be absolute if it changes, if something comes out of it. However, from the phenomenal point of view, the world is there, and we are obliged to speak of its creator. The creator is called Prajapati or Brahma. He is the first step in creation. We should be careful as the two words 'Brahman' and 'Brahma' sound similar.

The simile of an ocean is often used to describe Brahman, and that of a wave to describe the mind. The ocean is calm deep down, but on the surface the waves go on rising and falling. We can imagine

The Yogavasishtha of Valmiki

the sea without waves, but we cannot imagine waves independent of the sea.

Just as waves arise in the mighty calm and silent ocean;
The supreme self becomes the cause of the world and individuals.[14]

Coming back to creation, once the absolute non-dual reality imagines, it becomes many (plural). This results in the multifarious objects of the world, and innumerable individual beings.

While Brahman is non-dual, unchanging and blissful, the mind is plural, ever-changing, and because of this it is all the time in a state of agitation. It must be noted that not just sorrow, anxiety and fear, even joy is a state of agitation.

The Yogavasishtha sometimes identifies the mind with Brahma the creator, and sometimes, with the individual self, jeeva. It does so because anything other than the absolute Brahman is mind. So from Brahma, the creator, to the speck of dust, whatever the mind creates is of two kinds: illusory (*bhrantimayi*) and absolute-like (*Brahmamayi*). The one that is born out of seed, womb or cell-division, is called illusory because it is born out of association with something else. Brahma, the creator, is also born out of something (Brahman), but since he was not born out of a womb his birth is called absolute-like (Brahmamayi).[15] Brahma was born out of the imagination of the absolute reality, Brahman.

MULTIPLE UNIVERSES
Since the universal self has unlimited powers of imagination, it imagines not just one universe but millions.

Like the layers of the banana stem, there are worlds within worlds;
And like leaves of the banana tree, many spread outwards far and wide.[16]

Another important factor is that although there are trillions of creatures in these worlds, all of them do not experience the world the same way. Each creature, being subject to the law of coincidence (*kakataliya nyaya*),[17] creates a world according to its desires, vasanas. Because of this, there are innumerable worlds. As there is no end to the creative and imaginative power (*kalpana, sankalpa, viranchittva*) of Brahman, all sorts of unimaginable things and events happen in the universe.

Further, there are millions of universes within each universe, just as there are dreams within dreams.[18] There are huge galaxies, and each galaxy has millions of stars and planets. At the microcosmic level, there are hundreds of such worlds in each atom.[19] These worlds are governed by different physical laws, and the creatures that exist in them also have different modes of living. Some can see in the dark but not in the light. Some have no sense of smell, while others cannot hear anything. Some live on poison, and some die if they consume nectar. Some are sexless, and some are emotionless. All these worlds, however, are oblivious of each other as they are windowless. This means each individual creates a private world which is not accessible to others.[20]

Similarly, each living being exists simultaneously in different worlds at the same time.[21] They are subjects of our dreams, just as we are subjects of their dreams. Each being creates its own world according to its desires. For instance, in the Vetala story from the Yogavasishtha, it is shown that there are several worlds existing simultaneously like dreams within dreams, just as a banana stem consists of layer within layer.

What is the truth behind these illusory worlds and dreams? Although there are millions of suns and stars like dust specks in a beam of light, pure consciousness is the reality behind them, as these worlds are lit up by the light of consciousness alone.[22]

Thus, consciousness or Brahman is the one underlying unifying factor behind all these illusory universes. In truth, however, Brahman and the world are identical.

Brahman, however, is without attributes like the hollow of the banana tree;
Although there are hundreds of leaves, they are no different from the tree.[23]

WHY DOES THE WORLD APPEAR TO BE REAL

Even if we agree for a moment that the world is illusory, why does the experience of it look so real and solid? Why does it have qualia, that 'raw feeling', as modern philosophers and psychologists put it?

In the Yogavasishtha, King Shikhidwaja asks Kumbha if everything from Brahma to the pillar is an illusion, why this illusion generates sorrow.

Kumbha replies that just as hardness and dryness are not the properties of water, in extreme cold water becomes hard and appears to be dry; the same is true of the phenomenal world. It is not there but it appears to be there. Ignorance creates the illusory world and knowledge dispels it. If Brahma, the creator, is himself unreal, how can the world created by him be real? If the cause of the world does not exist, how can the effect exist? The effect that does not have a cause is nothing but an illusion, although it might appear to be real.

The world looks real because that is the nature of dream; it must look real, otherwise the dream ends. Even when we daydream, everything feels real although we are awake. To dream, two things are essential: imagination and ignorance. It must be remembered that an illusory thing can create misery for us, just as the illusory snake that we see in a rope generates fear. This is because we have taken it for granted that material objects actually exist, and the materialist would go to the extent of saying that only matter exists, as only matter can be perceived by the senses.

Vasishtha questions the very idea of calling any object 'real' or 'unreal'. He argues that all worldly objects are forever unreal (asadroopa) as well as real (sadroopa) because their reality depends upon perception. When not perceived they do not exist, and when perceived they exist.[24]

The phenomenal world depends upon the imagination (kalpana) and will (sankalpa) of the supreme primal consciousness (*samvit*). It is the inherent characteristic of consciousness. It imagines the body, and through this, everything else becomes manifested. This creates the contradictory result (*virudhaphala*) of the world being existent and non-existent at the same time.

For this reason, we experience the consciousness of the body as well as the grossness of consciousness simultaneously, as body is nothing but consciousness grossified.[25]

We shall now examine what is meant by reality in the Vedantic sense. 'Real' and 'unreal' are both relative terms. What is 'real' from the phenomenal level is 'unreal' from the transcendental and vice versa.

Vedanta says that anything that has a beginning and an end (momentary existence) is 'unreal'. When we hear the word 'momentary', we think in terms of seconds or minutes but fifty billion years is also momentary on the cosmological timescale. The technical name for momentary existence is maya. Whatever we see around us is maya because everything is changing all the time.

Maya has three properties (gunas) called sattva (purity, balance), rajas (kinesis), and tamas (inertia). The whole world is governed by these three gunas. Rajas is the dynamic quality of maya. It keeps the world and the living beings in it in a state of agitation or unrest. It makes us run after worldly objects, and keeps us involved in incessant action.

Tamas is inertia, laziness, rest. It makes us negative and generates sloth in us. Sattva is purity and balance. It binds us to good things, happiness and peace.

All the three properties are equally important and everything in the world has them in varying degrees. Anything that had only one property would perish immediately. Rajas, makes us move, but without tamas, we would go on moving endlessly, and without rajas, we would not be motivated to do anything at all. In sattva there is balanced attitude towards life.

We are told that we must rise from tamas to rajas, and then attain sattva, as the first two create bondage. The fact is that sattva also creates bondage. It makes us hanker after the good things in life. It is a better state than rajas and tamas, but it also creates bondage. It is a golden cage, but a cage nevertheless. Sattva is also part of maya. It is only after transcending all the three gunas that we attain moksha.

Maya appears different to each of us depending upon our viewpoint or level. From the transcendental level, it is not there at all; from the intellectual viewpoint, it is indefinable, and from the phenomenal viewpoint, it is real.

If all things come into existence and dissolve after a certain time as they are part of maya, there must be something 'real' behind this momentariness, otherwise change would not be possible. In fact, maya cannot exist without absolute reality, just as for a fake coin to circulate, there must be a genuine one around. Thus, maya is proof of absolute reality. A wheel cannot move without a fixed axle, a film cannot be projected without a fixed blank screen. How do we look for this unchanging reality?

The most practical thing to do would be to begin with the phenomenal universe, as we are familiar with it.

Classical Indian theorists hold that the entire world is made of five elements: earth (*prithvi*), water (*jala, apah*), fire (*agni*), air (*vayu*), and space (*akasha*).[26] All these elements are subtle, and because of this they cannot be perceived. However, when they are combined in a certain way, they give rise to multifarious phenomenal objects (see Chapter IX). In the former state they are subtle, and in the latter they are gross in varying degrees. Water, for example, is subtler than rocks, and air is subtler than water.

The gross (*sthoola*) or subtle (*sookshma*) nature of a thing depends upon its permeative quality (*vyapakata*).

Any object requires space to exist, and the amount of space required varies from one object to another, depending upon their grossness and subtleness. The grosser an object, the lesser space it occupies, and the subtler it is, the more space it occupies. Simply put, the more subtle an object, the more permeative it is.

Earth (solid matter), the grossest of all elements, is the least permeative; hence it has a relatively stable and solid form. Since the capacity of solid objects to permeate is highly restricted, they do not move or expand until external force is applied to them.

Water (liquid), the next element, is subtler than earth; hence it can penetrate the earth and co-exist with it. It can move forwards, backwards, sideways and downwards. It takes the shape of whatever it is contained in.

Fire is subtler than water, and it has an additional capacity to move upwards. As it is subtler than earth and water, its form is even more unclear, and it can permeate both earth and water. This is inferred from the fact that, upon heating, both earth and water become hot.

Air is subtler than the first three, and it permeates all of them. Being very subtle, air cannot be seen but it can be felt.

Finally, there is space, the subtlest of the elements. It is so subtle that it cannot even be felt. It permeates the first four, and all of them exist in space.

Although space is not perceivable, it is also an element. This means it also undergoes change and perishes. We infer this from the fact that in deep sleep space disappears, and so do all objects that it contains. This is the reason we do not remember anything that we have experienced in deep sleep. We shall explain in a while that space is also not absolute.

All objects that emerge from the combination of the five elements do not have the capacity to move until acted upon. What is it that acts upon them? To act upon all of them, it must be all pervasive and it must also have qualities not present in the elements.

Philosophers divide the cosmos into two kinds of things: insentient (matter) and sentient (matter plus consciousness). Insentient objects do not have the capacity to think, feel and know, whereas sentient ones do. Insentient things do not move of their own accord, but sentient ones do. This is because they possess an additional quality called consciousness. Devoid of consciousness, they too would be insentient like a dead body.

It is consciousness, the sixth factor, which acts upon matter and moves it. It is again consciousness that allows us to experience objects and talk about them. Finally, from the Vedantic perspective, it is consciousness that creates the phenomenal world.

THE VEIL OF IGNORANCE

Vedanta says that anything that has a beginning and an end (impermanent existence) is 'unreal' or 'illusory'. The technical name for illusion is maya, also known as *avidya* (ignorance), *adhyasa* (nescience,) *vismarana* (forgetfulness), and *khyati* (error). Maya is the power of absolute reality (Brahman) to create the illusory world through the three qualities of nature (*triguna*s): rajas (kinesis), tamas (inertia), and sattva (balance). Maya generates the world through its veiling power (*avarana* shakti) and projecting power (*vikshepa* shakti). It hides our true self from us and makes us think we are limited beings. It is this feeling of being limited in space, time and resources that makes us miserable.

The Cosmos: A Figment of the Imagination

Ignorance is generally understood in the negative sense of lack of knowledge. This view is not fully correct. Ignorance or nescience is negative and positive, passive and dynamic. Mere ignorance does not qualify as maya. We may be ignorant of who our parents are, or we may not know what quarks and quasars are. This is mere ignorance not maya. The blueness of the sky and the rainbow that we see so clearly are maya because they are optical illusions. They are passive maya for they do not compel us to react in any way other than perhaps to appreciate their beauty. According to Vedanta, not just rainbows and mirages, but everything in the world is illusory because we perceive the world through our senses, and senses always mislead, as they are incapable of presenting reality in its entirety. External input is infinite; the senses filter it out for us. If our ears had the capacity to hear all the sounds in the world, we would go mad. We see only a certain range of light called the visible spectrum. We do not see X-rays, Gamma rays, or Ultraviolet rays, but they pervade the whole world all the time. We may say this is a red rose, but is the rose red? It is just absorbing all other colours and reflecting red. Truly speaking, it is anything but red. The rose does not look bright red all the time; in late evening it looks darker, and at night it looks black. We call it red because we take bright daylight as standard, although we have no valid reason for accepting it as such.

To mistakenly take a rope for a snake and then run for our lives or try to kill it, is an example of the dynamic force of maya. Once we are sure it is just a rope, do we still go on running away from it? Since the fear generated in our minds after mistaking the rope for a snake arises out of ignorance, the sole purpose of Vedanta is not to teach us how to kill the snake, but how to kill ignorance. All efforts to kill the illusory snake will not only be futile, but also generate greater misery, as no amount of effort can kill an illusory snake. This is why the Yogavasishtha and Vedanta stress self-knowledge so strongly.

How does it do this?

We have discussed that all things which emerge from a combination of the five elements exist in space. The question is where does space exist? This is important, because if space also needed another space to exist, that space would need another space, and so on ad infinitum.

Space and all the objects that it contains ultimately exist in another dimension called consciousness. This is because it is consciousness that creates space. All matter exists in space, but space exists in consciousness. Without consciousness, their existence or non-existence has no meaning.

Most modern scientists hold that consciousness is a by-product of matter. Many Indian systems, on the other hand, say that matter is a by-product of consciousness.

It may be asked where consciousness exists. Who created consciousness? The word 'exist' does not apply to consciousness because consciousness is not in the domain of space, time and causality. It is consciousness that creates space–time causality. How can it be subject to them?

There is another point to be understood. Cosmologists say that there are millions of galaxies, and many more are being born, and that the entire universe is expanding at a tremendous speed. This leads us to believe that space must be infinite to accommodate this ever-expanding universe.

Suppose, for a moment, that all the galaxies disappeared. What would be left? Common sense would say infinite space would be left, just as if all furniture is taken out of a room, we would have an empty room. This view is wrong. The emptiness of the room is experienced because of the four walls and the roof. Without the walls and the roof, what can we say about the emptiness of the room?

Without objects, space collapses into nothingness. This is because, being a by-product of consciousness, space expands or contracts according to the imagination or will of the supreme conscious reality. In dreams, for instance, there can be no end to the objects we dream of. Space goes on expanding according to the number of objects we dream up. Space, in other words, is relative. When nothing is imagined, space disappears. In deep sleep, for instance, as we are not conscious, we do not will anything, so we imagine nothing. Because of this, space disappears in deep sleep. Thus, it is consciousness that creates space (*chidakasha*). Consciousness itself occupies no space.[27]

Not just space, but time is also relative according to the Yogavasishtha. Sometimes a moment stretches into an era, and there are times when eras shrink into a moment. There are, for example, several varieties of insects that die a few hours after they emerge. Those hours are a life-time for them. In the story of Gadhi, a Brahmin takes a dip in the river and experiences a long life during the few moments when his head was in the river.[28]

Many survivors of drowning accidents report that when they believed they were about to die, their entire life flashed by in a second.

Since space and time are not absolute, they are also not real in the Vedantic sense. And if space and time are both unreal, how can the objects that are supposed to exist in them be real? Everything is false and illusory. Everything is relative, so there is no universal constant except supreme consciousness.

How can we assert that consciousness is universal?

Let us begin with matter. Scientists now say that there are billions of universes and they are constantly expanding. No matter how many of them there are, and how far they expand, the consciousness of those who talk about this will always encompass them. It will also be greater because it is observing the entire expanse. The consciousness of the scientist, in this case, will always be encompassing and total. Here total means undivided or undiminished. The idea will be elaborated later.

Let us now move in another direction. Scientists also say that matter is divisible. Earlier, they were only able to divide it up to the molecular level, but now they can divide it up to quarks. There is a possibility that they may one day be able to divide it even further. No matter how much further they manage to divide matter, the consciousness of the scientist who divides it will always remain total and it will also encompass all matter.

We can take space now. We discussed that it expands or contracts according to the amount of matter. Space disappears totally in deep sleep, in coma, or when we are unconscious, but when we wake up or regain consciousness, we have memories of the past. We know that we are the same person who slept. This is because in deep sleep or coma, consciousness does not disappear. However, we do not remember anything as there is nothing to remember. Deep sleep and coma are states in which there is no subject–object duality. Because of this there is no experience, and as there is no experience, there can be no memory of it. There is no experience because the ego is nearly dormant in these states. Without an ego, experience is not possible.

We now come to consciousness itself. Can it be multiplied, divided or changed in any way? When we were children, our bodies were small, and the intellect was not fully developed, but our consciousness of our own selves was total. Now as adults, we have larger bodies; our intellect may have developed but consciousness has not grown with the body and intellect. It has remained as total as it was when we were children. Even if we lose a limb or two, there will be no reduction in our consciousness.

What about deep sleep, unconscious state and coma? In these states, it is the mind and the body that sleep or become unconscious, not consciousness itself. This is why, when we return to the waking state, we remember our past. Consciousness remains total even in these states. The body and senses are like a television set and consciousness is like the television signal. When the television is switched off or if it is faulty, we do not see the image, but this does not mean television signal has also gone dead.

Thus, the conscious self is always total, and it encompasses whatever we experience. It is larger than the largest thing we can imagine, and smaller than the smallest.

Tinier than the tiniest and larger than the largest, atman is situated in the cave-like heart of the individual being.[29]

Therefore, consciousness is the unchanging universal constant.

THREE STATES OF CONSCIOUSNESS

Vedanta, like other Vedic traditions, divides consciousness into waking (*jagarat*), dream (*svapna*), and deep sleep (*sushupti*). It further says that these three are interlinked, so to explain human nature and the world, we must take all three into account, otherwise we get a distorted view. Most systems the world over, however, base their explanation only on the waking state. This is not correct according to Vedanta. How can we ignore the sleeping and dreaming states which constitute nearly 50 per cent of our lives?

We may begin with waking and dream states, as we cannot say much about deep sleep. Explaining the unity between the waking state and dream state, Vasishtha says that just as the entire lotus, along with its petals, is present in the seed, the dream is an inseparable part of the supreme self. However, both states are ultimately the same.

The inner dream of the self manifests as the illusory external world,
But like milk placed in two pots, there is no difference between them.[30]

The waking world is exactly like the dream world we see.

The Yogavasishtha of Valmiki

Each person's dream world is their private creation, as others have no access to it.

Once it gets individuated, the self sees the world as a dream;
But the duality between the individual self and the other is as false as a dream.[31]

There is no difference between the dream world and the waking world;
Just as there is no difference between liquidity and water, movement and wind.[32]

Many find the dream world to be nonsensical and unreal. In the present age, until Freud, no one took the dream state seriously. Vedanta says that the dream experience is as important as the waking experience for it is as real or as unreal as the former.

No matter how many times we have dreamt in our lives, never did we believe that it was a dream. Everything looked so real, just as real as in the waking state. Only upon waking up did we realise that it was a dream. Going by this, how can we ever be sure that the state we call 'waking state' is not another dream?

We should either give the status of reality to the dream state or accept that the waking state is also another dream. Maybe what we call the 'waking state' is a dream of another state to which we will return. Do we not see dreams in a dream?

Vasishtha says it is true that the things and events of the waking state seem real to us, and the dream state unreal, but essentially both are equally unreal.[33]

Objects in a dream appear to be real because we forget the so-called waking self for a while. Similarly, once the self is known, all states become part of the self because there is nothing except the conscious self.[34]

Once the illusion of the world ends through self-knowledge, all that remains is the pure conscious self. Since that self is beyond the dimensions of space and time, we can neither say it exists nor say it does not exist. On account of this, it is said to be beyond the scope of language.[35]

Listening to these counter-intuitive statements, Rama says it is not right to say that there is no difference between the waking and dream states because when the dream ends we wake up and realise it was a dream. How does this lead us to conclude that the waking state is also a dream?[36]

Vasishtha answers this by saying that the dreamer has several experiences in a dream, interacts with relatives and friends, but after he dies in the dream, the dream ends and he comes back to the waking world. Only then does he realise that what he saw in the dream was not real. Similarly, after his death in his so-called real life, he wakes up in another world to see another dream.[37]

The one who dies in a dream, upon waking is called awake;
And who dies in the waking state is called alive in the dream state.[38]

It is generally believed that the waking world is external to us and the dream world internal. Vasishtha says this belief is also false, as even the dream world is external to the dreamer. They are both like identical twins.[39]

It is also believed that the waking and dream worlds are different because the former is longer and the latter shorter. This is also a relative experience, because in the waking state a dream seems short, but in the dream the waking life seems short.[40] We also believe that while there is continuity in the waking state, that is, after the dream ends, we wake up in the world we left before sleeping. We do not return to the dream once it ends. This is also incorrect, says Vasishtha, because after death, we do not come back to the present waking life.[41] We enter into another life, another dream, another world.

These two states are imaginary like events in a story;
And thus they serve as metaphors for each other.[42]

The Yogavasishtha of Valmiki

Although the dream world is private, individuals can enter the worlds of other individuals after self-knowledge dawns.[43] This is because it is the ego that creates a private world for us. Once the ego is vanquished through self-knowledge, all walls are torn down, and we gain access to the worlds of other individuals.

THE TROUBLE WITH SPACE, TIME AND CAUSALITY

Questions such as who created the world, how it was created, and what will happen to it in the future, arise because the mind cannot think without the categories of space, time and causality.

This was also pointed out by the German philosopher Immanuel Kant (1724-1804), who argued that our understanding of the world is structured with forms of experience and categories that give a phenomenal and logical structure to objects we experience. We cannot go beyond these categories of understanding. In other words, the world is not mind-independent. These categories are necessary for the experience and understanding of spatio-temporal objects. This means we perceive the world in a restricted way through categories of space and time. What we see is not a true picture of reality as it is beyond these categories, and because of this we will never know how things are in themselves.

Kant called the world perceived through the categories of understanding 'phenomenal', and the unknowable reality beyond these categories of understanding as 'noumenal'. For example, we see a rose as red. This is because we are experiencing it through the categories of understanding that mind uses. However, beyond the categories of understanding, what the rose is really like can never be known.

Let us examine the problem of causality briefly here, as it will be discussed in depth in the next chapter.

Whatever moves or transforms something is called cause, and the result is called effect. For any cause to bring about an effect, there must be space, otherwise change would be impossible. All movement and transformation require time. Thus, space, time and causality are all interlinked and inseparable.

Brahman is the cause of the world, but you cannot ask what the cause of Brahman is, as Brahman is not a part of cause–effect. If you include Brahman in cause and effect, you will have to say what the cause of Brahman is. This would lead to infinite regress.

Brahman is beyond all causality and other natural laws, so the metaphor of seed and tree does not apply to Brahman. It cannot be compared with anything because it is the conscious witness.[44]

Although the witnessing self is as vast as the sky, it cannot see itself;
Great is the illusion, the eyes can see the world but not themselves.[45]

The world may be an illusion, but why is it there in the first place? Why should the absolute non-dual reality become plural? Why should it create the mind? Such questions have been raised and answered at several places in the Yogavasishtha.

Questions such as these suggest that the absolute should have remained absolute itself. Why create plurality and the problems that arise with it?

We have already discussed that absolute means all pervasive and all knowing. It must include non-duality as well as duality, no-change as well as change. It should be perfect as well as imperfect; otherwise it would not be absolute. Absolute does not mean monotonous or static.

Vasishtha tells Rama that such questions dissolve after self-knowledge arises because then we know that the world does not really exist. At this point, the illusion of the phenomenal world ends, just as a dream ends upon waking. However, it is only ignorance that is destroyed after self-knowledge, not Brahman. Whatever we see in the world gets destroyed at the end of an aeon (*kalpa*). If with

The Yogavasishtha of Valmiki

the destruction of the phenomenal world, Brahman is also destroyed, how can we call it absolute and unending?[46]

In the same way, if we could change it or take some part out of the absolute Brahman, it would mean the absolute is no longer absolute. Thus, whatever emerges from it has to be absolute. When we say the world 'emerges' from Brahman, it gives an impression of Brahman as one entity, with the world coming out of it like a sprout. Truly speaking, if Brahman is all pervading, how can we speak of anything emerging or coming out of it?

Imagine we are in the deep sea. We can take some water out of it and throw it on the shore, but deep down what would be the meaning of taking some water and placing it elsewhere? No matter how hard we tried, the amount we moved would still be part of the sea, hence total.

DISSOLUTION OF THE WORLD

Any discussion about the creation of the world would be incomplete without talking about its dissolution. Whatever comes into existence must necessarily go out of existence at some point.

According to the scriptures, dissolution of the world is of four kinds: diurnal, natural, occasional and absolute.

We experience diurnal dissolution (*nitya pralaya*) every day in deep sleep. All our joys, sorrows, tensions and conflicts dissolve for a few hours. However, in deep sleep bodily functions such as respiration and blood circulation continue. Although we forget the conflicts of our waking state in sleep, their impressions remain. This is why upon waking, we remember what we did the previous day.

When the effect of the karmas of the past ends, it is called natural dissolution (*prakrit pralaya*). When Brahma dissolves its creation, it is called occasional dissolution (*naimittika pralaya*). Absolute dissolution (*turiya pralaya*) happens when one gains self-knowledge, achieves moksha, and becomes free of the cycle of birth and death.

In the same way, each individual creature, each particle that we see is nothing but absolute as it is within the absolute.

From absolute emerges absolute, and being a part of it, it is also absolute,
The world was never created, and whatever appears to be created is
absolute itself.[47]

The upshot is that causality applies only to the world of the imagination, but it does not apply to the one who imagines it, i.e., Brahman, the absolute.

This leads us to a paradoxical situation: consciousness or Brahman, which is real, is without a cause, and the world which is an illusion, is subject to causality.

In such a situation, is there any point in asking who created the world, as Brahman and the world are one and the same? The seeming difference is created out of ignorance. If the phenomenal world were different from Brahman, it would mean the world is outside Brahman. In that case there would be two domains: Brahman and the world. Then we would have to accept duality. If this is accepted then we cannot say that Brahman is absolute and all-pervading. Vedanta does not accept this view. For it, whatever there is, is Brahman alone.

Once self-knowledge dawns, we realise that in the ultimate sense the world never was, never is and can never be. It is just a figment of the imagination. It is just a thought.[48]

There is nothing that holds the world, neither any subject nor any object;
Neither is there any cosmos nor its creator, not even the disputatious.[49]

But the disputatious will never be convinced so easily, which is why in the next chapter we deal with the problem of causality, using rigorous logic alone.

ENDNOTES

1. English theologian, William Paley (1743-1805) argued in *Natural Theology: or, Evidences of the Existence and Attributes of the Deity, Collected from the Appearances*

of Nature, first published in 1802, that the nature of God could be understood by reference to His creation, the natural world. A watch, for instance, does not get assembled accidentally. It is designed and made by someone, and if it is designed, it means it has a purpose. Living organisms, he reasoned, are even more complicated than watches. Only an intelligent designer could have created them, just as only an intelligent watchmaker can make a watch. Thus, design implies there should be a designer, and that designer, Paley concluded, is God.

2. Rig Veda, Mandalam, X:129:6
3. Rig Veda, Mandalam, X:129:7
4. Param (ultimate) + atman (self) = Paramatman
5. VIB:149:16; From the absolute perspective, the phenomenal world does not exist at all; Because that which illuminates the presence and absence of things can itself never be non-existent. Ashtavakra Gita, VIII:4)
6. VIB:25:1
7. The Brihadaranyaka Upanishad, I:V:12
8. The Amritabindu Upanishad, Mantra 2
9. Jyotirbindu Upanishad, Mantra 6; According to Samkhya philosophy the entire creation (prakriti) is governed by three properties (gunas): sattva, rajas, and tamas. Sattva is balance, order, or purity, rajas stands for change, movement or dynamism, and tamas signifies darkness, inertia, and lethargy.
10. III:3:34
11. III:64:25
12. VIB:186:65
13. Other words used are: pulsates, vibrates, imagines, dreams, and creates.
14. III:100:25
15. VIB:136:22-26
16. IV:18:17
17. The law of coincidence (kakataliya nyaya) will be explained in the next chapter.
18. VIB:176:1-25
19. See Pashanopakhyana, VIB:58:1-23, VIB:59:1-63
20. VIB:63:13-19; Readers might compare this with the concept of 'monads' which was formulated by the German philosopher, Gottfried Wilhelm von Leibniz (1646-1716). His monads are independent entities that have no windows through which something can enter or leave.
21. Contemporary physicists also speak of parallel universes, multiverses or meta-universes. These universes are a hypothetical set of possible universes including the one we live in.
22. VIA:70:1-18; VIA:71:1-21; VIA:72:1-11
23. IV:18:18
24. The Anglo-Irish philosopher, George Berkeley (1685–1753) advanced a similar theory called 'immaterialism' or 'subjective idealism'. He held that objects like

tables and chairs are merely ideas in the minds of perceivers. They exist only when they are perceived, and do not when not perceived.

25. VIB:195:1-70

26. From pre-Socratic times, the Greeks also held the view that the universe was made of earth, water, air, fire, and the aether.

27. Swami Bhoomananda discusses this in detail in his book *Quietitude of the Mind: Its Science and Practice*, Narayanasrama Thapovanam, Trichur, 1985, p 266-269 and 193-196 in the 2010 edition.

28. V:44:1-40

29. The Shwetashvatara Upanishad, III:20; the same verse is also in the Katha Upanishad, I:2:20

30. VIB:31:32

31. III:1:4, see also Tripura Rahasya, Chapter XIII

32. III:57:47

33. VIB:31:33

34. VIB:31:34

35. VIB:31:36

36. VIB:105:19

37. VIB:105:20-28

38. VIB:105:29

39. VIB:161:27

40. VIB:165:5

41. VIB:165:7-8

42. VIB:105:31

43. IV:18:3

44. IV:18:25

45. IV:18:29

46. VIB:52:1-10

47. III:10:29; There is a similar verse in the Brihadaranyaka Upanishad (V:1:1) which says: That which is absolute and whole, from it only the absolute arises When the whole is taken out of the whole, the whole still remains.(I:1)

48. It is interesting to note what Sir James Jeans, the British astronomer, wrote in 1932: 'Today there is a wide measure of agreement, which on the physical side of science approaches almost to unanimity, that the stream of knowledge is heading towards a non-mechanical reality; the universe begins to look more like a great thought than like a great machine. Mind no longer appears as an accidental intruder into the realm of matter; we are beginning to suspect that we ought rather to hail it as the creator and governor of the realm of matter–not of course our individual minds, but the mind in which the atoms out of which our individual minds have grown exist as thoughts.' (*The Mysterious Universe*, Cambridge University Press, 1932, p 186.)

49. III:13:50

CHAPTER VII

THERE CAN BE SMOKE WITHOUT FIRE

Being rational beings, it is a natural tendency among humans to look for the purpose of life and world. This is because there seems to be an order to life, and laws that govern it. It is believed that this cosmos is not chaos — there is an underlying harmony in it.

How does one find the underlying harmony in the mindboggling vastness of the world? Looking at the sheer magnitude of whatever little we see of the universe, we often wonder who made this world, why he made it, and what the cause behind this astonishing complexity is.

The 'why' question dogs our lives as no one expects things to happen without a cause. Only miracles happen without a cause, and miracles happen only in fairy tales or dreams. Modern science does not believe in miracles. It says that if something appears to happen spontaneously, it only means we do not know its cause, just as we did not know how a magnet attracts iron filings until we discovered the law of electromagnetism. Since our age is dominated by rationality and scepticism, we are trained to find an answer to the 'why' question. Until we find the answer, we remain restless.

Modern science rests on the pillars of cause and effect. Science utilises reason, mathematics and logic to explain the laws of nature, but paradoxically, if we have the courage to stretch reason and logic far enough, we land in a situation where the pillars of cause and effect become shaky and then collapse altogether. However, most of us do not have the courage or the capability to go along with logic that far, as we know it might take us into an abyss of uncertainty. We stop before things make us uncomfortable.

Some Indian thinkers took the bold step of stretching logic to its limits even if it led them to absurdity. Absurdity, they felt, was preferable to comfortable ignorance, as it is only after realising the absurdity of it all that the real meaning of life can be understood.

At this point, we might say that Indian thinkers go on reminding us that the ultimate truth is beyond the senses, language and logic. If this is so, why do they rely so heavily on logic? This is because language and logic are indispensible in communication; without them, communication is vague and confusing.

The Logic of Kanada and the Grammar of Panini are indispensable tools of every branch of inquiry.

They are, however, just tools, not an end. They ought to be given up after the goal is reached. After reaching the goal, we realise that they are nowhere near the truth, although they help us realise it.[1]

We must first understand what we mean by 'cause' (karana) and 'effect' (karya). Tarkasangrha by Annambhatta (seventh century AD), a treatise on the Nyaya-Vaisheshika school of Indian logic, defines 'cause' as something that invariably precedes an effect (karyaniyatapoorvavrittih karanam[2]). The word 'invariably' is stressed for we ought to exclude all accidental things and activities that have no significant part to play in bringing about an effect. 'Effect' can be defined as anything which had no existence before coming into being (*karyam pragabhavapratiyogi*[3]).

In Western philosophy too, 'causality' is defined as the relation between an event 'one' and an 'event two', where event two is understood as a consequence of 'event one'. Aristotle was the first in the West to write systematically on this subject. To him, finding a 'cause' of something meant trying to answer why something happened. We shall mention his ideas briefly, as his terminology is similar to the one used in Indian theories of causation.

Aristotle proposed four aspects of causation. He called the first 'material cause'. Things are made of some material; for example, a statue can be made of bronze. Here bronze is the material cause. The second is the 'formal cause'; the shape of the statue. 'Efficient cause' is the third. Since things do not appear out of the blue, there must be someone who made them. In the case of the bronze statue, the sculptor is the 'efficient cause'. Lastly, we have what is called the 'final cause'. We do not make things without a purpose. Knives are made for cutting, shoes are made to be worn, and chairs are made to be sat upon.

As mentioned already, according to the law of causality, for everything that happens, there must be a cause. The buck does not stop here because if everything must necessarily have a cause, it follows that every 'cause' must also have a cause, and that cause another cause ad infinitum. In other words, every cause itself is an effect of some previous cause which itself was an effect of a previous cause, ad infinitum. If that is the case, how can we say that 'effect' had no existence before coming into existence?

There has been a long debate among Indian theorists whether effect exists in the cause or not. Those who say that the effect does not exist in the cause are called *Asatkaryavadin*s, and those who say it does are called *Satkaryavadin*s.

According to Asatkaryavadins, if the effect already exists in the cause, to talk about it would be a redundancy.

If the pot already exists in the clay, why do we need a potter to make the pot? If the cloth already exists in the fibre, why do we need a weaver to weave it? Nyaya-Vaisheshika, Hinayana Buddhists and some Mimamsakas belong to this camp.

In opposition to this, Satkaryavadins say the effect does exist in the cause. They argue that without a material cause, a thing can never come into existence. Without the clay, the pot can never be made. Further, if the effect was not in the material cause, then anything could be the cause of anything, and anything could spring out of anything. In that case, an apple tree might grow out of a mango seed, we could get curd from water, gold from stone and milk from bulls. But we do not see this happening in real life. Satkaryavadins, therefore, conclude that cause and effect are two aspects of the same thing. Cause is nothing but an effect that has not yet manifested, and effect is a cause that is manifested. The seed is a potential tree, and the tree is a seed that has realised its potential.

Here again there are those who believe that the effect or transformation is real or actual, and those who say it is not real but apparent. The former are called *Parinamavadins* and the latter are called *Vivartavadins*. The Samkhya and Yoga schools believe that the effect is real, while Advaita Vedantins, *Shoonyavadin* Buddhists and *Vigyanavadins* believe that the effect is illusory. They believe that cause produces effect without itself undergoing any real transformation.

The Yogavasishtha, which belongs to the Advaita Vedanta school, holds the contention that not only is the effect a manifestation of the material cause, the cause is also a manifestation, an effect, of a previous cause. Hence, both the cause and effect are appearances connected through unconditionally invariable antecedence and consequence. This view is similar to that of Shoonyavada Buddhists, but according to the Shoonyavadins, the appearance called 'cause' must totally cease to exist before the appearance called 'effect' jumps into momentary existence.

This seemingly small technical difference between Vedantins and Shoonyavadins leads them to a totally different world view, mode of living and way of dealing with the phenomenal world.

Advaita Vedanta strongly opposes Shoonyavada because according to Advaita Vedanta, appearances are not the appearance of 'nothingness' (shoonya) but rather of 'something' that underlies all appearances. 'Appearance' is technically called maya or mithya (illusion, unreal) by Vedantins. They argue that it is impossible for an illusion to arise without something real behind it. We see the waters of a mirage only because there is real water on earth. We might see a rope in a snake only because there are snakes in the world. Appearances, therefore, presuppose an underlying reality. This underlying entity or substance, called 'Brahman', is the cause of all changes or effects that we see, but it itself does not undergo any change. What this leads to is that the effect is a mere appearance; it is not a real change from the absolute underlying reality called Brahman. This view of Advaita Vedanta is called Vivartavada. The word *vivarta* in this context means something illusory, apparent, changing, fleeting or seeming.

We might consider a few other schools before coming back to the Yogavasishtha. *Svabhavavada*, or innatism, believes that things are as their intrinsic nature made them. It acknowledges the universality of causation, but traces all changes to the thing itself to which they belong. The cosmos is not chaos, but there is no external principle governing it. The phenomenal world is self-determined. Advaita Vedanta acknowledges this view but goes further.

Another school, called *Adrishtavada* (*adrishta* means unseen), believes that everything happens because of an unseen supernatural agency. Opposed to this are those who we might call the 'spontaneitists' or 'accidentalists', and they are represented by the Charvaka school, the Indian materialists, who dismiss anything that is not perceivable by the senses. They do not believe in God or any supernatural agency. Because causation implies an entity behind it, they do not accept it, saying that everything happens spontaneously.

Yadricchavada and *Animittavada* also contend that all this mindboggling complexity is without a cause.

We shall later see that Advaita Vedanta also denies causation, meaning things happen spontaneously, but they are philosophically opposed to the materialists.

Lastly, we touch upon yet another Buddhist theory called *Pratityasamutpada*, which could be roughly translated as 'dependent origination' or 'dependent arising'. This school says that there are multiple causes and conditions behind whatever happens in the world. Nothing exists as a singular, independent entity. A traditional example used in Buddhist texts is of three sticks standing upright and leaning against each other, supporting each other. If one stick is taken away, the other two will fall to the ground.

THE CAUSATION SYNDROME

The problem with causality is that no matter what view you take, if you go along with your own argument to its conclusion, you end up in trouble. Most of the time we walk along only until it is convenient. We do not have the temerity to walk to the edge of the precipice.

Gaudapadacharya[4], Shankaracharya's guru's guru, showed that causality is useful for pragmatic purposes, but if it is examined thoroughly, it leads us into absurdity. He is mentioned here because, like the Yogavasishtha, he holds the view that the world has no cause; hence you cannot ask how it was created. The world

The Yogavasishtha of Valmiki

was never created; it is eternal. This view, as we discussed in the Introduction, is called Ajativada.

Gaudapada strongly argued in favour of Ajativada in Gaudapada Karika, also known as Mandookya Karika.[5] It is a sort of commentary on the Mandookya Upanishad. Gaudapada Karika is generally regarded as the first known philosophical exposition of Advaita Vedanta and Ajativada. In it, Gaudapada argues that if you take causality seriously, you end up with the conclusion that the theory of causality is untenable, and that the phenomenal world is an illusion. In other words, it has no independent existence of its own. This view is called Ajativada, which is generally translated as theory of no-origination. Some people are misled by the word 'no-origination'. They think it means something that does not exist. We must be careful to make a distinction between non-existence and no-origination. 'Non-existence' means a thing never existed. For example, as far as we know, flying horses and Centaurs do not exist.

'No-origination', on the other hand, means a thing was never born or created. It means it exists always (eternal). Only a thing that perishes can be said to have been born. The world has no origin because it was always there (eternal).

In Vedanta, the word 'asti' (to exist or to be) is used in a special way, and not in the way we say a table exists or a tree exists, although in general parlance it could be used that way too. The word 'exist' in the Vedantic parlance means something that is present in three periods of time: past, present and future. It means a thing was always there in the past, is there now, and will be there forever. In other words, something that is eternal.

The table that we see did not exist before it was made, and it will cease to exist after it gets destroyed. Even during the time it has its so-called existence, it goes on changing. Its existence is, therefore, temporary, and in Vedanta anything that has a temporary existence is considered to be *asat* (false, untrue, illusory).

The Sanskrit word *aja* means that which exists always or that which is eternal (That which is unborn, eternal, free of distortions and ever-new).[6] All things in the world are born, and are bound to perish sooner or later. But 'aja' means something that exists always; in other words, it was never created, and by the same logic, it will never perish. We shall discuss Ajativada in some detail as that is also the fundamental contention of the Yogavasishtha.

The fundamental argument of Ajativada, no-origination, is that anything that exists cannot have something non-existent as its cause. In simpler terms, nothing can come out of nothing. A tree cannot grow out of a seed that does not exist. The existent cannot be the effect of something non-existent, and the existent cannot be an effect of the existent. Although all this may sound confusing, we can follow the argument if we progress step by step.

Gaudapada knows that it is normal for people to believe in causation and creation, but he tries to show that if causation is critically examined, it collapses under its own weight. However, to participate in the affairs of the world, it is necessary to uphold causation, otherwise we become unsure, confused and unable to get on with our lives.

Gaudapada begins by saying that those who argue for or against origination should be treated as friends, as they actually end up proving the idea of no-origination (Ajativada).[7]

Arguing against those who believe that the order of cause and effect can change, he says that if that is the case we will be faced with the situation where son might be the cause of the birth of his father.[8]

To those who believe in serial cause and effect, he asks them to clearly state the order in which cause and effect arise.

Further, if it is said that cause and effect originate simultaneously, there can be no mutual connection between them, just as the left horn of a cow is not the cause of its right horn. The horns of a cow grow simultaneously, but one is not the cause of the other.[9] If the cause is produced from an effect how can we claim it is a cause? And how can the cause that is not itself established be said to be the producer of the effect?[10]

Gaudapada says, suppose we accept that the cause emerges from the effect and the effect emerges from the cause, which of the two arises first, and on which does the emergence of the other depend?[11] If the upholders of causation do not satisfactorily answer this question, it is tantamount to ignorance of the order of succession. Since no school of thought can establish this, no-origination is the only conclusion: the world is just an imagination of Brahman, and to talk of causation in absolute Brahman is meaningless. When we wake from a dream, do we ask why certain things happened in the dream? Says Gaudapada:

The incapability of proving the order of cause and effect;
No-origination has been proclaimed by the wise.[12]

When people talk about cause and effect, they cite the example of seed and sprout (or tree). Which came first: the seed or the sprout? Gaudapada argues that the seed–sprout (cause–effect) relationship is of equivalence, and if the cause is equivalent to the effect, it is of no use in proving anything.[13] Seed and sprout are equivalent because a seed is nothing but a potential tree, just as a child is nothing but a potential adult. Do we ask which came first, the child or the adult?

If we accept that cause and effect are equivalent or identical, then one cannot be the cause of the other, and if we say they are not identical, then we would have to prove how an unidentical thing can produce something different from it. It is a law of nature that a mango tree cannot grow out of an apple seed.

Further, the seed that we have now can neither be called non-eternal nor eternal because, in both cases, the relationship of equivalence becomes established.

Suppose we say the seed is non-eternal; what happens? As we

know the present seed came from a certain sprout or tree, the sprout that would grow out of it would also be considered non-eternal, as an eternal thing cannot come out of a non-eternal thing. If we take the sequence backwards, it would amount to the same. The present seed came from a sprout which was non-eternal, and it came from a seed that was again non-eternal like the present seed. We could go back endlessly but the same argument would hold. This forces us to conclude that both seed and sprout are non-eternal. In other words, their relationship is of equivalence. According to the law of causation, there cannot be a cause–effect relationship between equivalent things.

On the other hand, if we hold that the seed–sprout relationship is eternal, they cannot be the cause of one another, as both are eternal and therefore the relationship between them is once again of equivalence. Since both are similar in this aspect — eternal — there cannot be a causal relationship between them. Gaudapada says:

Inability to establish antecedence and succession of causality proves no-origination;
Because if the effect (world) were truly existent, why would we not find its cause.[14]

A cause cannot be born out of an effect that is eternal;
Similarly, an effect cannot be born of a cause that is eternal.[15]

Thus, nothing is ever born either from itself or something else.[16] In his commentary on Gaudapada Karika, Shankaracharya explains this point further by saying that a thing that is said to exist cannot be said to have been born because only that can be said to exist which exists in the three periods of time (past, present, future), according to the scriptural definition. Such a thing is never born and never does it die, because it is eternal. If a thing does not exist, it can never come into existence, as it never existed in the first place like the horns of a hare.[17]

The Yogavasishtha of Valmiki

The Yogavasishtha is in agreement with Gaudapada, except that its canvas is much wider. While the Gaudapada Karika is a very short and telegraphic treatise consisting of only 215 verses, the Yogavasishtha is a gigantic tome, running into 23,734 verses. They both give thorough arguments, but while Gaudapada Karika is very logical, terse and brief, the Yogavasishtha is logical, poetic and voluminous.

It must be pointed out here that the concept of no-origination is not peculiar to the Yogavasishtha. We see similar views in other scriptures and schools, although they are articulated differently, according to their own epistemological and metaphysical positions. Most of these theories are called theories of illusion (maya) or theories of error (khyati). They are also called theories of superimposition (adhyasa).[18]

Since the question about causality ultimately takes us back to how this world was created, the question arises whether the cause (the creator) of creation is absolute or non-absolute. If it is absolute, this means it cannot change; hence it cannot be a cause for anything. If it is non-absolute (limited), this means it has parts. A thing that is limited means it is gross, and if it is gross it means it changes, and if it changes means it has parts. And if it has parts, we have to determine which particular part is the cause of creation.

For example, in the creation of a pot, is it the solidity of the clay that is the cause or the form of the pot? Is the kneading of the clay the cause? The solidity of the clay cannot be the cause, as it itself undergoes change. The form of the pot cannot be the cause, as this would mean it is the cause of itself. The kneading of the clay cannot be considered the cause either, because this follows the first two. Further, if you consider the kneading of the clay to be absolute (non-dynamic), kneading becomes unchangeable (*kootastha*), therefore, it cannot be the cause. If you consider it to be dynamic, we would see pots being made everywhere all the time, as kneading would be present all the time and everywhere.[19]

NAGARJUNA ON CAUSALITY

Like Gaudapada, the Madhyamaka Buddhism exponent Nagarjuna also refutes causality in Moolamadhyamaka Karika and Vigrahavyavartanee.

Nothing whatsoever arises, not from itself, not from another, not from both itself and another, and not without a cause. (I:1) He argues further:

There are just four conditions of existence of anything: efficient cause, supporting condition, precipitating condition and dominant condition.

Among the four conditions of the existence of a thing, there is found no substantial essence of the thing. If things have no substantial essences, then there can be no real relations between different things.

There are no causes with conditions; there are no causes without conditions. There are no conditions without causes; there are no conditions with causes.

Things arise from conditions, but if there is no arising, aren't conditions not conditions?

There are no conditions of existing things, nor are there conditions of that which does not exist. How can the non-existent have a condition? If something exists, does it need a condition?

If there are no existents, nor non-existents, nor existent non-existents, how can there be any causes? If there were a cause, what would it cause?

If there are events (for example, mental states) without supporting conditions, why should we speak of supporting conditions at all?

If things do not begin to exist, then they cannot cease to exist. If things do not begin to exist, how can they have precipitating conditions? If something has ceased to exist, how can it be a cause of anything else?

If things have no substantial essences, then they have no real existence; and, in that case, the statement, 'This is the cause or condition of that,' is meaningless.

An effect cannot be found in a single cause or condition, nor can an effect be found in all causes and conditions together. How can something not be found in causes and conditions arise from them?

> **If an effect arises from causes or conditions** in which it does not pre-exist, then couldn't it arise from no causes or conditions at all?
>
> **If an effect is created by its conditions**, but the conditions are not self-created, how could the effect ever come to be?
>
> **Therefore, effects cannot arise from causes or conditions**, nor can they arise from non-causes or non-conditions. If there are no effects whatsoever, how can there be any causes or conditions.
>
> *Courtesy: George Cronk © 1998*

As far as the Yogavasishtha is concerned, Brahman is absolute; in other words, without parts.

Listening to this, Rama says that if Brahman is absolute, it means it is perfect, and if it is perfect, it cannot undergo any change. If this is the case, how did the world come into existence from Brahman?

If no creation and modification is possible in Brahman;
How does the existent and non-existent become manifested?[20]

This is a natural question. If ultimate reality is absolute and unchanging, how did this world come about? To explain this, Vasishtha takes up the nature of effect first, and says that effect (change) is brought about in five different ways.

The first way an effect is brought about is when the cause or the first state is destroyed totally just as when milk turns into curd. In this case, the change is irreversible, as we cannot turn curd back into milk.

Irreversible modification means it is not possible to revert to the original state;
Just as milk undergoes a change after becoming curds, dear son.[21]

The emergence of the world from the absolute cannot be considered of this kind, as it would mean Brahman is not absolute, and the definition of Brahman is that it is without a beginning, middle or end;

hence, it is immutable.[22] This would also mean that Brahman and the individual are no longer one and the same. And if the creation of the world from Brahman is irreversible, it means liberation (moksha) is not possible. We would never regain our state of pure bliss.

What kind of change is brought about in Brahman to create the world? Let us examine four other ways in which things can be modified.

The second way the effect is brought about occurs when the cause or first state becomes restricted. For example, a pot that is made of clay undergoes a change but we still recognise that it is made of clay. The clay it was made from was soft, while the pot is solid, as it is baked. But the change is not total. The clay has retained some of its original characteristics, otherwise we would not realise that the pot is made of clay.

The third way an effect is brought about happens when the original state undergoes a change, just as when water turns into ice. Ice looks and feels different from water, but it turns back into water when it melts.

The fourth way is when the earlier state does not get hidden, just as when waves are seen, water is also seen. The fifth occurs when the earlier state becomes hidden, just as the rope gets hidden when we take it for a snake.

In these examples, only in the case of milk turning into curds is the change permanent. In all other cases, the change is not total or permanent. For the purposes of Advaita Vedanta, in the case of the rope and snake, the change is only illusory. No change has been brought about. We are just cognising the rope wrongly. The snake that we see in its place is illusory. The snake got created without the rope undergoing any change, and this change was brought about by our own faulty cognition.

The Yogavasishtha of Valmiki

Vasishtha says that the change brought about in the creation of the world is of the fifth kind, in which the world is an illusion, because there can be no change in absolute Brahman.[23] Since it is an illusion, we cannot assign any cause to it except faulty perception.

In the absence of a cause the world can never be said to have come into existence
Because the effect never comes into being in the absence of a cause.[24]

It is one thing to disprove the creation of the world through logic, but doing so does not convince us, as we certainly do live in a world whose reality cannot be denied. Do we not see things and feel them? How can anyone say that the mountains, plains, sea, buildings and people are an illusion? Rama naturally asks:

How does the world of the seeing subject and the seen object become apparent?[25]

To answer this, Vasishtha says that if this phenomenal world is taken to be existent, it would mean it came into existence at some point in time and will get destroyed at some future point in time. If before the creation there was nothing, then how did this world come to be created, as nothing can come out of nothing? If before the creation, there was something, then we have to concede that the world is eternal. By the same logic, if after the total annihilation of the cosmos nothing remains, how will the next creation begin? Obviously, something is there before and after the creation. This something is the absolute Brahman, which is formless, without parts and timeless.

Furthermore, according to the laws of causality, an effect can never be brought about by a cause in isolation. For example, to create a pot, the potter himself is not enough; he needs clay, a potter's wheel, water and other things. These are called contributory (*sahakari*) causes. But if before the creation of the world only Brahman existed and nothing else, it means no other cause existed except Brahman. In that case, how did Brahman produce anything? Therefore, nothing can ever be produced.

In the absence of a contributory cause, cause and effect are not different;
Therefore the illusory world is not different from the absolute.[26]

The creatures that are born out of that non-dual pulsation;
In absence of contributory causes, cannot be different from it.[27]

Vasishtha says that, in the absence of contributory or secondary causes, a belief in the creation of the world is like talking about the daughter of a barren woman.[28] If you say that the world was created without contributory causes, you have to accept that the efficient cause of the world itself has manifested as the illusory world.[29] If before creation, formless Brahman remains in its own state, where is the question of the creator and the created?[30]

If there is a seed we can talk about cause and effect;
In the formless, how can there be seed and the order of birth and death?[31]

Cause and effect are not two separate processes but two aspects of the same process.

There is no difference between seed and sprout, fire and heat;
Understand seed to be the sprout and karma to be the man.[32]

Causeless Brahman appears as phenomenal world to the uninformed;
And they alone are deluded by the laws of cause and effect.[33]

Thus, the entire causal phenomenal world;
Exists for the one who takes it to exist.[34]

The conclusion of this argument generates fear in the minds of the weak. It is for this reason that Gaudapada says that the wise preach the doctrine of origination (creation) for those who contend that things exist, because such people are afraid of the idea of no-origination.[35]

ORDER IN THE COSMOS

If the phenomenal world is just an imagination of Brahman, why do we see so much order in it? Why do the stars go about their paths? Why do seasons change? Why is nature the way it is? There must be a reason or purpose for it.

Rama asks if this dreamlike world arises out of Brahman without any cause, and if all other objects can also arise without any cause, why do crops not grow without a cause? That is, without ploughing the fields and planting seeds. Vasishtha says, the way a particular world is imagined, it becomes subject to unbreakable laws (cause and effect) because, without these imagined laws of causality, their creation cannot even be imagined. The way the mind imagines a thing, it is experienced accordingly.[36] Just as the people in the home of our imagination live according to our imagination, so do the beings and objects exist according to the imagination of Brahman. Natural laws are not universal; they are different in each universe.[37]

Whatever the purified mind wills becomes likewise immediately;
Just as flowing water turns into a whirlpool.[38]

Everything in existence has a reason, but existence (the absolute Brahman) itself has no reason, so we cannot ask who created it. Brahman is both infinite and finite, whole and part, both cause and effect. All talk of the cause of the absolute Brahman is meaningless because the absolute was neither created, nor can it be destroyed. We may call it ever-existent or eternal, although these terms are also misleading because no word can describe it.

As Brahman encompasses everything, there is no possibility of any change in it or the possibility of taking any part out of it. It is not possible, for example, to take some space out of space and place it elsewhere. To do this, we would need space again, which is impossible. We can cite the example of infinity. We cannot take anything out of the infinite, because if it were possible, the infinite would not remain infinite. What emerges from the infinite has to be infinite.

THE QUESTION OF PURPOSE

We have argued that it is natural for us to assume that all things must necessarily have a cause, and if things have a cause, they must also have a purpose. Thus, if the world has a cause, it must also have a purpose. Vedanta says that this world was not created for a purpose, because if we say that there is a purpose behind it, there must be a cause, and that cause must have another cause.

Vedanta says that the world is just a game (*kreeda, leela*) of the supreme self, and no game can be played without rules. This is why we have laws of nature, otherwise the game of the supreme self would collapse.

Karma, causality, destiny and fate are all imagined concepts and not ultimately real. Whatever happens in the world cannot be explained by any kind of logic. But if this is the case, we might ask how the world is governed. There must be laws behind the order we observe in nature. The scriptures say that no one ever knows or will ever know how it is governed, but it goes on all the same, according to the law of coincidence (kakataliya nyaya). '*Kaka*' means 'crow', '*tala*' means 'palm tree' and '*nyaya*' here means analogy.

It is said that a crow perched itself on a palm tree at the same time as the fruit was falling. There were certain pundits who happened to be watching this event, and soon they started giving reasons to explain the event. One said the fruit fell down because the crow perched on the tree. Another said that it was because the fruit was falling that the crow perched on the tree; someone else said that there was neither crow nor fruit, nor even a tree. He said they were imagining them, so the question of cause was meaningless.

The Yogavasishtha says that there was no connection between the crow perching on the tree and the fruit falling down. These were two events which happened independently of each other. Things happen in this world without any connection with each other, but we try to impose causal laws upon them, as the intellect cannot function otherwise.

Without a reason and without any desire, everything goes on happening
According to the law of coincidence just as whirlpool forms in water
effortlessly.[39]

The illusory world comes into existence, because of the law of coincidence
Like a mirage and the illusion of seeing two moons, it gains its illusory
existence.[40]

All things come into existence without a cause and
As they are without a cause, they cannot be said to exist.[41]

Non-existent like horns of a hare and the water of a mirage
Never found in the light of knowledge, how can there be a cause of the world?[42]

Those who look for the cause for the horns of a hare are like those
Who try to sit on the shoulders of a barren woman's grandson.[43]

CAUSAL RELATIONSHIP

Causal relationship between things and events can be of several kinds, according to Naiyayika theorists. One of these is *samavaya sambandha* or inseparable inherence. This is the relationship that exists between the whole and its parts, the qualified and its essential qualities, the agent and his activity, the genus and the species. The relationship between a tree and its branches, fire and heat is of this type.

The second kind is called *samyoga sambandha*, incidental relationship, such as that of a table and the material it is made of. A table can be made of any material, such as wood, steel or plastic. The material used is incidental.

Other than this, there is also *adhyasa sambandha* — superimposed or illusory relationship, which occurs when we take a rope for a snake or nacre for silver. The relationship between Brahman and the world is of this kind — it is illusory.

Although the Yogavasishtha and Gaudapada refute causality like the Charvakas, they are philosophically poles apart. Charvakas believe in matter alone. They rely totally on sensory perception and deny the existence of the mind and consciousness. To them, consciousness is an illusory by-product of matter. Shoonyavada Buddhism also refutes causality, using the dialectical method.

Vedanta in general and the Yogavasishtha and Gaudapada in particular hold that consciousness is the only reality and matter is an illusory by-product of it. The world comes into existence because of consciousness. In other words, the phenomenal world has no independent existence. It is just an imagination of the supreme consciousness. Its reality is only as good as the reality of a dream.

Vasishtha says that this proves that Brahman is neither the efficient nor the material cause of anything.[44] If there is an effect, there can be a cause, but that which is absolute has no causality, so how can it be the cause of anything?[45] It is only because of maya that we think the world arises.

The supreme consciousness (the supreme self) is the cause of all causes, but is itself not the effect of any cause. Vasishtha says that those who try to find the cause of Brahman are wasting their effort, because when cause and effect are both within Brahman, it is foolish to talk about cause and effect.[46]

So far Gaudapada and Vasishtha have been talking about the unreality of the so-called physical universe. Now they extend the logic to the mind itself. We shall first take up what Gaudapada says about mind.

The mind does not come in contact with objects or their appearances;
As the objects do not exist and appearance of objects is no different from mind.[47]

The mind cannot come in contact with anything external. But we certainly touch things in the world, and surely our hands get burnt when we touch fire. This can be countered by saying that even in a dream we touch things and our hands get burnt in fire, but can we consider these experiences to be real? No, because upon waking we find that our hands never touched anything. However, it is the nature of the mind that it can see things that do not exist at all. This is because absolute consciousness has unlimited powers of imagination. The mind itself is part of that imagination. Hence it, too, does not have real existence.

Thus the mind is never born, nor the things that it cognises;
Those who take it to be real are like those who see footprints of birds in the sky.[48]

Vasishtha continues by arguing that this means that the waking state is as false as the dream state. The body that goes about doing things in a dream cannot be considered to be real, because at the same time, there is a body of the waking state lying in the bed. Just as the body in the dream is considered to be unreal, the body in the waking state is also unreal, and the phenomenal world, too, is unreal.[49]

No matter how many times we may have dreamt in our lives, everything looks real in the dream and other states false, and in the waking state the dream looks false. In this case, what grounds do we have to insist that only the waking state is real?

Other than their spatial location, the objects of the waking state too are unreal;
Just as they are unreal in a dream, they are unreal in the waking state too.[50]

Vasishtha says that which appears to be stable is called the waking state, and that which appears to be unstable is called the dream state. If the dream is taken to be real, it is as good as the waking state, and if we experience the waking state as unstable, it is as good as a dream.[51]

Except for the appearance of stability and instability, there is no difference between waking and dream states, as the experience of both is always similar.[52]

Hindu philosophers talk of three states of consciousness: waking, dream and deep sleep. This is called *avasthatraya*. Most of us take the waking state to be real and others to be false, but this thinking is flawed. A world view that considers only the waking state is incomplete and misleading because we sleep and dream nearly half of our lives. How can we ignore the other two states, and take only the waking state to be real?

These three states do not succeed each other in time as is normally thought, and they also do not exist in the same place as they have their own order of space and time. The waking and dream states have separate space and time scales, and in deep sleep both space and time disappear. Hence, it is not correct to assume that the same ego operates in waking and dream states. Waking and dream states have their own independent egos, which is why often in dream we do things which our waking ego would not permit.

The dream state appears false only upon waking. While we are dreaming, it is as real as the waking state. In sleep there is absence of the ego. This is the reason we do not remember anything about it upon waking. In the absence of the ego, the subject–object distinction is lost. Because of this, we experience nothing, and without experience there can be no memory.

These three states have independent parallel existences, and they do not overlap each other. For example, I might say I woke up at seven in the morning, had breakfast at eight, went to work at nine, came back and had dinner at eight, went to sleep at eleven, had dreams, went into deep sleep, and woke up the next morning at seven. There seems to be a sequence of events until I went to sleep, but what happened after sleep cannot be considered to be a part of the same waking experience. This is because the waking state ceased before the sleep state, and it was absent until the morning. Therefore, it is wrong to speak of waking, dreaming and deep sleep as occurring serially. However, we are able to speak about these three experiences because although the ego in them is different, the witnessing consciousness in all three states is the same. It is neither dynamic nor static. It is beyond all states: it is the unchanging and uninvolved witness of all states. All states arise out of the vibration of consciousness. All states are equally false or illusory; only the witnessing conscious is real.

This is what both Vasishtha and Gaudapada argue. The phenomenal world seemingly grows out of the pulsation or vibration of the absolute consciousness. It lasts as long as the vibration continues, and disappears when the vibration stops. There is no question of causation in it, as it is illusory. It is not surprising that both Vasishtha and Gaudapada use the metaphor of a burning torch to explain how this worldly illusion is created.

At night, when we move a burning torch in circular or zigzag motion, we see circular or zigzag forms. These forms exist only as long as we go on moving the torch. When we do not move the torch, the forms disappear. Vasishtha says:

Just as rings of fire are seen when a burning torch is moved in the dark;
The world too appears when the mind vibrates, and disappears when it does not.[53]

Gaudapada echoes the same metaphor.

Like the illusion created by the circular or irregular motion of a burning torch;
Vibration of consciousness creates the illusion of the subject and object.[54]

Just as the stationary torch does not create the illusion
When the consciousness does not vibrate, the illusion of the world disappears.[55]

Having examined the nature of causation, and its relationship with matter and mind, we are now better prepared to examine the questions that deal with personal identity, mind, human action, karma and final liberation.

ENDNOTES

1. Ludwig Wittgenstein says at the end of *The Tractatus Logico Philsophicus*: My propositions are elucidatory in this way: he who understands me finally recognises them as nonsensical, when he has climbed out through them, on them, over them. (He must, so to speak, throw away the ladder, after he has climbed on it.) He must transcend these propositions and then he will see the world aright. (6.54)
2. Tarkasangrha, 24
3. Tarkasangrha, 25
4. As in the case of Shankaracharya, there is no general agreement about when Gaudapada lived. Going by various scholars, he could have lived anytime between 300 and 820 AD.
5. At one time this was also known as Agamashastra.
6. The Bhagavad Gita, II:20
7. Gaudapada Karika, IV:4
8. Gaudapada Karika, IV:15
9. Gaudapada Karika, IV:16
10. Gaudapada Karika, IV:17
11. Gaudapada Karika, IV:18
12. Gaudapada Karika, IV:19 (The word 'buddha' means the one who knows, but here it is used with an inflection that indicates it is used as a plural noun in the third vibhakti: 'buddhaih', which generally means 'by the enlightened persons' or 'by the wise men'. As Ajativada resembles no-origination of the Buddhists, some of the early Tibetan Buddhist scholars assumed that Gaudapada was a Buddhist. Gaudapada, however, makes it clear that he is not a Buddhist, and that belongs to the Vedantic tradition.)
13. Gaudapada Karika, IV:20
14. Gaudapada Karika, IV:21
15. Gaudapada Karika, IV:23
16. Gaudapada Karika, IV:22
17. 'Rabbits have no horns' is a Sanskrit metaphor to talk about a non-existent thing.
18. The theory of the Apprehension of Subjective Cognition of the Yogachara School is called *atma-akhyati*. The Buddhist nihilistic Madhyamika theory is called *asat-khyati*; that is, apprehension of the non-existent, shoonya. Prabhakara theory talks about non-apprehension (*akhyati*), Nyaya talks about misapprehension (*anyatha-khyati*), and the Advaita Vedanta school proposes a theory of apprehension of the indefinable or indescribable (*anirvachaneeya-khyati*).
19. VIB:142:6
20. VIA:49:1
21. VIA:49:2
22. VIA:49:3
23. VIA:49:5

24. VIB:106:26
25. VIB:106:33
26. III:14:13
27. III:14:12
28. IV:2:3
29. IV:2:4
30. IV:2:5
31. VIB:54:25
32. VIB:28:15
33. VIB:144:49
34. VIB:144:48
35. Gaudapada Karika, IV:42
36. VIB:177:1-12
37. VIB:208:1-7
38. IV:17:4
39. VIB:144:46
40. IV:54:7
41. VIB:22:6
42. VIB:22:8
43. VIB:22:9
44. VIA:97:9
45. VIA:100:2
46. VIB:37:18
47. Gaudapada Karika, IV:26
48. Gaudapada Karika, IV:28
49. Gaudapada Karika, IV:36
50. Gaudapada Karika, II:4
51. IV:19:9-10
52. IV:19:11
53. III:9:58
54. Gaudapada Karika, IV:47
55. Gaudapada Karika, IV:48

CHAPTER VIII

YOU ARE THE NAVEL OF THE COSMOS

The cosmos is changing every moment. If this fact is accepted, it follows that all change can only take place against something that itself does not change. The wheel can move only on a stationary axle; and if the axle also started rotating, movement is impossible. The movie is a projection of a series of photographs on a blank stationary screen. If the screen also moved and changed, projection would be impossible.

What the Upanishads and the Yogavasishtha call Brahman, Paramatman or atman is nothing but that unchanging axle, around which the entire cosmos moves.[1] However, this is just an analogy, and is only partly applicable to Brahman and the world. Any analogy is true only in part; it should not be stretched too much.[2]

The ultimate reality has no name or form, but for practical purposes, the knowledgeable call it *rita* (supreme law), *atman* (self), Brahman or *satyam* (the ultimate truth).[3]

The word 'Brahman' is derived from the Sanskrit root *brih*, which means to grow, to expand or to evolve. It is the ultimate cause of the cosmos. All things are born out of it, supported by it and finally return to it.[4] It is the mind of the mind, the life of life, the ear of the ear and the tongue of the tongue.[5] It is the hidden reality behind all things, just as a child is hidden in the womb of its mother.[6]

Although everything is supposed to have been born out of rita, in truth, nothing is born out of it. The phenomenal world is an inherent quality of Brahman, like the waves are inseparable from the sea, or the lustre of a conch shell from the shell.

The ultimate truth can be observed or viewed at several levels. From the general, or what we call pragmatic viewpoint, it is natural to speak in terms of creation and creator, but from the ultimate perspective such statements are meaningless.

Among the enlightened, statements such as, 'This is created from Brahman And this is not created from Brahman,' do not seem appropriate, Raghava.[7]

If this is the case, why do the scriptures and the learned preach the doctrine that the world emerged from absolute Brahman? Vasishtha says that it is merely for the purpose of instruction. How else can one teach? The scriptures provisionally assume duality to teach us about the non-dual, because we are only familiar with the dual. Because the non-dual is beyond our comprehension, the guru speaks in terms of duality until we comprehend it. Once the understanding seeps in, duality is abandoned.[8]

We might ask, how do we know that Brahman is absolute? Why should it matter to us? The answer to that since the phenomenal world, which we take to be real is actually like a dream, the misery it creates is also false like a dream (We have discussed this thoroughly in the last two chapters). We are miserable because we have taken it for granted that the world is real. If we realise the ultimate truth, our misery disappears, just as the misery we experience in our dreams disappears upon waking.

The Yogavasishtha says that contemplating Brahman does not harm us. It is worth the effort because if there is no Brahman, by contemplating it we lose nothing, but if there is Brahman, contemplating it makes us cross the ocean of the world.[9] Either way, contemplating it is beneficial.

It has to be stressed here that contemplation should not be a mere mental exercise. Hair splitting will get us nowhere; in fact, it might compound our misery. We ought to use reason, but there comes a time when reason exhausts itself, as Brahman is beyond the senses and the intellect. At that point, we ought to be bold enough to take a leap into the unknown.

How did the ancient sages get the idea of Brahman if it is beyond the senses and the intellect? To answer this, the Yogavasishtha begins by suggesting that the universe we live in must have come into existence at some point in the past and will cease to exist at some point in the future, because anything that comes into existence has to go out of existence one day. If this is the case, the question arises as to what it is that remains after the dissolution of the universe and before the creation of the new one.

If nothing remains, how can a new universe come into existence, as nothing can come out of nothing? If something remains, we cannot call it total dissolution. We have dealt with this point in the last chapter.

Vasishtha tells Rama that what remains after annihilation is formless, so it is neither light nor dark, neither nothing nor something, neither the seen nor the onlooker, neither matter nor non-matter, neither manifest nor non-manifest. It is neither temporal nor non-temporal.[10]

Hearing this, Rama says that it is understandable that after annihilation, what remains is formless, but how can it be neither light nor darkness, neither nothing nor something and so on.[11]

If everything is annihilated, then only a void ought to remain, otherwise how can we say that everything has been annihilated?

Vasishtha replies that what remains after annihilation cannot be nothingness as nothingness cannot be the basis of any new creation.[12] Like an uncut sculpture in a stone slab, this universe is neither nothingness nor non-nothingness. It is beyond dualities.[13]

'Nothing' can be imagined only in opposition to 'something', and 'something' can be imagined only in opposition to 'nothing'. 'Something' and 'nothing' cannot be thought of without their opposites.[14] This is why it becomes difficult to talk about it.

Nothingness has grown in nothingness, Brahman has grown in Brahman;
Truth is being reflected in truth, and the whole is situated in the whole.[15]

The truth is that this universe never gets created out of Brahman;
Nor does it get dissolved; Brahman alone exists in itself.[16]

EVERYTHING IS BRAHMAN

As it is difficult for most disciples to think about the abstract reality, Vasishtha uses poetic metaphors and similes to describe Brahman and the creation of the universe. He says that just as there is no difference between the Bilva fruit and the Bilva creeper;[17] just as there is no difference between the water and the wave, there is no difference between Brahman and the world.[18]

On several occasions, Vasishtha says that the cosmos is like the stem of the banana tree. The stem of the banana tree has several layers. Similarly, the universe has several dimensions, and there are worlds within worlds.

The closest metaphor that we have to describe Brahman is space. Everything is within space; space has no form and no colour. It does not wither with time, and it is all pervading. However, space is also one of the gross elements, as it disappears during deep sleep.

Brahman is like space, it is unchanging, formless, unsullied and all-pervading, but in addition to that, it is conscious and blissful.

One of the super statements (mahavakyas) proclaims: 'Pragyanam Brahman'. Pragya means awareness or consciousness. Hence, this super statement means consciousness is Brahman. The entire universe is pervaded by consciousness, as the universe is a product of consciousness. Without consciousness, all talk of the existence and non-existence of the universe would be meaningless. Who would then say that the universe exists or not? This is the reason why it is said that the universe gains its existence only in the light of consciousness.

In the phenomenal world, there are things that are luminous (*bhati*) like the sun, and others that are not luminous (*anubhati*), like the earth, moon and other planets. All the planets shine because of the light of the sun, but the sun shines on its own. However, even the bright sun disappears if we close our eyes, go to sleep or become unconscious.

From this, it follows that all objects of the world are illuminated by consciousness. Thus, consciousness is self-luminous and everything else is lit by it.

Yogavasishtha says that consciousness lights up everything. It resides in the individual self, associates with the phenomenal world, creates maya and becomes bound.[19] As it is the one that cognises everything; it can never be an object of cognition.

We know the world through the intellect and the mind only in the background of consciousness. Even an extremely intelligent person cannot perform any intelligent function during sleep.

Although the intellect and the mind can help us know the world, they cannot help us know the conscious self. For example, the eyes can see the whole world but they cannot see themselves. In the same way, the 'witness' or Brahman can see everything, but it cannot see itself. It is not an object; it can never be cognised.

THE LIGHT OF CONSCIOUSNESS

Describing Brahman, the Vicharabindu Upanishad says that Brahman shines by its own light, and everything else is illuminated by its light (Mantra 3). In the phenomenal world, we have things that are luminous (bhati) like the Sun, and there are things that get illuminated (anubhati), like the earth, moon etc. All the planets are seen because of the light of the Sun, but the Sun shines because of its own light. Even the bright Sun disappears if we close our eyes or go to sleep. From this, it follows that all the objects in the world are illuminated by consciousness. Consciousness is self-luminous (bhati) and everything else is lit (anubhati) by it. Consciousness lights everything. It resides in the individual self; it is the one that makes an association with the phenomenal world, and it is the one that creates maya and becomes bound. As it is the one that sees, it can never become an object of cognition.

Yet we know it because Brahman is self-evident. In fact, the knowledge of Brahman is the only direct knowledge we can have. All worldly knowledge is indirect as we gain it through the medium of the senses and mind. Knowledge through any medium is always indirect, hence distorted.

That which is known directly is Brahman.*

*The Brihadaranyaka Upanishad, III:4:1

From the Vedantic perspective, to know things through the sense organs is called ignorance (*agya*). To acquire special knowledge through analysis and contemplation is called *vigyana*. But the absolute truth, of which the various forms of knowledge are relativistic in comparison, is called pragya.

DEFINING THE INDEFINABLE

Since the beginner has no clear idea of Brahman, the process of elimination is employed. This process is called 'not this, not this' (*neti-neti*). Many translators have called it the process of negation, but elimination[20] (*parishesha apavada*) is a better word. The guru begins by saying that Brahman is absolute and unchanging. It is the subject and not the object. Since the entire universe is an object of our cognition, the guru eliminates the universe or the phenomenal world first, saying that it cannot be the self or Brahman. Then he argues that the body which we take to be the self also cannot be the self because we can see it, touch it and feel it. It is thus also an object, albeit a live one. It goes on changing, and it is subject to birth, old age and death. Thus, the body cannot be Brahman.

After this, the guru asks if the mind and thoughts could be the self or Brahman. He points out that since our mind and thoughts change all the time, they also could not be Brahman. By this process, he leads us to realise that only the witnessing consciousness within us is Brahman — the true self — as it never changes, never becomes old, never suffers disease, old age or death.[21]

How does he prove this? He says that we experience many things from the time we are born. We change places, friends, professions and ideologies several times. Our body, too, goes through change. The one who witnesses or experiences all this change, however, undergoes no change at all.

If the subject, too, changed with time, how would we remember we are the same person who went through all those experiences?

Since we are discussing absolute reality, we ought to define it. To say that it is indefinable is also a definition, although this definition does not help much. Absolute reality is indefinable because it is the subject and the rest of the world is the object. We cannot point to any object in the world and say, 'Brahman is like this,' or 'It is not like this'.

Things are distinguished by putting them in opposition to what they are not. Light is distinguished from darkness, solid from liquid, heat from cold, and so on. Even similar looking things are distinguished by pointing out some distinguishing feature. A horse and a donkey have similar features, yet they are quite different. In a particular class, too, there are differences. Among horses, there are small horses, big horses, black horses and white horses.

In Indian philosophy, a thing can be defined in three ways: One way we define something is by distinguishing it from others. This method is called 'vyavartaka lakshana'. For example, to point out my house in the street, I might say that it is situated between the red house and the green house. Here I am distinguishing my house from others.

Second, I could point out the apparent attributes of my house. This is called 'tatastha lakshana' (incidental qualification). I might say it is the one with the yellow car parked in front of it. The yellow car will not remain parked there forever, but for the time being it would serve the purpose of identifying my house.

The definition of an object that helps us to provisionally identify something, but which is discarded later for a better definition or explanation is called tatastha lakshana, incidental qualification. Once you have identified my house, the yellow car would be unnecessary. Later, if you wish to show my house to someone else, and if incidentally there is a black car outside it, you would say it is the house with the black car parked in front of it. Here what sort of thing is in front of the house is immaterial. Anything in front of the house would serve the purpose of identifying it — a motorcycle a tree or even a bird perched on the gate. Vedanta, too, discards the earlier definition to take us further into the inquiry of Brahman.

At the third level, we define a thing by describing its essential or intrinsic nature. This is called 'svaroopa lakshana'. I might say my house is the two-storey one made of red bricks.

We could define Brahman through the same process. At the first stage of discourse, the guru says that Brahman or atman (the self) is distinct from *anatman* (non-self). This is an instance of vyavartaka lakshana. This is easy to understand, as a distinction is being made between what Brahman is and what it is not. The phenomenal world of matter and ideas is not Brahman (anatman, non-self) and the one who sees the phenomenal world is Brahman (atman, the conscious self).

Shankaracharya uses this method at the beginning of his commentary on the Brahmasootra. He says that the subject and the object—the self (atman) and the non-self (anatman)—are as different as darkness and light. The attributes of one cannot be the attributes of the other.

Although he says the self and the non-self are contradictory entities, the ultimate purpose of Shankaracharya's literary corpus is to prove that the self and the non-self are ultimately one; that there is nothing other than Brahman, who is both the self and the non-self. In the beginning, however, duality between them is temporarily assumed.

After the disciple is more mature, the guru goes a step further. He says that Brahman is the substratum of the phenomenal world (tatastha lakshana). Here the phenomenal world serves the same purpose as the yellow car served in identifying the house.

In the third stage, the intrinsic or inherent nature (svaroopa lakshana) of Brahman is described by saying consciousness is Brahman (pragyanam Brahman); the self (atman) is Brahman (ayam atman Brahman) or truth or knowledge is Brahman (satyam-gyanam-Brahman).

Thus, the guru leads the disciple to the conclusion that consciousness is Brahman and Brahman is consciousness. This means that anything possessing consciousness is Brahman. He says that consciousness is both a necessary and sufficient qualification for Brahman. Pragyanam Brahman means that consciousness and Brahman are identical. This method of defining is called svaroopa lakshana (intrinsic nature of something).

There are other literary devices also through which the meaning of the super statements (mahavakyas) can be conveyed. Sentences can often convey more than their literal meaning. It was generally accepted by Indian grammarians that words have two meanings: primary meaning (abhidha) and secondary or implied meaning (lakshana).

We see a lion and say, 'This is a lion'. Here, we mean what we say literally. But suppose we say of a man, 'He is a lion'; here, it is obvious that we are referring to his fearlessness and bravery. The first sentence is an example of primary meaning and the second of secondary or implied meaning.

The implied meaning of words is conveyed in three different ways: *jahad lakshana*, *ajahad lakshana* and *bhagatyaga lakshana*.

In a sentence, if the literal meaning is given up and another meaning is implied, it is called jahad lakshana. In the sentence, 'He is a lion', the primary meaning that he is a man is abandoned, and another meaning, that he is fearless, is implied.

When the primary meaning is not abandoned, but an additional meaning is suggested, it is called ajahad lakshana. In the sentence, 'Man is a rational being', the word 'man' does not refer to males alone. Here, women and children are also implied by the word 'man'.

In bhagatyaga lakshana (also called *jahadjahal lakshana*) some part of the meaning of a sentence is given up and some not. This will be explained later.

It has earlier been shown that, in the statement, 'You are that' (tat tvam asi), we know 'you' refers to you, the person, and the word 'that' stands for Brahman, who is absolute, infinite and blissful. The very proposition sounds preposterous. 'How can I, a limited being in body, with a limited mind, intellect and resources, be the all-powerful, all-pervading, boundless Brahman?' The guru counters these objections and proves that the individual and Brahman are indeed one. He reconciles this seemingly impossible state of affairs through bhagatyaga lakshana.

In the term 'bhagatyaga lakshana', 'lakshana' means a symbol or property, *'tyaga'* means 'to discard', and *'bhaga'* means 'part'. It, therefore, means 'identification' or 'definition by division and elimination of certain properties'.

WHEN A SPADE IS NOT A SPADE

We use words to express, but often the words we use, express more than their literal or dictionary meaning. Indian linguists speak of two basic types of meaning: primary (abhidha) and secondary (lakshana). While primary meaning is literal or dictionary meaning of a word, the secondary meaning is metaphorical or allegorical. It conveys more than what the word literally means. However, the secondary meaning is not totally different from the primary meaning as it is based on it. In the traditional example 'the hamlet on the Ganges' (*gangayama ghoshah*), it is obvious that a house cannot exist on a river. Here, the indication is that the house is on the banks of the Ganges.

In the ninth century, Anandavardhana realised that there was more to words than primary and secondary meanings. He introduced a third kind of meaning into poetics which he named vyanjana or the suggested meaning. Vyanjana is the third power of language that conveys all the elements that constitute poetry. It is the capacity that suggests a meaning other than the literal and metaphorical meaning.

He held that apart from the words possessing a literal meaning, they carry and convey a socio-cultural import that includes everything other than the literal meaning. One has to be familiar with the social background to grasp the meaning of what is being said.

In this connection, Anandavardhana introduced the concept of dhvani (suggestivity) in his treatise Dhvanyaloka to include the emotional meanings of linguistic utterances. For example, the word 'summer' evokes different responses from people all over the world. While it evokes unpleasant feelings in warm countries like India, it generates feelings of joy in the polar countries.

Anandavardhana agreed that primary and secondary meanings were important, but to him suggestivity was the soul of poetry (*kavyasyatma dhvanih*). He argued that the purpose of poetry was to evoke the universalised emotions that are present in men (*sthayi bhava*). This is possible with dhvani or suggestion.

This suggested meaning cannot be understood by merely knowing the rules of grammar and word meaning. One needs heightened or refined poetic sensibility to grasp the suggested meaning of poetry.

We have discussed these concepts because nearly all Indian texts were written in poetic form; even those written in prose are essentially poetic. It is, therefore, important to understand what poetic devices are and how they are used.

The standard example of this is coming across a person called Devadatta, whom you knew in your childhood. You see him now, years later, in a different place. He has changed physically over the years. When you saw him last, he was a teenager, but now he is a man, has a beard, and dresses differently. In spite of all this, you recognise him after speaking to him and asking some questions. You then conclude that 'this' Devadatta is 'that' Devadatta of your childhood — 'Soyam Devadattah'.

We shall now see which of these three lakshanas conveys the identity of the individual self and Brahman through the statement, 'You are that'.

It cannot be jahad lakshana, as in jahad lakshana, the literal meaning of the sentence is abandoned. Here, we cannot abandon either the meaning of 'you' or 'that', as they both possess consciousness. If the meaning of one of them is abandoned, the identity between the individual and Brahman cannot be established.

The same problem arises if we try to use ajahad lakshana, in which part of the meaning is retained and part added. If we did that, the equivalence between 'you' and 'that' would be lost.

The reconciliation of 'you' and 'that' is achieved by bhagatyaga lakshana through a unity of the two meanings of the pronouns 'you' and 'that', and by showing that both pronouns refer to the same person. Once the equivalence is established, we can drop both the pronouns as we do not need them any longer. In the process of understanding, we eliminate the unnecessary and accidental characteristics and look for the essential.[22]

The same method can be employed to understand other super statements such as *Sarvam hyetad Brahman* — all this is Brahman; Ayam atman Brahman — this atman is Brahman; Aham Brahmasmi — I am Brahman.

Let us take the statement 'All this is Brahman'. The universe is made of multitudinous objects: galaxies, stars, planets, rivers, mountains, rocks and living beings. How can these diverse things ultimately be one?

The mindboggling diversity of the universe is seen by us because of the differentiating characteristics of each object. What happens to this immense plurality when we try to identify all things with a single reality?

The plurality of the world is perceived because all things are distinguished from others by their names and forms (*nama-roopa*). However, Vedanta holds that the physical distinctions of all things in the universe are accidental.

We distinguish one thing from another by certain distinctive characteristics (*vishesha*s). Without these unique characteristics, the thing we are trying to identify would be indistinguishable from others. For example, each drop of water is different from the other. Their difference is due to their being different in space and time, but when these drops merge into the sea, they lose their differentiating characteristics. Now they can no longer be called water drops. We are compelled to call the collection 'ocean', as they have lost their individual distinguishing position in space and time.

Brahman transcends space and time, so it cannot have the characteristics of things located in space and time. Brahman is the essence, and, therefore, it can be equated only with essence.

The essential Brahman cannot be identified with the accidental attributes (nama-roopa) of the objects of the world.

In Indian philosophy, they talk of five characteristics called nama, roopa, asti, bhati and *priyam*. Asti, bhati and priyam mean existence, luminance, and bliss (beauty, endearing), respectively, and they are used to describe the nature of Brahman.

The first two refer to the phenomenal world, and the last three to absolute reality, Brahman.[23] Nama and roopa mean name and form. All things have form and they are called by some name,[24] but as they could have had a different form and name, these are just incidental characteristics. For example, a knife could be called by any other name, and we could give it any other shape. Shakespeare reflected the same sentiment when he said, 'What's in a name? That which we call a rose, by any other name would smell as sweet.' As names and forms have an incidental existence, they are called name-and-form-complex (nama-roopa-prapancha).

We are in a strange situation. Although we perceive only names and forms, and run after name and forms like wealth, friends and material goods; what we really seek is that which is beyond names and forms — existence, luminance and bliss. For example, most of us are attracted to money. In fact, it is not money that is of importance, but what we think money can give us. If we suspected that the currency we are carrying in our bag was counterfeit, we would try to get rid of it immediately because, far from deriving any benefit from it, we might land up in jail. Similarly, we treasure our family and friends, but what we actually treasure is the love and security we expect from them. If they did not give us love and security, we might not value them so much.

We do not actually pursue people, relationships and things, but something we think might follow from them. If that something does not follow, we reject them. This is why friends can turn into enemies, wealth can become a curse and home can become a prison.

The upshot is that it is not the name and form we seek, but a desirable consequence that follows them. What is this consequence?

It is permanent bliss that we actually seek out of these names and forms. We hope that by having a certain person as a friend or spouse, by having a certain amount of wealth, and by achieving a certain status, our stress will be reduced. Stress, however, can be external, as well as internal. We think this tension can be removed by fulfilling our desires, and desires can be satisfied by acquiring worldly objects (names and forms). Our logic is that by acquiring names and forms, we will attain lasting bliss.

We, however, forget that it is the nature of desires that they can never be fulfilled, as one fulfilled desire gives birth to a hundred new desires. This vicious cycle is known as samsara.

Why do desires arise? Desires arise out of ignorance. They arise out of our false belief that we are incomplete and limited beings, that the ephemeral world is real. We try to satiate our desires by acquiring the finite objects of the ephemeral world. We erroneously think that by accumulating finite objects, we will one day acquire infinite fulfilment. This is an erroneous line of reasoning, as no amount of finite things can give us infinite satisfaction. Names and forms, therefore, can never give us supreme bliss.

THE ULTIMATE GOAL OF LIFE

Hinduism talks of four goals of human life: dharma, artha, kama and moksha. Each one of us ought to do our duty (dharma); each one of us ought to earn wealth (artha) so that we can fulfil our desires (kama), and ultimately gain freedom from misery (moksha). If we look closely, it transpires that there are not four goals but just one — ultimate freedom or moksha. Unknowingly, all our worldly pursuits are only for freedom from misery. The mistake we make is that we think by pursuing names and forms, we will gain freedom from misery, and this erroneous logic is the root cause of human misery.

All this discussion has been to prove that this astonishing world of names and forms is ultimately Brahman. How do we go about proving this?

The astounding variety of things in the world is made of substance or matter, and matter exists in space. Rivers, tanks and oceans are different, but the essence of them is water. The same applies to all other worldly objects; they are structurally different but substantially one. All matter is made of parts, and if we go on dividing the parts, in the end we reach a point where there is nothing. This so-called 'solid' matter is, in the ultimate sense, subtle.

Furthermore, we have already argued that if we take the things of the phenomenal world to be real, we will have to grant the same status to the objects of dream, for they also look real. If we say the objects of dream are unreal, how do we defend the reality status of the world in the waking state?

All objects, whether of waking or dream state, are the creation of the imagination power of Brahman; hence the mahavakya: *Sarvam khalu idam Brahman* — all is Brahman. The one who imagines and whatever is imagined cannot be said to be different from each other. Thus, we establish the unity between the world and Brahman.

Asserting the same identity between Brahman and the world, Vasishtha tells Rama:

I tried to imagine the gold bangle without gold
But never found anything other than gold.[25]

In a wave I see nothing but water;
And when there is no wave, I see water alone.[26]

Thus, behind all this amazing change, there is one unchanging reality, which we call Brahman. It is the navel of the cosmos, and that navel is you.

We shall see if Vasishtha proves this impossibility in the chapters that follow.

ENDNOTES

1. See Shwetashvatara Upanishad, Chapter I, for a detailed discussion
2. III:10:12
3. III:1:12
4. The Chandogya Upanishad, III:14:1
5. The Vicharabindu Upanishad, Mantra 3
6. The Vicharabindu Upanishad, Mantra 4
7. III:95:4
8. III:95:5-7
9. II:13:35
10. III:9:45-50
11. III:10:1-4
12. III:10:8
13. III:10:10
14. III:10:14
15. VIA:3:11
16. III:10:13
17. The name in English for Bilva is Bael. It is also called 'stone apple' or 'wood apple'. In Hindi it is called Bel or Bael Shriphala.
18. III:10:19
19. VIA:36:4
20. The knowledge of Brahman is known through the phrase 'not this-not this'; After illusion and ignorance are removed, the self shines in its own light. (The Vicharabindu Upanishad, Mantra 6)
21. I am a body, I am the senses, I am the mind, I am the intellect, I am happy, I am sad, I am a Brahmin, I am lean, I am black, I am deaf, I am poor, she is my wife, he is my son, this is my house – dissociate yourself from these associations and know that the self is beyond all of them. (The Jyotirbindu Upanishad, Mantra 10).
22. Since the terms 'this' and 'that' imply their total identification, jahal(d) lakshana cannot be employed; neither can we employ ajahad lakshana, as there would be a total difference between the two; Here we can employ bhagatyaga lakshana without fear as we say 'He is that man'. (Ramagita: Mantra 27). The Brahmanubhava Upanishad also says:
That I am the very Brahman is indicated by the method of 'not this-not this' by employing jahadjahal(d) lakshana (also called bhagatyaga lakshana) – The Brahmaubhava Upanishad (Mantra 27); see also Vedanta Sara Chapter IV.

23. Existence, luminance, bliss, form and name are five aspects of all reality; of these the first three belong to Brahman, and the last two to the phenomenal world. Drig Drishya Viveka, XX:20.
24. It is true that all things do not have names, but still we talk about them by using the words like 'something' or 'X'. Here 'something' or 'X' is also a name (nama).
25. III:9:31
26. III:9:32

The Yogavasishtha of Valmiki

CHAPTER IX

THE BIRTH OF
THE INDIVIDUAL SELF

We might have doubts about the existence of Brahman, the universal self, but we cannot doubt the existence of the individual self; that is, of our own existence. Do we need any empirical or logical proof that we exist? Everything else could be illusory but not our own self. If we did not exist, who is asking these questions?

The existence of the self is the only self-evident truth in the world. Having said this, all that is required is to see if there is a universal self, and how it is related to the individual self.

Most Indian systems illustrate the relationship between the universal and individual self through the analogy of the ocean and the drop. The universal self is like an ocean, and the individual self is like a drop.

At this stage we might extend this analogy further because we also have to accommodate the creator of the world (Brahma). We can now say that waves are like individual creatures, the ocean is like the creator of the world. Both are limited and both change. The unchanging reality behind them is water (absolute Brahman).

According to Vedanta, individuals have a body, an ego, a mind, a brain and the universal self. Our liberation or suffering depends upon which of these we identify ourselves with. If we identify with the body, mind or ego, we become limited beings, subject to change and misery. However, if we identify ourselves with the universal self, we become united with it and do not feel limited and miserable. For example, if a drop thinks it is different from the ocean, it is naturally going to feel insignificant and limited, but if it realises it is essentially an ocean and ultimately water, it is going to feel significant and free. Whatever the truth might be, life is affected by the way we think about it.

It has been argued that if the individual and the universal were not one and the same, moksha would not be possible. A gold bangle when melted becomes gold; it would not if it had not been made of gold.

Brahman is eternal and there is no second, while individuals (jeevas) are innumerable. Billions have been born and billions have perished; billions are being born, billions will be born and later perish. Once born out of Brahman, they become involved in the world and experience its joys and sorrows.

Just as a rock gains momentum as it rolls down a mountain;
Separated from the supreme self, the dream of the individual gets reinforced.[1]

As mentioned earlier, the words 'Brahman', 'Paramatman', 'atman', 'chit' are used to talk about the universal self. For the individual self, Vedanta uses two words such as 'jeeva' and *shareera*. When the individual self seemingly separates itself from the universal self but has not yet taken a physical body, it is called jeeva. When it takes the form of a body it is called shareera, *kaya* or *deha*. It must be noted that at times the word 'jeeva' is also used for the gross body, and in the sense of 'person' or 'individual'. The context in which it is said must be considered.

Not just humans, but all organisms that exist are jeevas; in other words, they are essentially nothing but the universal self. They have acquired different kinds of bodies according to their past deeds (karmas) but, sooner or later, they are bound to be reunited with the universal self. This reunification is called liberation, moksha, nirvana or *kaivalya*. Until liberation is regained, the body is a means to perform actions in the world.

It must be remembered that the body is just a vehicle or an instrument which we use to go about doing things in the world. It is not our real self. We could use it to do good things or bad things; the body itself does not insist on anything. For example, we might use a knife to take a bullet out of someone's body or we could use it to kill someone. The knife remains neutral in both cases. Similarly, we could use the body to perform good or bad actions. However, if we took the body to be the self, we would think it was the body that was responsible for our good and bad actions, and we might then reward it or punish it. Because of this misidentification of our real self with the body, some neglect it or torture it.

When the scriptures say that the body is not the self, it is to show that the drop is essentially an ocean and not a mere drop. It means that as an individual self confined to a body, we are limited, but essentially we are not. This does not mean that the body is to be looked down upon and neglected. It merely means that if you take the body as your true self, you will never understand your true self, as you will limit your understanding to the body alone.

THE GLORY OF THE BODY
In the initial chapters of the Yogavasishtha, we see the young prince Rama making the common mistake of deprecating the body. He says he cares little for the body as it is an abode of all sorts of diseases,

and is subject to old age and mental afflictions.[2] The body is nothing but a pack of bones, nerves, jellies, urine and other detestable things, so what is the point in craving for it. As it is finally going to perish, why should he bother about it?

In reply, Vasishtha tells Rama that it is only the uninformed who see the body as a place of infinite misery. For those who know the self, it is a source of inexhaustible happiness.[3] After attaining liberation, the body becomes 'Amaravati', the abode of the gods for the enlightened.[4]

In the scriptures, the body is often likened to a city, *pura*; hence the word purusha is also used to mean 'human being', the one who resides in a city. Vasishtha says that this beautiful city of the body is illuminated by the light of supreme consciousness, and for the wise person it is a source of joy, not misery.[5]

Just as a city is composed of buildings, roads, houses and thousands of human beings and animals, the body is composed of sense organs, veins, muscles, internal organs, body cells, blood, brain and mind. Hindu scriptures say that the universe is extremely complex and the body is equally so, because whatever is in the universe is in the body. The body is thus a microcosm and the universe a macrocosm. By understanding the microcosm we can understand the macrocosm, so to take it as a mere bag of bones and veins would be a monumental mistake.

In fact, Vasishtha draws an analogy between the individual body and the universe. Unbounded space is the forehead of the individual (jeeva), earth is its feet, middle space its stomach and the entire cosmos is its body.[6] The heavenly bodies are its body parts, water is its blood, the mountains are its muscles and the rivers are its veins.[7]

If you see it as mere flesh and bones, the body becomes just a means of hedonistic pleasures. The wise, however, use it to their advantage but do not cling to it. When the body is destroyed, it is a small matter for the enlightened, but as long as it is there, it is a source of unlimited pleasure and joy for them.[8] The wise do not

The Yogavasishtha of Valmiki

rue when the body becomes old and dies because the self within it neither gets old nor does it perish with the death of the body.

Like the space within the pot does not get destroyed when the pot is broken;
The self does not get destroyed with the destruction of the body.[9]

However, some people do not appreciate the importance of the body, and they neglect it, torture it or even end it by committing suicide.

In the story of Chudala from the Yogavasishtha, when King Shikhidwaja tries to give up his body, his wife Chudala says: O King! Why are you throwing the innocent body into such a great abyss? You are like the ignorant ox that kills its own calf. This body is gross and dumb, it has committed no sin. Do not give it up.[10]

Having said this, it must be remembered that we should neither get too obsessed with the body, nor torture it by fasting, penance and other mortifications.[11] Instead of torturing and disfiguring the body, we must remember that it performs actions according to the dictates of the ego, so the solution is to do something about the ego.

The ego creates the world; the body is just an instrument of all activities;
With the ego gone, the world becomes quiet like the wind without motion.[12]

THE INDIVIDUAL SELF AND THE INDIVIDUAL BODY
We shall now see exactly what Vedanta means by the individual self (jeeva) and how it is created.

Vasishtha defines the individual self and the body through various examples and analogies. When the universal self first becomes individuated, it appears in a subtle form called 'jeeva'. Later, it assumes a gross form and gains a physical body called 'deha' or 'shareera'.

When the supreme self becomes sullied because of its own will,
The entity that grows out of its desire is called the individual self (jeeva).[13]

Describing the nature of jeeva, Vasishtha says, that which is subtler than the subtle, grosser than the gross, that which pervades all is called jeeva by the learned.[14] In the beginning it is like the faint imagination an artist has of the image he wishes to paint. It has not yet taken a physical form. Once it gains a form, it acquires a complex of mental and physical characteristics.

Thus, by acquiring life (*prana*) it is called jeeva. By acquiring the idea, 'I am this', it is called *ahamkara* (ego). When it starts discriminating between objects, it is called *buddhi* (intellect). Finally, by making choices or by willing, it is called *manas* (mind).[15]

Taking another angle, Vasishtha says that when the ego is dictated to by the mind (*chitta*), it is called the doer (*karta*), and when it is predominated by pulsation (*spanda*), it is called action (kriya). When these combine, they are called jeeva. Essentially, there is no difference between them.

We must never forget that it is Brahman who, by being the cause of body, ego, intellect and mind, is called prakriti. Because of the power of growth, it is called body (deha), by predominance of ignorance it is called gross (*jada*) and, as it is conscious, it is called chaitanya.[16] Vasishtha says that the body, however, gets decayed, destroyed or dissolved with time.

Giving a physical explanation, Vasishtha says, like a snowflake, the jeeva is created out of sperm through the pleasure of intercourse, and through the same pleasure other creatures are created. Then the jeeva gets a gross form through quintuplication (five-fold combination, *panchikaranam*) of the elements.[17]

The five elements are not available for perception in their pure form; we only see them when they combine with other elements. The jeeva, after taking solid form because of five-fold combination, assumes a human form. It is then called man (*nara*).

As we observe nature, we see that there are things that are conscious and those that are not. The body is unique—it is gross matter (jada) as well as conscious. The gross body comes alive because of the life-element (*jeevadhatu*), which is also called breath (prana).

HOW THE ELEMENTS COMBINE

Panchikaranam (quintuplication) is a process by which each of the five gross elements (*panchamahabhootas*) is formed out of the five subtle elements (*panchatanmatras*). Explaining the process of grossification Shankaracharya writes in *Panchikaranam*:

The learned talk about the quintuplication of elements. To begin with, the earth is divided into two equal parts. Then one half of every other element is divided into four equal parts. Then the four parts of each element have to be distributed among the other four elements. This way, the gross space constitutes five parts, including four parts of other elements beginning with the wind. The knowers of truth call this the process of quintuplication (Panchikaranam).

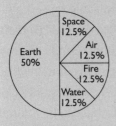

The pie chart shows how the Earth combines with others elements. Others combine in the same way.

The five elements cannot be seen in their pure state; they can be seen only after they combine with each other.

Element	Nature	Characteristic	Organ
Akasha	Space	Gravity Shabda (sound)	Ear
Vayu (Wind)	Kinesis	Sparsha (touch+sound)	Skin
Agni (Fire)	Radiation	Roopa (form+sound+touch)	Eye
Apah (Water)	Electricity	Rasa (taste+sound+touch+form)	Tongue
Prithvi (Earth)	Magnetism	Gandha (smell+all other four)	Nose

It must be noted that behind all these elements is the mind because the elements are a creation of the mind.

In fact, the body is also subtle but appears to be gross because of ignorance.[18] If everything that is there is consciousness alone, how can body not be conscious? For the sake of instruction, and to avoid initial confusion, the body is said to be matter.

DIMENSIONS OF THE BODY

Common sense tells us that the physical body is the only body that we have, but in Hindu, Buddhist and Jaina philosophy, this body is not the only body we possess.

The word 'body' has a much wider meaning in Indian philosophy: it is not limited to the physical body. We do not exist merely on the physical plane; there are three other planes or dimensions on which we exist.

Before we understand the other dimensions of the body, we must know that whatever there is exists at four levels: *Virata* (phenomenal level), *Hiranyagarbha* (subtle level), *Eeshwara* (causal level), and a fourth level, which has not been given a name. It is just called 'The Fourth'. These dimensions are symbolically represented by the letter ॐ which is composed of three syllables: *A-U-M* (अ-उ-म).

'A' is the primal sound, and it pervades all other sounds that can be uttered. It represents the physical dimension of absolute reality. In most of the languages around the world 'A' is the first letter of the alphabet. Thus, 'A' stands for all the sounds that can be uttered to name the things of the phenomenal world (Virata).

Among the three levels of consciousness, the Virata belongs to the waking state. Since it is the basis of all that is visible, it is called Vaishvanara. This is why, talking about the importance of the sound 'A', in the Bhagavad Gita, Krishna tells Arjuna: Among the letters, I am 'अ'.[19]

The next dimension, called Hiranyagarbha, is represented by the letter 'U', and this is a higher dimension. It is called the 'raised' (*utkarishta*) level, and since it is between 'A' and 'M' levels, it forms a bridge between the two. It is the subtle dimension of absolute reality, and its psychological state is dream (svapna). Here everything exists in subtle form. Everything is at the mental level. It is characterised by brilliance (*taijasa*).

The Yogavasishtha of Valmiki

The third state is Eeshwara, the causal dimension, and it is represented by the letter 'M'. It stands for 'measure', as it is the upper limit of whatever can be uttered. To utter the sound 'M', the mouth has to be closed, and in doing so, the earlier states 'A' and 'U' merge into it. It is called the causal state because the other two states arise from it.

Now we can take up the doctrine of three bodies (*shareeratraya*). Hinduism says that each one of us has three bodies: *sthoola shareera*, the gross body; *sookshma shareera* or *linga shareera*, the subtle body, and *karana shareera*, the causal body. In terms of modern psychology, we could say that each of these bodies represents the physical body (biological), mind (mental), intellect, and beyond.

To understand the concept of three bodies, we would also discuss the corresponding concept of five sheaths: the food sheath (*Annamaya kosha*), the vital sheath (*Pranamaya kosha*), the mental sheath (*Manomaya kosha*), the intellect sheath (*Vigyanamaya kosha*), and the bliss sheath (*Anandamaya kosha*). For clarity, see the chart that follows.

Since our gross body depends upon food for survival, and since it is also food for other creatures, it is named the food body. The gross body comes into existence when the five elements: space, air, fire, water and earth become gross through a process called five-fold combination, panchikaranam. The gross body undergoes six kinds of changes and distortions (*shadvikara*). It comes into existence, it is born, it grows, it matures, it decays, and finally perishes.[20]

It is through the gross body that we experience the joys and sorrows of the world. The gross body is also said to be a city of nine gates, *navadvare pure dehee*.[21] The nine gates are: the mouth, two eyes, two ears, two nostrils and two excretal organs.

The gross body is an object of perception and the preceptor is the self (atman). Because in deep sleep all consciousness of the body is lost, the gross body cannot be the self. For this reason, the psychological state of the gross body is considered to be the waking state. Just as the space within the pot is in no way affected by the destruction of the pot, the self (atman) is not affected in any way with the destruction of the gross body.

The subtle body, sookshma shareera (or linga shareera) is a product of the subtle elements that have not yet split into five gross elements (panchamahabhootas). In their subtle from they are called *tanmatra*s. They are called subtle because they cannot be perceived by any of the five senses.

It is because of the subtle body that we pulsate with life. The subtle body incorporates the mind, the intellect, emotions, and it is the subtle body that experiences joy, sorrow, heat and cold. The subtle body is associated with three of the five sheaths: vital sheath, mental sheath and intellect sheath. This body is in the dream state. The vital sheath (Pranamaya kosha), consists of five life forces (pranas) and five organs of action. Without this life force, we would be dead. Even in dream and deep sleep states, the vital force exists but it is almost insentient because in sleep the body does not react to external stimuli or threat. This is why the characteristic of this state is dream. Atman, on the other hand, is fully conscious, so the vital sheath cannot be considered to be the atman.

Now we come to the causal body (karana shareera), which is the subtlest of the three. It is the cause of sthoola and sookshma shareera, and pervades them both. It is indescribable, as it has no shape, colour or weight. It consists of the mind and the five organs of perception (*gyanendriyas*). But the causal body is also not the real self because its nature is ignorance (deep sleep). It has a beginning and an end, and is subject to change and distortion. Since this body is also witnessed by the atman, it cannot be called the atman.

Ek aeva tridha stithah (The one that pervades the three)				
Virata Consciousness + Gross world	Sthoola shareera	Annamaya kosha (5 external organs)	Vishva sangya Vaishvanara	Jagarat (Waking)
Hiranyagarbha Consciousness + Subtle world	Sookshma shareera	Vigyanamaya kosha (Intellect+Ego)	Taijasa sangya	Svapna (Dream)
		Manomaya kosha (Mind+ 5 senses)		
		Pranamaya kosha (5 external organs+ 5 pranas)		
Eeshwara Consciousness + Causal world	Karana shareera	Anandamaya kosha (Emotions)	Paragya sangya	Sushupti (Sleep)
The Fourth Cannot be described	Shuddha atmatva	Gyanaprakasha (Light of knowledge)	Atmajyoti	Turiya (The fourth)

The chart shows four dimensions or aspects of the absolute reality. The first level is called Virata (phenomenal world), the second is called Hiranyagarbha (subtle world), and the third is called Eeshwara (causal world). The fourth has not been given any name because it is beyond the realm of the mind and language. The Mandookya Upanishad says that absolute reality is symbolised by the letter ॐ (which has three syllables A-U-M, and represents three dimensions of the self (atman). The symbol ॐ is pronounced A-U-M, and covers all sounds that can be uttered. 'A' represents the primal sound and pervades all other sounds. 'U' represents the superior and intermediate sound. It stands for the reality between waking and sleep. 'M' represents the third dimension of reality of deep sleep. The fourth dimension cannot be represented by any sound or letter.

The karana shareera is blissful; hence it is associated with the bliss sheath. We do not have a parallel for this in most schools of psychology, especially the contemporary ones.

At places, Vasishtha uses the word *'para shareera'* for the causal body. He says there are three kinds of jeevas: sthoola, sookshma, para, and a seeker of self-knowledge must go for the third one, and ignore the other two.[22]

Explaining the nature of the three bodies, Vasishtha says that the body, which consists of limbs and other parts, and craves for enjoyment, is the gross body (sthoola shareera).[23] The one that wills and desires is the subtle body (sookshma shareera).[24] Lastly, the one that is free of all desires, is untouched by what the other two bodies do, and is the one that creates the whole world for us is the causal body (para shareera).[25] This body is in 'the fourth' (*turiya*). It is final liberation.[26] Turiya is the one which is beyond the three states of waking, dream and deep sleep, is free of the ego, truth and untruth. It is the impartial witness of everything.[27]

It must be noted that at times, possibly for the sake of simplification, the Yogavasishtha treats the causal body and mental body as one. It says that from Brahma onwards, all creatures have two bodies: the mental (*manah shareera*), and the physical (*mamsa shareera*), the one made of flesh. The former achieves what it wants immediately; while the latter, the physical is dependent and limited.[28]

At places, the Yogavasishtha uses the word *adhibhautika deha* for the gross body, and *ativahika deha* for the subtle body.[29] These are minor technical details, so we shall stick to the concept of three bodies, as this is consistent with the overall Vedantic literature.

THE INDIVIDUAL AND UNIVERSAL SELF
To explain the relationship between the individual and the universal self, the Yogavasishtha uses the metaphor of chariot and horses.

Gross like the stem of a tree, the gross body is a chariot, and the senses are
like horses running after the objects of the world;
Breath is like energy, the mind is its reins, the charioteer is the universal
self (atman) who is enjoying the ride.[30]

The Mundaka Upanishad uses the metaphor of two birds to illustrate
this relationship:

Two friendly birds live together on the same tree (body);
One (the individual self) experiences the joys and sorrows of the tree,
while the other (the universal self) just looks on.[31]

Elaborating on the relationship between the individual and universal
self, Vasishtha says:

Just as clouds and wind are related; the bee and lotus are related;
The self and the body are related similarly, Raghava.[32]

Since the jeeva is in essence no different from the absolute (Brahman),
each jeeva has the entire cosmos within it. The metaphor of a pot
and the space within it and outside it is also used to show the
relationship between Brahman and jeeva. Space is unlimited, but
within a pot it appears to be limited. It is the pot that is making it
limited, but that is just appearance. In fact, the space within the pot
is also not limited. As soon as the pot is broken, the space within it
loses its apparent limitedness because space is everywhere, totally
unaffected by the presence or absence of the pot.

There may be millions of pots all over the world, and they
would seemingly have millions of limited spaces within them, but
the fact is that space is indivisible. Similarly, when the universal
self associates itself with the mind, ego and body, it becomes
limited and comes to be known as jeeva. This way of explaining the
nature of the jeeva is called 'Avichchedavada', which is attributed
mainly to Vachaspati Mishra, one of the commentators on the
Brahmasootra.

DIMENSIONS OF THE BODY

The concept of the sheaths is explained in the Moksha Gita thus:

The food sheath is made up of the five elements. It has a beginning and an end. It is inert, made of parts, and is an effect of the five elements.

Because it is full of impurities, you are not the body sheath. You are the witness of this body. So remember, 'I am not the body but Brahman.'

The vital sheath is a product of Rajas guna. It also has a beginning and an end, it is inert, and it is an effect. Therefore, you are not the Pranamaya kosha. You are the witness of this sheath. So remember, 'I am not the Pranamaya kosha. I am Brahman.'

The mental sheath is a product of Sattva guna. It also has a beginning and an end, it is inert, it is an effect. Therefore, you are not the mental sheath. You are the witness of this sheath. So remember, 'I am not Manomaya kosha. I am Brahman.'

The intellect sheath is also a product of Sattva guna. It, too, has a beginning and an end, it is inert, and it is an effect. Therefore, you are not the intellect sheath but a witness of this sheath. Remember, therefore, 'I am not the Vigyanamaya kosha. I am Brahman.'

The bliss sheath is full of ignorance, as it is a modification of prakriti. It is the effect of past karmas; it is transient, it is gross and insentient. Therefore, you are not the bliss sheath but a witness of this sheath. So remember, 'I am not the Anandamaya kosha. I am Brahman.'

Shankaracharya uses another metaphor for explaining the relationship between Brahman and jeeva. He says we see the world through the senses, and this creates ignorance. It is like seeing the image of the world in a mirror. Although it looks the same as the original object, this is not the case, as it is a reflection. This school is called Pratibimbavada (*pratibimba*=reflection, *vada*=ism).

HOW THE UNIVERSAL SELF BECOMES
THE INDIVIDUAL SELF

In reply to Rama's question about how the universal self becomes the individual self, Vasishtha says that being endowed with all

The Yogavasishtha of Valmiki

powers, Brahman is capable of doing anything. One of Brahman's characteristics is the unlimited power of imagination. Because of this, whatever it imagines is manifested.[33]

We showed that there is no causal relationship between Brahman and the creation of the world in Chapter VII. Creation is the very nature of Brahman, and of its own accord it takes the form of gross elements and becomes the illusory jeeva.[34]

Vasishtha says that just as a learned man loses his noble character by associating himself with a lowly woman, the universal self loses its true nature and becomes individual self.[35] The subtle or mental body becomes different from the supreme consciousness by imagining it is different from it, and it regains its true nature once again by associating itself with supreme consciousness.[36] This separation, it has to be remembered, is only imaginary.

It is often asked what the purpose is behind Brahman becoming the individual self. Hinduism does not see a purpose behind the creation of the universe. It sees it as mere game of the universal self. There is no purpose in the game; it is just for the sake of playing. In a game of chess, for instance, we limit ourselves by the rules of the game, and see the other player as an opponent, although the other person might be dear to us. If a game has no limits of any kind, the game becomes chaotic and players as well as spectators lose interest in it.

This is why, when willingly forgetting its true nature, the universal self acquires the idea of 'me' and 'mine', it is called ego; when it develops the power of will, it is called mind, and when it gains the power to make decisions, it is called intellect. For cognising and enjoying the objects of the external world, it develops the five senses. When it is predominantly conscious, it is called jeeva, and when it is predominantly gross, it is called *puryashtaka deha* (a body of eight constituents).[37] These eight constituents are: five senses, vital force (prana), mind and ego (ahamkara).[38]

To fulfil its desires, the mind creates four kinds of organisms:

svedaja, ones that grow in sweat, *udbheedaja*, ones that grow out of the earth, such as trees and plants, *andaja*, oviparous, ones that grow out of eggs and *jarayuja*, viviparous, ones that grow inside a womb.[39]

Coming back to the analogy of the chariot, Vasishtha says that the individual self (jeeva) is the chariot of the universal self (chit), ego is the chariot of the jeeva, the intellect (buddhi) is the chariot of the ego, and mind is the chariot of the buddhi.[40] The vital force (prana) is the chariot of the mind, the sense organs are the chariot of prana, the body is the chariot of the sense organs, and the physical limbs are the chariot of the body.[41] Thus, pulsation and activity go on in a body on the ever-rotating wheel of the unreal world. As long as there is prana, the mind wills, just as the trees of the forest sway as long as the wind blows.[42] When the mind is still, there is no pulsation or will.[43]

It is the will to be something other than the self and look outwards that creates the body, and it is the vital force that gives it life. Vasishtha says that mind and body grow out of two seeds: life force (prana) and desire (vasana).[44] The life force creates vibration in the mind and then manifests itself in the body the way a whirlpool is created in water.[45] Just as a faint fragrance can be smelt when the wind blows, the subtle mind becomes known through the vibration of the life force.[46]

THE IDEA OF PERSONALITY

Once the absolute self (atman) becomes individuated, innumerable individual selves are born, and each of these has a unique personality. Human personality is not static and one-dimensional but dynamic and multi-dimensional. Although the real self or atman is pure and undergoes no change, our personality certainly does. The persona that we don is like a mask that a theatre artiste wears. This pure consciousness wears five masks or layers of energy (*panchakosha*) at different levels of grossification.

The Yogavasishtha of Valmiki

The word panchakosha is made of two words: *pancha*= five, and *kosha*=sheath, envelope, cover or layer. The sheaths or layers are used as a metaphor to describe the individual self in different dimensions. The five sheaths are: Annamaya kosha (food sheath), Pranamaya kosha (vital sheath), Manomaya kosha (mental sheath), Vigyanamaya kosha (intellect sheath), Anandamaya kosha (bliss sheath).

It is these five koshas that result in individual personality traits, just as seven notes of music result in endless compositions. This is because every moment, these koshas determine our thoughts, emotions, words and actions.

The five sheaths also correspond to the three bodies: the physical body (sthoola shareera), the mental body (sookshma shareera), and the causal body (karana shareera). The gross body corresponds to the dense physical dimension, the subtle body to the mind, and the causal body to the core in which the archetypes reside (see chart).

An interesting characteristic of the five sheaths and the three bodies is that they are hierarchical, so that each level transcends and includes the lower one.

If we do not learn to transcend these sheaths and bodies, we can never know our true self, and until we know our true self, we will remain stuck at whichever layer we take to be our true self. For example, those who take the gross body to be their real self, will not rise above eating, drinking and being merry; those who choose to live at the subtle level will be engulfed by mental and intellectual turmoil all their lives, and those who graduate to the causal level will attain higher mental peace. Total freedom is realised by those who transcend all these levels and unite with the absolute self or Brahman.

It must be noted that the concept of the five sheaths and three bodies may give us the impression that they are compartmentalised. This is only partly true because there is a continuum among them, as they coexist at different levels of energy, and energy is found at every level.

When the mind focuses on external objects, it experiences joys and sorrows, and by control of the breath (*prana nirodha*) it becomes free.[47] In order to quieten the mind, yogis practise breath regulation (*pranayama*) and other methods.[48]

The second seed is desire, which gets reinforced and keeps the jeeva trapped in the cycle of birth, death, old age, disease and misery.

Rama asks, 'Of the two seeds, which one has to be destroyed first in order to be free of misery?'[49] Vasishtha says that desire is the main seed. If we could give up desire through maturity, effort and constant practice, liberation would immediately be the result. However, giving up desires is a gargantuan task, because desires cannot be given up until the mind is active, and until the mind is active, self-knowledge is not possible.[50]

We need not be disheartened by this daunting task however. With patience, persistence and help from a guru, we could put an end to both of them, as they are closely interrelated. Just as the presence of wind is known only by its movement when the movement is not there, it is not felt, the same way the jeeva has its existence as long as there are desires. Without these, it disappears and becomes one with Brahman.[51]

THE CAUSE OF BONDAGE
Why and how does the supreme self (atman) become an individual self? Advaita Vedanta says that the cause of bondage is ignorance (avidya, *agyana*) or forgetfulness (*vismarana*). The question may be asked, if the atman is absolute and free, from where do bondage, ignorance and forgetfulness come from?

We have wrong ideas about absoluteness. We think it has to be complete, perfect and unchanging. If that were so, such an absolute would be dead, and further, how would we explain limitedness and change, truth and untruth, good and evil? It would mean limitedness and change, evil and ignorance are not part of the absolute, and in that case the absolute would not be absolute.

Advaita Vedanta says that absolute Brahman incorporates all plurality. It is both absolute and limited, free and bound, large and small, light and dark, good and evil, life and death.

Freedom means to have choice, the choice to be unbound or limited, happy or miserable, knowledgeable or ignorant, good or evil. Otherwise, freedom would be no freedom at all; it would be bondage of the worst kind — bondage from which there is no escape.

For example, the ocean is both ocean and droplet at the same time. It is up to the droplet to see itself as different or not different from the ocean. When it sees itself as different, it becomes limited, but when it immerses itself into the ocean, it becomes free and unlimited.

Arguing on similar lines, the Yogavasishtha says that jeeva comes into existence because of the imaginative power of Brahman, and because of its own nature of being both unlimited and limited. Because of this imagination, it seemingly loses its unbounded and limitless nature and becomes confined. Anything that is limited can never have a sense of liberation, and can never be happy.

Because of its self-imposed limitation, it begins to consider itself different from other jeevas; and it begins to cooperate or compete with them, as it sees them as friends or foes. Those who help the individual self in its pursuit of worldly desires are seen as friends, and those who create obstacles in its path become enemies. The supreme self is absolute and thus has no desires, but the jeeva, being incomplete, has unlimited desires. Each fulfilled desire gives rise to hundreds of new desires, making it impossible to fulfil them all. Happiness in this limited world of jeeva, therefore, is an impossible goal.

When desires predominate, the jeeva takes the form of several species (*yonis*) and takes birth as plants, animals, worms and humans in order to fulfil those desires.[52] As a result of this, it gets caught in the cycle of happiness and suffering, birth and death. Just as a monkey jumps from one tree to another, the desiring body leaves one body and is born again in another.[53]

We might ask why the universal self generates imagination in itself and becomes the individual self. Such questions cannot be answered. Why does fire burn? Why is ice cold? Why is the sun bright? What answer can one give for such questions? Things are as they are because of their nature. Why they are like that? No one can ever give an answer to that because whatever answer is given, in the end someone will again say, 'Why?' This is the reason such questions are called ultimate questions, atiprshnas.

It is the nature of the universal self that it can become an individual self by imagination; there is no other answer to this question. Everything goes on happening according to some unknown law of coincidence called kakataliya nyaya.

KINDS OF IGNORANCE AND UNAWARENESS

As previously discussed, jeeva comes into existence because of the veil of ignorance that is created through the ego. This ignorance is of seven kinds, and thus there are seven kinds of jeeva according to their state of consciousness. It should be noted that, traditionally, consciousness is divided into three states. The first is the jagarat state, the conscious state, or when we are awake. The second is the dream state, svapna; here, we are partly conscious. The third is sushupti, the state of deep sleep.[54]

The Yogavasishtha adds four more states to the first three. These are also called states of ignorance.[55]

Beejajagarat (initial-waking state): In the beginning of creation, the consciousness, in its core or initial form, which is devoid of a name, which will be later called mind, and individual self. The word '*beeja*' means 'seed' or the initial state. The word 'jagarat' means 'wakefulness'.[56]

The Yogavasishtha of Valmiki

Jagarat (waking state): Immediately after dissociating from the supreme state of consciousness, the idea of selfhood 'I' and 'this is mine' arises. This is the waking state. At this stage, there is no memory of the past, as it is just the beginning of the individual consciousness.

Mahajagarat (super wakefulness): With the passage of time and many cycles of birth and death, the idea of 'I' and 'this is mine' becomes reinforced.

Jagaratsvapna (waking dream): The above-mentioned feelings of selfhood and possession become so strong that the individual begins to take them for real. This is like the illusion of seeing a mirage or, owing to a defect in the eye, seeing two things in the place of one.

Svapna (dream): We dream in the super wakefulness state, and upon waking we realise that what we saw was unreal.

Svapnajagarat (dream-wakefulness): Over a long period of stupor, the dream state begins to appear as real.

Sushupti (deep sleep): As the name suggests, it is the experience of deep forgetfulness. In this state, all the above six states disappear, and the individual consciousness becomes gross and unconscious, although the earlier six states are still present in a much diminished form. This state gives rise to future miseries, as it is gross and unconsciousness.

Further, depending upon the level of their wakefulness, there are seven kinds of jeeva mentioned in the Utpatti Prakaranam.[57]

Svapnajagara: This is a state when the jeevas of a past age begin to dream. The world in which we live is a dream of those beings. We are the beings of their dreams, and our desires are nothing but their desires.

Sankalpajagara: When jeevas of a past age awaken out of slumber and become so contemplative that they forget their wakeful world, and only their will (sankalpa) becomes their awakened state.

Kevalajagara: They are the first jeevas born out of Brahman.

Chirajagara: When Kevalajagara get involved in the process of cause and effect.

Ghanajagara: When they become sinful as a result of their misdeeds.

Jagaratsvapna: When, as a result of good company and contemplation, they begin to see the world as unreal or a dream.

Ksheenajagara: Those who have attained supreme knowledge, who have gone beyond jagarat, svapna and sushupti and are now in turiya (liberation).

Depending upon the mixture of the three gunas (sattva, rajas and tamas), there are fifteen types of jeeva in fourteen planes of existence (Bhuvanas).[58]

Idamprathamta: Those who do good deeds immediately after their first birth;

Gunapeevaree: When the above kind find liberation after indulging in worldly affairs after a few births;

Sasattva: Those who realise what is good and bad, and try for moksha;

Adhamsattva: Those who become engulfed in worldly affairs and attain moksha after many births;

Atyanta tamasee: Those for whom moksha becomes nearly impossible even after several births;

Rajasee: They are in between, and they attain moksha after a few births;

Rajasasattvikee: Those who are not pure at birth, but become so after doing good deeds;

Rajasarajasee: Those who are not born in fortunate circumstances but, owing to their good deeds, attain moksha quickly;

Rajasatamasee: Those who are not born in fortunate circumstances and are so full of desires that it takes hundreds of births for them to attain moksha;

Rajasa atyantatamasee: These are an even more extreme type of the former;

Tamasee: Those who have lived hundreds of lives and are not likely to attain moksha soon;

Tamasasattva: Those who become worthy of moksha immediately after birth, owing to their good deeds;

Tamorajasee: Those who attain moksha after a few births;

Tamas tamasee: Those who have lived thousands of lives, and will live thousands more before they attain liberation;

Atyanta tamasee: Those who have lived millions of lives, will live millions more and are unlikely to attain moksha.[59]

STRANGE WORLDS OR STRANGE CREATURES

Not only are there millions of worlds, they are also inhabited by creatures that are unlike any on earth. Vasishtha tells Rama that, although there are many kinds of organisms all over the universe, they experience joys and happiness the same way as we do. Even the tiniest organism has desires and expectations like us, and they, too, strive to realise them as we do. For example, an extremely tiny organism named 'Timi' is as active in the sky as a vulture looking for its prey.

Just as we have the notion of 'this is mine', all the creatures of the world have the same, depending upon their level of consciousness. Rocks and other non-living things are in a state of deep sleep, the plant kingdom is partially awake, and micro-organisms, the animal kingdom and humans are partially asleep and partially awake.[60]

Through external sense organs, the individual self sees the external world, through internal sense organs it sees the inner world, and through its sensitive mind, it sees both the external and internal world.[61] When these organs see the external world, it appears gross. During this experience, internal cognition is there but it is feeble so the internal appears subtle in comparison with the external. When the organs focus on the internal, this appears gross. Now the perception of the external world is feeble, so the external world appears subtle in comparison.[62] Whatever is seen becomes an object, hence gross. In fact, nothing is gross, as everything is a creation of the mind, and is thus dreamlike.

Vasishtha reminds Rama that all these jeevas may look real, but they are illusory. When there is not even one jeeva, how can the possibility of many arise?[63] That the jeeva is born out of Brahman is said just for the sake of instruction.[64]

It may be asked, if all jeevas arise from one Brahman, why do all of them not think and wish alike?[65] Why do they not know what is happening in the minds of other individuals?

When Brahman playfully imagines itself as jeeva, it creates rules, as no game can exist without rules. The rule is that one jeeva should not know about the minds of others, otherwise what would be the point in creating many jeevas? The game would collapse, as one jeeva would pre-empt others. At this rate, nothing would ever happen. Suppose in a game of chess, you know what move the opponent is going to make, and the opponent also knows what move you are going to make, all the fun of playing would be lost. This is why it is no fun playing chess with oneself. For the game of the world to progress, one jeeva should not be aware of what the other desires and intends.

As long as jeevas remain individuated and separate, they are unable to see the worlds created by other jeevas, but once they break the barrier of individuation, they are able to see the individual creations of other jeevas.[66] This is done by overcoming the ego and purifying the mind. Once the mind is purified, it can see the worlds of other jeevas, as the wall of ego which separates one organism from another is broken.[67]

In conclusion, it is out of its own imagination, determination and ignorance that the supreme self takes the form of an individual self, and becomes encased in a corporal body. But Vasishtha repeats endlessly that bondage is only an illusion. All the individual has to do is to understand through self-knowledge that his individual self is no different from the universal self. For this realisation, only self-knowledge is sufficient. We do not need to resort to ascetic discipline or penance.

The body may be unreal, but since we have it, and as long as it is there, we must give up likes and dislikes and perform duties and actions.[68] As long as we are in the game, we must play it to the best of our ability.

The ultimate truth is that Brahman alone exists in its purity, and whatever it imagines, it becomes that.[69] After the mind is quietened and after all desires are given up, all that remains is Brahman in its original purity:

Duality seen among Brahman, individual, mind, illusion, doer, karma, world
Is not real in any way, as it is mere imagination of the mind.[70]

ENDNOTES

1. VIA:65:6
2. I:18:34
3. IV:23:18
4. IV:23:29
5. IV:23:4-17
6. VIB:19:25
7. VIB:19:26
8. IV:23:19
9. III:122:21
10. VIA:93:18,19
11. VIA:118:6
12. VIB:3:15
13. VIA:55:41
14. VIB:19:4
15. V:71:54
16. V:71:55
17. VIB:20:10-12, see also VIB:22:32-37, VIB:87:7-36

18. VIA:6:26
19. The Bhagavad Gita, X:33
20. These six-fold changes are: *jayate* (born), asti (has a being), *vardhate* (grows), *viparinayate* (undergoes change), *apaksheeyate* (decays), and *vinashyati* (perishes).
21. The Bhagavad Gita, V:13; there is also a verse in the Atharva Veda that says: Ayodhya is the city of powerful gods that has eight chakras and nine gates. (X:2:31)
22. VIA:124:17
23. VIA:124:18
24. VIA:124:19
25. VIA:124:20
26. VIA:124:21
27. VIA:124:23
28. III:92:9-10
29. III:3:7,8
30. II:12:22; The metaphor of the chariot is also found in scriptures such as the Bhagvad Purana VII:15:41-42; the Katha Upanishad, III:3; the Bhagavad Gita is a supreme example of this metaphor.
31. The Mundaka Upanishad III:1:1; The same analogy is also found in the Rig Veda I:164:20, Atharva Veda IX:14:20, and the Shvetashvatara Upanishad IV:6,7
32. III:102:16
33. III:67:2
34. III:1:13
35. VIA:124:1
36. III:67:56
37. VIA:50:14-17
38. VIB:19:23
39. III:1:16
40. VIA:31:39
41. VIA:31:40
42. VIA:31:44
43. VIA:31:46
44. V:91:14
45. V:91:19
46. V:91:20
47. V:91:22-23
48. V:91:26
49. V:92:1
50. V:92:3-20
51. VIB:19:8
52. VIA:51:66
53. V:71:67

54. In addition to these three, there is also turiya, which is just called 'the fourth'. This is the enlightened state; nothing can be said about it as it is beyond the senses and the mind. It can only be experienced.
55. III:117:1-29
56. This classification is also found in the Brahmarahsya Upanishad, in which the first stage, Beejajagarat, is named differently as Bindujagarat (Mantra 16).
57. III:117:12
58. The fourteen worlds or planes of existence are: Bhooh, Bhoovah, Svah, Mahah, Janah, Tapah, Satya, Atala, Vitala, Sutala, Talatala, Rasatala, Mahatala, and Patala.
59. III:94:1-18
60. VIB:99:3-26
61. VIB:145:1
62. VIB:145:2-3
63. III:14:18
64. VIA:51:9
65. III:14:28
66. IV:18:3-4
67. IV:18:11
68. IV:62:10
69. III:14:21
70. III:65:3

CHAPTER X

THE MIND AND
ITS CREATION

In the story, 'Chittopakhyana' from the Yogavasishtha, Vasishtha tells Rama an allegoric tale about a dark and dangerous forest where he saw a demon wandering. The demon was gigantic, with hundreds of eyes and hands. His behaviour was that of a mad man. Through his numerous eyes, he would see many things in the forest, and would run hither and thither to get hold of them. If he failed to get what he desired, he would begin to beat his body wildly. Fearful of his own self, he would retire to a dense corner of the forest where there were thorny bushes. Sometimes he would retire to a banana grove. In neither place was he peaceful. He would get bored and begin to scream wildly. One day, when his anguish was too much to bear, he jumped into a deep well, not knowing that it was full of poisonous creatures.

He began to live in the well. At daybreak, he would emerge from it and roam about in the pleasant surroundings of the forest, but would soon become bored.

'Whenever I came across him,' Vasishtha said, 'he would change direction, but one day I managed to confront him. I looked him in the eye, and soon his demoniac body began to disappear. He then entered my heart and became quiet and peaceful. I met several such demons in the forest and quietened them merely by looking at them, but those who avoided me, are still miserable.'

After listening to this strange story, Rama asks Vasishtha where was the forest he described, and who the demon was. Vasishtha replies, 'The forest is this world, and the demon is the mind. The hundreds of hands and eyes that he has are nothing but desires (vasanas). The dark well is the household. The thorny bushes are hell, and the banana grove is heaven. I am wisdom (*viveka*). When I look at the mind it becomes quiet. Through contemplation and wisdom, the mind becomes quiet, and the person attains supreme bliss.'[1]

This story not only captures the nature of mind, but also hints at how it can be quietened. Nothing has to be done to quieten it except understanding its nature and being aware of its activities. The mind is like a servant who misbehaves when the master is away.

We have already discussed how the mind and the world are created when absolute Brahman pulsates or imagines. One may be convinced by this explanation or one might not. It does not matter how the mind was born, and why it has certain characteristics. The fact is that it creates misery and bondage, and if we wish to be happy, we ought to make an effort to understand the mind and set ourselves free.

For the Yogavasishtha, anything other than Brahman or absolute consciousness falls in the domain of the mind. In its view, the mind, intellect, ego, emotion, life-force, body and entire cosmos, including space and time, are mind.

This entire world is created by the mind; the heavenly bodies are the mind; The sky is the mind, the earth is the mind, and the wind is also the mind.[2]

If the mind does not illuminate the heavenly bodies,
There will be no light, even after the Sun has risen.[3]

Just as all the activities of the world begin after the Sun rises;
The world comes into existence in the light of the mind.[4]

If the entire cosmos is a creation of the mind, it follows that all the laws of the cosmos and the properties of all matter are created by the mind. This is because all that is visible or imaginable is produced by the mind. Mind is all — earth, stars, sky, living creatures and anything else we can imagine.

Vasishtha says that there is nothing real or unreal in the world. It is the mind that takes something for real or unreal.[5] The mind imagines the gross body and the world; therefore, it is the mind that is responsible for the illusion.[6]

The world gets created like the illusory water is created by a mirage;
Its existence is momentary like the illusion of seeing two moons.[7]

It makes a small thing appear big, a real thing unreal;
Makes a bitter thing tasty, and turns a foe into a friend.[8]

Following this, we could say that when the supreme consciousness (atman) vibrates, it can be called 'mind'. Mind is not a thing; it is merely a name of the absolute consciousness that is imagining or pulsating of its own free will. When the absolute consciousness stops pulsating, the mind disappears. When it pulsates, it appears to be gross.

The gross appearance of the formless is called mind;
Other than this, the mind has no existence at all.[9]

In the Yogavasishtha, the mind is named variously as manas (mind), buddhi (intellect), ahamkara (ego), chitta (individual consciousness), karma (previous deeds), kalpana (imagination), samsriti (flow, worldly life), vasana (desire), prayatna (effort), smriti

The Mind and Its Creation   177 (memory), *indriya* (sense organs), prakriti (nature), maya (illusion), kriya (actions), jeeva (living thing or being), and antahkarana (the internal organ).[10]

We might ask why the mind is known by so many names. Vasishtha says that just as an actor assumes different roles on the stage, so the mind engages itself in different activities and roles. For example, when a man cooks, he is called a cook, when he teaches, he is called a teacher, and when he leads a village, he is called a village head. Similarly, when the mind performs various actions, it is known according to the relevant role it plays.[11]

However, in Indian philosophy and more specifically in the Yogavasishtha, the mind is generally called 'manas' and 'chitta'.[12]

The word 'chitta', which stands for individual consciousness, should not be confused with a similar sounding word, 'chit', which is another name for absolute Brahman or supreme consciousness. While 'chit' is absolute, all change—happiness, misery, and action—take place in the realm of 'chitta' (mind or individual consciousness).[13] Although the Yogavasishtha uses 'chitta' and 'manas' interchangeably, at places it uses 'chitta' for the first stage when the mind is formed, and 'manas' as a general term for anything other than Brahman. In contrast to this, chit is the absolute self.

BIRTH OF THE MIND

Rama asks Vasishtha several times how the mind is born, whether it is gross or subtle, what its characteristics are, and how it works.[14] Vasishtha replies that the mind is neither gross nor subtle; it is both.[15] On the one hand, it is associated with supreme consciousness and, on the other hand, to the phenomenal world.[16] It arises between truth and untruth, grossness and consciousness.[17] The existence of the mind is nothing more than a name. Just as the void is both subtle and gross,[18] the mind is neither subtle nor gross, but pervades everything like space.

So what exactly is the mind? Vasishtha says:

Out of ignorance, the mind arises from Brahman
The ultimate power, just as a wave rises from the ocean.[19]

This analogy illustrates the relationship between the universal mind (chit) and the individual mind (chitta).

For the learned, the mind is nothing but Brahman;
As they know that the wave is no different from water.[20]

Mind is just will, and the nature of the will is to pulsate;
From pulsation arise actions and the consequences that follow.[21]

Where there is will, there is mind, and that is how it is sustained;
It is not possible to differentiate between the will and the mind.[22]

Since the mind is just an imagined thing, and the world it creates is called an illusion (maya). The concept of maya leads people to conclude that the world does not exist. If that were the case, whom are maya theorists talking to? Maya just means that we are perceiving things wrongly, that we are taking our true self to be other than what it is or, as per the famous example, we are taking the rope for a snake. Maya theory reminds us that the snake is not there; it does not say that there is nothing there. Something is definitely there—the rope, but we are seeing it wrongly. This is because of erroneous perception (ignorance). If there were no rope, there would be no snake. It is this ignorance that creates problems. Once ignorance is cleared with self-knowledge, the illusion disappears like the darkness of the night disappears at sunrise.

This is how the mind becomes the seed for the entire worldly creation;
And this happens when consciousness directs itself outwards.[23]

In Europe, following the Scholastics of the Middle Ages, Franz Clemens Brentano (1838–1917) describes consciousness as 'intentional', which means whenever we think, we think about something. This view has now become a standard definition of consciousness in Western philosophy. In Indian philosophy, 'intentional' consciousness would be called 'mind'. It is the mind that is intentional not absolute consciousness. Absolute is not conscious of anything; it is consciousness itself.

Vasishtha tells Rama that, although the mind gives rise to thoughts and imagination, it is itself a product of imagination and hence a myth.

That is how this great long worldly dream comes to be;
And all creatures move from one dream to another.[24]

Once the false perception becomes strong, it becomes solid like a wall;
Then whatever the mind desires, it experiences it as such.[25]

When the will becomes reinforced, the mind experiences external objects as real;
Even so, whatever the mind experiences is just imaginary.[26]

The entire world is anchored in the mind, Rama;
Thus, bondage and liberation are also in the mind.[27]

CHARACTERISTICS OF THE MIND

Since the mind grows out of the vibration of the supreme self, it is highly mercurial. It keeps fluctuating like a barometer. If we identify ourselves with the volatile mind, we are bound to be in a perpetual state of unrest. If someone asks why the mind pulsates, all that can be said is that this is the very property of the mind. If it does not pulsate, it would not be mind.

Just as coolness is the property of ice, blackness of coal;
Extreme pulsation is the inherent nature of the mind.[28]

Vasishtha says that pulsation of the mind is called ignorance, and we must end this ignorance by contemplating our real nature.[29]

Because the mind survives on ignorance and forgetfulness, the purpose of the Yogavasishtha is to show how to end ignorance.

To do this, we ought to first remember that we are not the mind but pure consciousness. Then we have to verify if this claim is true.

It has been asserted repeatedly that the mind does not have an independent existence, that it is illusory because the mind depends upon Brahman (chit) for its existence. Vasishtha says that the mind is a parasite like a wild cat that eats an animal killed by a lion. 'How can the mind, which is gross, exist without the chit?' asks Vasishtha.[30] It may be possible for a block of stone to have the power to move, but without the aid of the universal self, the mind can do nothing.[31]

Explaining how the mind is both absolute and dynamic, Vasishtha says that the life force (*pranavayu*), is always pulsating, and thus is gross, while the power of the absolute self (*chit shakti*), is unsullied and all-pervading.[32] That which grows through the association of absolute power and vibrating life force (chit shakti and *pranaspandana*) is called mind.

The relationship between the conscious power (chit shakti) and the
pulsating power (spanda shakti) is called mind;
As there is no ground for its existence, it is called false knowledge.[33]

It might be asked if the absolute is perfect and unchanging, why does illusion arise in it. The Yogavasishtha says that just as the tree is hidden in the seed, illusory duality is inherent in every creature.[34] The supreme consciousness is absolute, omniscient and omnipresent, but since it is perfect and absolute, it must also include duality; otherwise it would not be absolute. The absolute has to be all-inclusive. It is perfect, but it has to include imperfectness; it is non-dual, but it has to include duality. No doubt the absolute is consciousness alone, but it must include matter too. It is pure bliss, but it must also include misery as well. It must have the desirable as well as the undesirable things otherwise we would have to give a parallel status to undesirable things. This would create duality or two domains: one of desirable things and another of undesirable.

Then we would have the problem of explaining how we can claim that the supreme power is absolute if it has no power over the undesirable realm. In traditional language, if God is all powerful, why can He not overpower evil?

Vedanta says, although absolute reality is pure bliss and without any modifications and distortions, it pulsates because this is a part of its nature, just as it is natural for the ocean to have waves. This pulsation is also known as imagination or creative power, viranchittva, forgetfulness or ignorance of the absolute.[35]

This is the illusory power, and it is also called maya;
This is the supreme ignorance that creates the miserable world.[36]

THE PROCESS OF INDIVIDUATION

Once the world comes into being through the willpower or desire of Brahman, the mind gets involved in its own creation because of the simultaneous birth of the ego (ahamkara) and intellect (buddhi). The mind either desires something or wishes to get rid of something. This tendency is called *raga-dvesha* (attraction and aversion). In this, it is the intellect that helps us choose between various options, and to find solutions to the problems we face every moment. Then there is the ego. This asserts its individuality by claiming — this is mine, this is not mine. Thus, the non-dual is divided, and this is the beginning of misery because limits mean bondage, and no one likes bondage.

Consider the ego to be the seed of the tree called universe;
From it are born rivers, mountains, lakes and oceans.[37]

Once the supreme consciousness becomes the mind, desires arise within it. Because of desires, it is the mind that enjoys things, suffers, dies and is born again, thus creating bondage for the individual. However, if the mind is illuminated by self-knowledge, it frees itself from bondage.[38] Until then, we are guided by the mind. Just as a charioteer steers the horses in whichever direction he wishes to go, the mind takes the body wherever it wants.[39]

Using another metaphor, Vasishtha says that the mind is like a bridge that can either take us towards the phenomenal world of misery, or towards the transcendental world of supreme bliss. Just as a child makes a toy out of clay, and then destroys it to make another one, the mind imagines a body, and then destroys it and makes another body.[40]

This creates a vicious cycle of life, birth and death. In the beginning of creation, according to the Yogavasishtha, gods such as Brahma, Vishnu and Shiva were consciousness alone, and were not subject to the cycle of life and death. It is only when the individual consciousness, under the influence of the ego, began to think it was different from the universal consciousness that the cycle of karma and births and deaths began.

The Yogavasishtha says that birth and death, and heaven and hell are creations of the mind. In fact, whatever is ascertained by whomever and in whatever manner is perceived by them likewise. Objects of the world in themselves are neither good nor bad, neither desirable nor undesirable, neither bitter nor sweet. It is the perceiving mind that makes us feel that they are so.

After the supreme consciousness begins to think falsely that it is the body, duality arises. Now the unbounded and infinite atman becomes limited. It begins to feel that it lacks certain things, and because of this, it begins to desire certain things and avoid certain others. To achieve or avoid things, action is needed. All actions arise only if we think we lack something, and the belief that whatever we lack can be acquired from the outside.

As the seed of action is the mind, it later experiences the result of its good or bad actions.[41] This is the beginning of our bondage and misery.

It may be asked why the free and blissful atman chooses

bondage and suffering. The answer is, first of all, that this bondage is not real; it is just a game of the universal self, and it is out of playfulness that the supreme self imagines itself to be bound and limited. In any game, we make certain rules and the players have to limit themselves according to those rules, otherwise the game cannot progress. We have discussed this in Chapters I, VII and IX. The same way, in a stage play, a perfectly healthy actor might play the role of a sick person, and a strong actor might play the role of a weakling. In both cases, the actors are just playing their roles without giving up their true nature.

Further, freedom means to have both options, to be free or bounded, to live or die, to love or hate, and to be good or bad. If we had the freedom to be good alone, it would not be freedom — it would be bondage, although we would be imprisoned in a golden cage.

Thus, when the atman, of its own free will, pulsates and becomes the mind, the illusory world of the individual mind (jeeva) comes into being (we have discussed this in Chapter IX). It must be noted that this transformation of the supreme self into the individual mind is only apparent, not real. Just as the moon is reflected in dozens of tanks and lakes, the supreme consciousness resides in different bodies.

Thus, there are individual selves in innumerable numbers;
According to the imagination of the supreme consciousness.[42]

Billions of individuals were born out of the universal self in the past;
And will be born in the future like the spray of vapour in a waterfall.[43]

It must be remembered that the true nature of the supreme consciousness cannot be polluted. Just as a mirror begins to reflect clearly after it is dusted, the mind regains its blissful nature with the dawn of self-knowledge.[44] Only when it limits itself by becoming a mind, does it seemingly become impure, limited and bound.

It is this ignorance which binds the mind and makes it think that it is different from Brahman or absolute consciousness. This ignorance is the cause of all misery and it creates the cycle of birth and death. At the rate this ignorance is dispelled, our bliss and freedom increase. Bliss can arise with self-knowledge alone, as bondage is created out of ignorance.

UNDERSTANDING THE MIND

It might be asked, if the mind is an illusion, why are we discussing it? Why are we trying to define it? Why are we trying to suggest ways of conquering it? If the absolute is non-dual, and if the world is unreal, why are we discussing the nature of duality? How will this duality end by knowing the fundamental truth?[45]

We are discussing illusion because we do not realise it is illusion. Although the mind is an illusion, maya, it is a dynamic kind of illusion. It is important to understand that it is an illusion because it affects our lives and makes us perform all sorts of actions. For example, in the popular example of the rope and the snake, if we are aware that it is just a rope that looks like a snake, we will not be afraid of it at all. This does not qualify as maya, for we are not affected by this perception. It would qualify as maya only if we were compelled to do something after we perceived the rope as a snake. We should either run for our lives or try to kill the snake.

Vasishtha says that the illusory power of maya is so strong and dynamic that the world is swallowed up by something which has neither a body nor any shape. Could anyone think of a greater absurdity?[46]

The mind is an illusion, and the world it creates is also an illusion because something real cannot emerge from an illusion. The myth survives the way dreams survive, as long as the person is asleep (ignorant of the self).

If we were not affected by what seemingly goes on around us, it would be foolish to discuss it. We discuss the nature of illusion because we take the whole chimera (*prapancha*) to be real. We are not only dreaming but are also taking the dream to be real. This is why those who are awake (such as gurus and wise men) teach; otherwise there would be no point in teaching.

Knowledge is stressed because duality emerges out of ignorance. If duality were real, knowledge would not have dispelled it and the thesis of Vedanta would have collapsed. In the popular example of rope and snake, if the snake were real, shining light on it would not have made it disappear. In fact, its reality would become established with certainty.

Vasishtha says it is just for the sake of instruction that duality has to be assumed initially, although there is no duality as such.[47] Brahman and the world, consciousness and mind, action and agent are not different, just as the flower and its fragrance are not different. It is only to make the uninformed understand that it is said that the world grows out of Brahman. Such doctrines are not preached to the knowledgeable. Until duality is presumed, discourse becomes impossible.[48]

Suppose some apparatus is malfunctioning; in order to repair it we would have to understand how it works. To understand how it works, we would have to rip it apart. This ripping apart is akin to assuming duality in the non-dual reality. By assuming duality, it becomes easy to understand reality.

All discussions about mind, ego, ignorance, free will and so on are only to awaken a person who is having a dream, whether it is a good or a bad dream. Therefore, in the phenomenal domain, discourse has meaning, but in the absolute domain, it has no meaning. Medicine could be beneficial for a sick person, but it could be harmful for the healthy.

Further, although absolute reality is one, it can be viewed from various levels. Whichever level we choose, we begin to identify ourselves with it, and that level alone begins to appear to be real to us.[49] This is why there is so much animosity between various doctrines, philosophies and religions.

Whatever is perceived by the mind in whatever manner;
It is experienced likewise in like manner.[50]

By taking nectar to be poison it becomes so;
And if you have a friendly approach, an enemy becomes a friend.[51]

We see that creatures live in all sorts of environment. We die by taking poison, but there are organisms for whom the same poison is food. This much is understandable. The point is, if by merely thinking poison can become nectar, why do we die after taking poison? The answer to this is that our conditioning is not strong and dense enough yet. The organisms that thrive on poison have been conditioned thoroughly. This is why for them it is not poison but food. The conditioning has to be dense and sustained long enough for it to work.

Although we have the freedom to view the world from any level, whatever level we view it from, our world becomes likewise. One of the main characteristics of the mind is that the way we think, our life gets affected accordingly — *Ya matih sa gatirbhavet*. As willpower (sankalpa shakti) is the fundamental nature of the mind, whatever sort of world the mind imagines, it creates that sort of world through its willpower.[52]

From the absolute standpoint, the mind and the world do not exist at all, but because of our own limited vision, we cannot view the truth from the absolute dimension; we see it from the phenomenal standpoint. From this viewpoint, the mind appears to be real and the absolute appears to be unreal, and because the mind appears to be real, it has a profound effect on our lives. For instance, when we see a beast attacking us in a dream, we get frightened; our heart begins to thump violently although the beast is not real. We realise the beast is unreal only upon waking up. While we were dreaming, it was as real as anything else.

Thus, the mind is the cause of all experience, as it is the mind that cognises the external world, as well as internal feelings. Whatever is experienced in the light of the mind alone is called direct cognition, pratyaksha.[53]

In all the joys and sorrows and in the creation of various objects;
The mind alone is the doer and the enjoyer; mind is man indeed.[54]

Lemon and sugarcane are neither bitter nor sweet, nor the moon cool and fire hot;
Whatever is imagined in whatever manner, it is experienced likewise by the mind.[55]

Look at the powers of the mind, without the need of space and time
It makes a white thing appear black, and a black thing white.[56]

If the mind is engaged elsewhere, the tongue does not
experience the taste even of well-chewed food.[57]

What the mind sees alone is seen, what is not seen by it is not seen;
The sense organs create them accordingly, as one sees forms in the dark.[58]

Since time is also created by the mind, it is not absolute. For example, it is a common experience that when we are in misery, time moves slowly, and when we are happy it passes quickly. Vasishtha says that it is only because of the mind that a single night appeared to be twelve years long for King Harishchandra, and an entire age passed in a moment for King Indradhyumna.[59] If the mind is happy, even the extreme torture of hell becomes pleasurable, just as handcuffs and chains become pleasurable for someone who believes he is going to become king next morning.[60]

The upshot is that it is the mind that is the enjoyer or sufferer, not the gross body and the supreme consciousness.[61] All this enjoyment or suffering is experienced because we forget our true blissful nature and identify ourselves with the mind–body complex. If an actor from a rich family, who is playing the role of a beggar, identifies himself with the character of the beggar, he takes the sufferings of the beggar as his own. He is then as miserable as a real beggar, although his sufferings have arisen out of forgetfulness of his true self. This is why Vasishtha says that it is the uninformed who suffer sorrows, not the enlightened.[62] The uninformed take the body–mind complex to be their true self forgetting that they are essentially absolute Brahman; the enlightened, on the other hand, realise that they are absolute Brahman and the body–mind complex is just a temporary attribute they have acquired because of their past karmas.

Although the senses operate because of the mind, and the mind needs the senses to cognise, the mind is independent of the senses, as it is the mind that creates the senses. When the mind wishes to see, it creates eyes; when it wishes to hear, it creates ears; when it wishes to touch, it creates the skin, and when it wishes to smell, it creates the nose.[63] When it wishes to taste, it creates the tongue. Just as an actor on stage performs various roles, the mind performs various functions in the body.[64]

Thus, constantly affected by likes and dislikes, the mind is always choosing from the unlimited options that the world presents.

A strange trait of the mind is that if it does not get the object of its desire it becomes miserable, and if it gets the object of its desire, it gets bored with it and later miserable. It wants to get rid of what it worked so hard to get, and begins to look for something else. Because of this, the mind is always fluctuating, always unsatisfied. It fluctuates because it desires something all the time.

If we could get over desire, the mind would quieten on its own. Is this possible?

ENDNOTES
1.   III:98 and 99
2.   III:110:15

3. III:110:16
4. III:122:52
5. IV:21:57
6. IV:11:18, IV:20:4
7. III:4:40
8. III:110:20
9. III:4:42
10. III:96:13,14; see also III:96:37-42 III:115:18; VIA:114:18; VIA:30:28-32; VIB:143:37
11. III: 96:43-44
12. Chitta is the mind from which distortions arise (the Yogasara Upanishad, Mantra 7).
13. III:14:57-76
14. III:96:36
15. The Chandogya Upanishad treats the mind as gross because it is a byproduct of food. If one does not eat food for fifteen days, the faculties of the mind stop working, (VI:7:1-6). Food is gross, so the mind that grows out of it is also gross.
16. III:96:37-42
17. III:112:13
18. In Indian philosophy, space is also one of the gross elements because we have no idea of it in deep sleep.
19. III:100:1
20. III:100:2
21. III:96:1
22. III:4:44
23. V:13:81
24. IV:18:47
25. IV:18:48
26. III:52:38
27. III:98:3
28. III:112:3
29. III:112:11
30. V:13:50
31. V:13:86
32. V:13:87
33. V:13:88
34. IV:17:6
35. III:4:36-51
36. V:13:89
37. VIB:7:11
38. IV:4:9
39. IV:10:44

40. IV:10:45
41. See also IV:11:25-27
42. IV:43:1
43. IV:43:2
44. VIA:31:25
45. VIA:33:2
46. V:13:101
47. III:100:4
48. III:15:1-8
49. You become whatever you take yourself to be. If you think you are a body, you become so; And if you take yourself to be Sachchidananda Brahman, you become so.
   (The Vicharabindu Upanishad, Mantra 8)
50. III:60:16
51. III:60:17
52. VIB:149:16
53. III:110:21
54. III-115-24
55. IV:21:33
56. III:110:33
57. III:110:34
58. III:110:35
59. III:110:22, 23
60. III:110:24
61. III:115:10
62. III:115:13
63. III:110:18
64. III:110:19

CHAPTER XI

THE NATURE OF DESIRE

What would life be without desire? For most of us, a person without desires is as good as dead. Life means to desire and to hope. We think a person without desires lacks motivation, and has no zest for life. Without personal desire, why would anyone do anything at all.[1]

There is some truth in this claim as desires keep us motivated, and give us respite from the miseries of life but we often forget that the desires that were fulfilled, later disappointed us, or just caused us to desire more. All fulfilled desires turn sour in the end.

This world has so many wonderful things to offer, why do we never derive any satisfaction from them? The answer is that the world is changing every instant. Some things change quickly while others take some time, but they change nevertheless. How can an ever-changing world satisfy us? First of all, we do not usually get what we want easily, and even when we get it, we want it to remain in the same state forever. This is impossible. The object of our desires changes, as constant change is an inviolable law of nature. When we see that the object (persons included) has changed, we feel let down; we feel we have been cheated, forgetting an important fact that we have also changed over time.

Disappointed, we look for the next thing, in the hope that it will give us happiness, but as that thing is also subject to change, we become miserable and again look for something else.

At some point, we begin to wonder if there is anything at all that can give us peace. At this point, for some of us, the journey to the self can begin, although it may not necessarily begin for all. Most of us continue to hanker after desirable things all our lives.

Before embarking upon the journey to know the self, the first task should be to understand the mind and its workings because the root cause of our problems is the mind. It is the mind that creates duality, and as long as duality is willed or imagined, misery will persist.

Why do they say that the world is nothing but misery? Do we not experience happiness sometimes?

We shall examine this claim in parts. If the world were nothing but abject misery, we would end our lives without hesitation. Those who lose all hope commit suicide but for most of us there is always hope, there is always a tomorrow, because the mind survives on time.

Time means either the past or the future. The present is not part of time, according to Vedanta, as the present is existence itself, and existence is beyond time. Time means memory. To 'exist' is not memory, it is a fact. We do not say, 'I remember I am'; we say, 'I am'.

Most of us, however, are always thinking either about the past or the future. The past is over; there is no point in reliving past glories or repenting for our mistakes. Dreaming about the future also does not help us. It simply wastes the present. It is the present that matters. If it is lived fully, our worries and conflicts disappear because those who live in the present become free of the mind.[2]

The Yogavasishtha of Valmiki

The mind is always thinking about the past or the future because the present is death for the mind. The mind survives by making us think that although things might be bad today, they will be better in the future. Some people, on the other hand, like to live in the past. Since the past can never come back, they are miserable.

If we examine this problem, we find that all the joys of the past have lost their lustre and, in most cases, have turned into misery. What has gone wrong? The fact is that it is not things that possess properties called 'joy' and 'misery'. It is our mind that attaches these properties to things. It is for this reason that no external object can give us joy. Even when it appears to, the joy is fleeting, as the mind is fickle and gets bored with everything after a while.

This is why the learned say that only the 'real' can give joy and the unreal can only bring misery. There is no greater 'unreality' than the mind.

As we have mentioned before, truth is that which exists always. It is unchanging, and an untruth is that which comes into existence for a short while and is ever changing. We notice that nothing in the phenomenal world has always been there. This is the reason nothing can give us lasting happiness. As King Janaka muses in the Yogavasishtha, 'My life comes into existence for a while in this seemingly timeless world, and shame on me for trying to pin my hopes on it.'[3]

The truth is that worldly objects in themselves can neither give us joy nor unhappiness. It is the expectation of deriving happiness from them that makes us miserable. This is why a gyani is immensely happy while we are miserable, although we live in the same world. Just as beauty is not inherent in a thing but in the eye of the beholder, happiness and sorrow are not innate in things but in our mind. This is why joy turns into misery and misery into joy, depending upon the state of our mind.

The Nature of Desire

KINDS OF DESIRE

Desire for the body (*Deha vasana*): Excessive attachment with the body is one of the mains reasons of our misery. We should take care of the body and use it to our advantage, but we need not be obsessively concerned about it. Nobody wants the body to grow old knowing full well that it will. Rarely are we happy with the kind of body we have.

Desire for recognition (*Loka vasana*): To be recognised, to be popular, to be powerful in society keeps people motivated. This desire, however, can become a mental affliction, and in extreme cases make us power hungry and dictatorial.

Desire for the scriptures (*Shastra vasana*): Excessive desire for a good thing can also become a problem. Reading scriptures to acquire knowledge is beneficial in the quest for bliss, but this to can become an obsession. Many people go on reading one scripture after another forgetting why they are reading it. Too much attachment to the scriptures can make us fanatical. After self-knowledge is gained, we should give up scriptures just as medicine is given up after regaining health. The desire for reading scriptures and quoting them is one of the most difficult to overcome.

As we have seen, the cause of misery is the volatile nature of the mind. We might ask why this is so. Why did nature not give us a stable mind? The fact is that a stable mind would be of no use at all. A cardiogram, the instrument that measures the vibrations of the heart, for instance, cannot give us accurate information unless it is highly sensitive to the slightest tremor. The more sensitive it is, the more accurate and useful it is. But if the doctor loses his calm by looking at the vibrations of the cardiogram, he will not be able to do his job well.

The mind, along with the five senses, is nothing but a mechanism that serves the body; it helps us survive in the world. It has to be extremely sensitive to the changes around us so that we can assess the situation. In order to analyse and make sense of the information that it perceives, it first has to break down the incoming information. This is why the mind cannot deal with anything that is not polar. The mind evolved to deal only with entities that are polar or dual.

Polarities or dualities create conflict, but they also create beauty. For instance, it is because of the contrast between various colours that we enjoy the beauty of a flower or a sunset. In fact, on the phenomenal plane, polarity (maya) alone is of use to us. Drawing on the analogy of clay, we notice that clay itself is not of much use to us, but the pot that is made of clay certainly is.

Coming back to polarities, the problem is not with the mind as such, but with our total identification with it. Thus, as long as there is mind, there will be polarities; there will be a sense of space and time, and there will be an ego. As long as there is ego, there will be misery. Even the seeming joys and pleasures that the mind gives us are nothing but misery in disguise. No one actually wants misery, but since everything in the world is made of polarities, joy is necessarily accompanied by sorrow, as it is the other side of the coin. We might want only one side of the coin but this is impossible; the other side will necessarily come with it. As Janaka muses:

Along with existence is destruction, along with beautiful, the ugly;
Along with pleasure is pain; this being the case, what can I ever desire?[4]

Further, the mind is never happy with one polarity for very long. After a while it seeks change. Since it is the mind that creates the world, and since it is this that creates desires and likes and dislikes, it is the mind that motivates all action through its willpower. Thus, only actions that are motivated by the mind are called actions, and not those that happen in spite of it.

Raghava, consider what the mind does alone as done;
And what the mind renounces, consider it as renounced.[5]

There are several functions that the body performs, such as

breathing, blood circulation and the rest, but these do not qualify as actions, as there is no intention or will behind them. Similarly, unintended actions performed by humans cannot be called actions. Only intentional actions that are guided by the mind and the ego are subject to blame and praise. Going by this logic, when we give up the ego, quieten the mind and begin to live according to the inner law (rita), we become free of sin, as well as piety.

The mind, when faced with a situation, first assesses it and decides on a course of action. Once the mental decision to act in a certain way is made, physical action follows. In other words, our body is the vehicle or instrument of mental actions. As mentioned earlier, the mind perceives the world, and is then either attracted to certain people or objects, or is repelled by them. When it has a desire for a certain person or an object, it makes a resolve to gain possession. However, life is not easy. There are others who wish to possess the objects of our desire, so there is cut-throat competition among humans for desirable things.

No matter how many things we seek and get, everything turns sour in the end. The solution is to drop the ego, drop the tendency to desire things, and accept whatever is the result of our actions.

Giving up desire does not mean to become totally uninterested in life. It just means to live life fully in the present. If we desire something, it means we do not have it now, for we cannot desire what we already have. In order to get it, we need time, we need to make an effort, and we need resources. Since we have no control over the future, we keep running to fulfil our desires. The moment we fulfil one desire, we run after another, and then another. This goes on as long as we are directed by the mind and the ego.

When we become masters of the mind by annihilating the ego, we become free of greed and desire. We become blissful, quiet, non-aggressive, polite, strong and possessors of a super body (*mahashareera*).[6]

The question, therefore, is how to become possessors of a super body by becoming the masters of the mind?

Right now, we are using only a tiny fraction of our mind and body complex because of the limiting factor called the ego. Once the limiting factor is removed, we gain access to the entire energy of the universe. Earlier, the body had only limited energy, and because of this it got tired and worn out easily. Now it becomes capable of performing things that we could not have imagined earlier.

After gaining self-knowledge, seekers become free of mind (*achitta*), as they become like blank space.[7] Does this mean that liberated people have no mind? How do they manage to get by in the world?

As long as the body is there, the mind will also be there. How else would we do our daily work? How would we communicate with others, and how would we associate with the world? All talk about conquering the mind, annihilating the ego and becoming a no-mind means we should become masters of the mind or ego. We have to learn to tame the wild horse, but we should not incapacitate or kill it. The enlightened also have a mind, but they are the masters of it.[8] Once we become the masters of our mind, we begin to use it to the best of our advantage. From being an uncontrollable wild horse, it becomes an obedient and excellent horse.

In the following chapters, we shall see how the ego operates, and what can be done to subdue it.

ENDNOTES
1. Even dumbheads do not do anything without a purpose.
2. V:50:16
3. V:9:6
4. V:9:41
5. III:110:14
6. VIA:116:1-12
7. V:91:47
8. V:50:24

CHAPTER XII

THE EGO AND ITS WORKINGS

Who am I? This is a question which even the least philosophical minded among us ask when in a pensive mood. The answer might seem obvious, but it is only deceptively so.

Most of us take for granted that we are the body. But we soon realise that the body constantly changes. It is susceptible to disease and old age, and finally dies. On the other hand, if a limb is severed, although we would be at a disadvantage in doing our worldly duties, our selfhood is in no way reduced. If a woman loses two limbs, we do not say she is half a woman, neither does she feel she is half a woman. Therefore, the body cannot be the self.

Some of us think we are the mind, and identify ourselves with the thoughts, beliefs and ideologies that we hold. The fact is that the mind and thoughts also keep changing. In childhood we have a certain set of ideas, and as we grow up, we might not hold those ideas any longer. We might also change our ideologies: a communist might become a liberal, a liberal might become a rightist, and a rightist might become a leftist.

From birth to death our world goes on changing, yet the one who experiences this constant change remains unchanged, otherwise who would notice the change? If I were different from the child I was many years ago, how would I remember the experiences of my childhood? There has to be something that has not changed all these years.

Throughout our lives, we see objects, other human beings, animals, trees, mountains, houses and cars. We experience joys and sorrows and ups and downs. In all this seeing and experiencing, we notice that the one who is seeing and experiencing all these things and situations is aloof from everything else.

It must be noted that even the body, mind and intelligence are part of the world, as they, too, go on changing. The self is independent of all these. In other words, there is the objective world and a subject that is experiencing it. We might ask which of the two (the self and the phenomenal world) has an independent existence; in other words, which of the two cannot exist without the other, and which will continue to survive in spite of the other.

There must be something that does not change in spite of this constant change. That something, according to Vedanta, is supreme consciousness (atman).

THREE STATES OF CONSCIOUSNESS

There are the three states of consciousness: waking, dream and deep sleep. When we wake from a dream, we notice that behind the dreamwork, there was someone who was seeing the dream. The dream world was unreal, but the subject experiencing it was not. After we get up from deep sleep, although we do not remember anything, it is clear that someone was there, having the experience of deep sleep, otherwise how could we say, 'I slept well'? Further, although there is a discontinuity in memory in deep sleep, upon waking we remember the events that happened before going to sleep. From this we infer that, even in deep sleep, our selfhood was not totally dissolved.

We take up the waking state now. It is quite possible that, just as the dream world appeared very real to us but was actually unreal, the world of waking state (jagarat) could be as unreal. Here again, although the waking state might be unreal, the experiencing subject is without doubt real.

The question then arises: Who is the common experiencing subject of these three states? It cannot be the body, as this is nearly unconscious in the dream and sleep states. It cannot be the mind, as this undergoes a change during the dream state. For example, a king might dream that he is a beggar. In deep sleep, the mind is not there at all, which is why we do not remember anything upon waking. If it is not the body or the mind, it has to be something beyond these. Vedanta says that it is the individual consciousness or the true self, as it experiences all three states without itself undergoing any change.

According to the Yogavasishtha and other non-dualistic Vedantic texts, there is one supreme conscious reality, which creates the world, preserves it and finally destroys it. This supreme reality is the real self, as it is absolute and unchanging. It exists in the three dimensions of consciousness and time; in other words, it is eternal. It is essentially pure consciousness (chit), but when it imagines the world, it is called by several names, such as the mind, the ego, or the individuating principle, depending upon the different functions it performs.

Being alive and conscious, it is called the individual self;
By getting oriented outwards, it is called the mind.[1]

When it makes clear decisions, it is called the intellect;
When it imagines, contemplates and becomes a knower, it is called the mind.[2]

The idea that 'I am somebody' is called the ego;
It is called mind by those who know the scriptures.[3]

The Sanskrit word, ahamkara, is generally translated as 'ego'. Having understood how the mind comes into being, we shall now try to understand the meaning of the term 'ahamkara' — what it stands for, how the idea of the false self or ego originates, what effect it has on our lives, how it creates misery for us, and how it can be quelled.

The Yogavasishtha says that as long as we are governed by the ego, we can never experience true bliss.

All distortions such as happiness and sorrow that arise,
Are the consequences of alterations created by the ego.[4]

The question then arises: If the ego is the cause of our suffering, why is it there in the first place? Why do we so strongly cling to it? Would we not be better off without it? The answer is 'no', because there are two realms, the phenomenal and the absolute, and they are governed by different laws. The ego is indispensable in the phenomenal world, because it is the ego that creates the world. This is the reason it is an indispensable tool for survival and progress in the physical world. It gives us a sense of identity by making us different from others. How would a creature defend itself if it did not have an idea of 'self', and if it did not have an idea of 'the other'? Without the idea of selfhood, when hungry, I would not feed myself; without the idea of selfhood, I would not defend myself in danger.

It is because of having a strong ego that humans have managed to dominate the world. However, it is also because of that same ego that humans seem to be the most miserable creatures on earth. Anything that can be useful can also be harmful if we allow it to become our master. The ego is the impediment in our quest for the true self, because in the non-dual realm, there is pure consciousness alone; there is no competition, no struggle to succeed — everything is pure bliss, *ananda*. The ego has no place there.

The Yogavasishtha says that whether it is the body of a sage or someone ignorant of the self, it cannot exist without an ego. There is a natural tendency to assert ourselves in society. No one in the world wants to be a nobody. However, the Yogavasishtha reminds us that the ego does not have an independent existence. It owes its birth to ignorance. It arises out of false identification with the external world and we begin to consider the ego as our true self.

How can we say that the ego is false, that it has no existence? If it is a myth, why does it create so much suffering in our lives? We have discussed earlier that even a false or illusory thing can generate misery. For example, if, owing to clerical error, a medical report says that we are suffering from a terminal disease, our world is turned upside down. The report is false, but the misery it generates is real. It could kill us.

The ego, or what we refer to as 'I', is a projection of the mind that arises out of our association with worldly things. The ego, along with the mind, is one of the main causes of misery and suffering, and the greatest obstacle in the path of ultimate freedom and bliss.

If the ego generates nothing but suffering, why do we not do something to get rid of it. The truth is that the ego is the prime cause of misery, but we do not realise this because the ego is also the source of all the joys we know, although these joys turn out to be nothing but misery in the end. If people around us tell us that we are beautiful, strong and intelligent, we are overjoyed. However, if they tell us that we are not beautiful, strong and intelligent, we feel miserable, although we might actually be beautiful and strong.

When we do well, make money and rise in position, people begin to respect and fear us. This is gratifying because it makes us feel we are 'somebody'. But when we lose our money and position, the same people ignore us—now we feel miserable. This is why it is said that the ego does not have an independent existence—it is created through the opinion of others.

When a child is born, we give it a name, otherwise how would we distinguish it from others? This name, however, is a mere label;

we are not born with it. As the child grows, this label becomes inseparable from the child's personality. Some people are so touchy about their name that they get upset if it is mispronounced or misspelt even slightly.

As we grow up, we begin to attach other labels to our self, such as education, profession, ideas and place in the society. In due course, all these acquired labels (*upadhi*) become so ingrained in our minds that we begin to see them as integral to our selfhood. Without them, we would lose our identity. Strip a king or a minister of their power, and they become totally miserable because of their strong identity with power. Strip a businessman of his wealth, and he is lost. Take away a person's religion, and the result could be disastrous.

All our lives, we attach one label after another upon ourselves. These labels, no matter how gratifying, will be snatched away sooner or later. The body, however strong and beautiful, will perish; our brothers, sisters, wives, husbands, and children are not permanent; wealth and status, too, are temporary. However, all these give us a sense of identity, and it is this false identity that creates the ego.

This is why the Yogavasishtha says that the ego which grows out of these associations is a myth, because none of these — body, wealth, power, status — is our true self. They are temporary adorations and assumed titles or roles (upadhi).

The ego does not have an independent existence, as it needs a body, wealth and so on to sustain itself. Anything that is acquired (upadhi), and anything that changes, cannot be our true self.

How does the ego create bondage and suffering? When we identify ourselves with our external possessions (the body, mind and intellect are also external) we get a sense of gratification, and we also begin to experience fear, for we might lose them. We get angry if someone hampers our progress; we become fearful of losing our possessions, and we become possessive of what we have. The greed to have more and more, the desire to protect what we have, and the fear of losing it creates bondage. This is how misery begins.

Of its own accord, the self imagines its separate illusory existence;
And this idea of selfhood becomes the cause of worldly bondage.[5]

This is how the ego operates. It creates sorrow, yet it also gives us some gratification. After all, what is more gratifying than the feeling of 'I am so and so', 'I did it', 'I am beautiful', 'I am rich', 'I am intelligent', 'I am humble and pious'? The main purpose of our lives seems to be to become 'something', to get noticed, to get recognition. The ego keeps our world going, and this is a good thing if we think this world is all there is, and if we are satisfied with the fruits it offers. But no matter how successful we might be, no matter how wealthy and powerful we might be, or how knowledgeable, we always seek more and more, and as long as we seek more, we can never be happy.

If we come to realise that our desires can never be fulfilled through worldly possessions, we might begin to look for something beyond.

What is beyond? It is certainly not the mind. The mind has the power to will, but it is gross and material because it gets affected by the intellect. The intellect which decides for us is also gross because it is controlled by the ego, ahamkara, and we have just argued that the ego is an illusory creation of the individual consciousness.

The Yogavasishtha says that there is one universal self (Brahman, paramatman, atman, chit). When the universal self identifies itself with a particular body, it becomes an individual self (jeeva). These two are essentially the same, just as the universal space and the space within a pot are the same, although they might appear to be different. Because the individual self is oriented towards the external world, it is gross. There is only one self, and it is called super consciousness, *mahachitti*. It is pure and unblemished.

Although the mind–ego complex is illusory, it is our greatest enemy. This is the reason gurus and scriptures repeat endlessly that we ought to kill the ego.

The phrase 'kill the ego' has generated a great deal of misunderstanding among the seekers of self-knowledge. Most of those who hear it think that one ought to become a non-entity, a nobody, an unfeeling person or a doormat. This view is totally wrong. We ought to 'kill' the ego, but not the sense of 'selfhood'. The idea of 'selfhood' is called '*asmita*', which means 'the sense of being', and it has to be distinguished from the word 'ego' (ahamkara). An enlightened person does not have an ego, or we can say, he has become a master of his ego, but he certainly has a sense of selfhood. When hungry, he feeds himself, not someone else; when in danger, he defends himself. Without an idea of selfhood, there would be no difference between a conscious person and insentient matter.

How does one conquer a foe that does not exist? How does one turn it into a friend? This is the whole science of self-knowledge or what is called *adhyatma gyana* or Brahmavidya.

ENDNOTES
1. VIB:188:4
2. VIB:188:5
3. VIB:188:6
4. IV:33:35
5. III:96:19

CHAPTER XIII

KNOWLEDGE: THE BEST METHOD

At the beginning of the Yogavasishtha, King Suteekshna asks Sage Agasti whether human effort (karma[1]) or self-knowledge (atma gyana), or both, brought about freedom from misery (moksha). The Sage replies:

Just as birds need two wings to move about in the sky
Both self-knowledge and effort are needed for final liberation.[2]

Knowledge alone or action alone does not lead to liberation;
Hence, the seers advocate both as a means to final liberation.[3]

When someone thinks of ultimate liberation, it is natural to ask how liberation can be attained. However, by asking 'how', we unknowingly accept that we are bound.

If we are unwell, it is natural to ask how we can regain good health. If we consult doctors in spite of being healthy, it can only mean we think we are ill. In such a case, the only thing the doctor has to do is to prove that we are in good health, or he might give vitamin pills so we feel we are being treated. In the same manner, Vedanta says we never lost our freedom, so the question 'how to become free' does not arise. All that needs to be done is to show us that our sense of bondage is mistaken.

Since the matter is not that simple, let us get back to the question of whether self-knowledge (atma gyana) or human effort (karma) is the means to attain liberation. It should be noted that, later in the book, Vasishtha tells Rama that there are two methods of quietening the mind: gyana and yoga.

The two ways of destroying the mind, Raghava, are yoga and knowledge; Yoga is regulation of mental distortions; knowledge is investigation of the self.[4]

Since we have a third word 'yoga' here, we must first be clear what the words 'gyana', 'karma' and 'yoga' mean.

We could begin with the words 'karma' and 'gyana'. The Vedas primarily consist of two portions: one is called Karmakanda and the other Gyanakanda. Karmakanda is also called Poorvameemamsa, and as the name suggests, deals with actions, duties, rituals and sacrifices. The author of this section of the Vedas is Jaimini.

The second portion, called Gyanakanda, is also known as Uttarameemamsa or Vedanta, and deals mainly with self-knowledge. Its author is Vyasa, who was the guru of Jaimini. The goal of Uttarameemamsa is final freedom, moksha, kaivalya or nirvana. It holds that the individual and the universal self are one, and bondage arises out of ignorance. Since ignorance can be killed by knowledge alone, no physical effort or method is required.

Poorvameemamsa stresses human action to achieve the goals of life, and goals can be achieved in several ways. To lead a comfortable life, one needs wealth. To earn wealth one could work hard, inherit it or acquire it by dishonest means.

Society applauds us for what it considers to be good actions, and punishes us for bad. If society did not reward or punish us, there would be chaos.

Poorvameemamsa is about how things ought to be done (dharma), and it does not stop at judging our actions in this life alone. It says, depending upon our actions, we either go to heaven or hell. However, there is a catch here: after we exhaust the results of our good or bad deeds in heaven or hell, we come back to earth and start afresh. Nothing more is promised by Poorvameemamsa. In other words, it does not talk about the possibility of final freedom.

Poorvameemamsa is important because not all of us are interested in ultimate liberation. Most of us would like to live in this world and be successful in our pursuits. As the knowledge of this section of the Vedas is about the phenomenal world, this knowledge undergoes change with time. With progress, old methods are replaced by more advanced science and technology. In prehistoric times, they used stones to start a fire, but now we have more efficient means. This is why most of the knowledge of this section of the Vedas is redundant now.

Vedanta or Uttarameemamsa, on the other hand, does not emphasise action, as human effort can, at most, give us a temporary stay in heaven or hell. This section of the Vedas stresses self-knowledge (atma gyana), which frees us from worldly misery.

Since the Yogavasishtha deals mainly with final liberation, it says throughout that self-knowledge is the only means of final liberation. At times, it advocates physical effort, as a preparatory step, to cleanse the mind, but the real emphasis is on self-knowledge alone. Vasishtha repeats this several times, stressing that ultimate freedom is attained no other way. In this chapter especially, the word 'knowledge' stands for 'self-knowledge' not worldly knowledge.

By knowledge alone misery ends; by knowledge alone is ignorance dispelled;
By knowledge alone is the final state attained; not through any other means.[5]

Since we have argued throughout that the supreme self and the individual self are not different, to know the supreme self, knowledge alone is the means, not any kind of physical effort.[6] This is because the idea of individuation arises only through ignorance of the true self. We merely have to realise that we are nothing but the supreme self. What effort would be required to do this apart from gaining self-knowledge?

Vasishtha says that the illusion created by a mirage cannot be dispelled even if you perform millions of actions. It is dispelled by knowledge alone.[7] The supreme self is neither far nor near, neither easy to attain, nor difficult: it is known through self-knowledge alone.[8] Penance, charity, fasting, worshiping a deity and other techniques are in no way helpful in knowing the self. Other than complete firmness (*vishranti*) in one's inherent nature, there is no way to know the self.[9]

The mind is quietened by one's own will and knowledge — austerities, rituals, sacrifices, charity, worship and the rest are a waste of time, says Vasishtha.[10] Even a sinner can become liberated through contemplation.[11] Ignorance is the only sin, and it can be dispelled by knowledge alone.

As the Yogavasishtha does not advocate the methods of Poorvameemamsa as a means of liberation, we may leave it aside, and take up the debate on whether liberation is gained by self-knowledge (gyana) or method (yoga).

Traditionally, the scriptures have advocated two methods to gain moksha: Samkhya and Yoga. In this context, it must be said that the word 'Samkhya' does not represent the Samkhya school of Indian philosophy alone. It is used for any school that stresses self-knowledge and understanding, rather than any kind of physical effort. The word 'yoga' represents any school that stresses human effort such as breath control, body and mind purification and meditation to attain liberation.

Differentiating between the two, Vasishtha says that those who have known the self through self-knowledge and are in a perpetual state of bliss are called Samkhya yogins,[12] while those who transcend the mind through breath regulation and other physical means are called Yoga yogins.[13] However, there is one occasion when Vasishtha says that they are ultimately one:

He who sees Samkhya and Yoga as one, he alone sees (the truth rightly);
For what is achieved through Samkhya can also be achieved through Yoga.[14]

Vasishtha elaborates by saying that one method of gaining liberation is that of self-knowledge, which is well-known, and the other is *pranasamrodha* (to stop, hold, regulate, curtail breath).[15] Rama then asks which of the two is easier and preferable. Vasishtha says both yoga and self-knowledge are equally useful in crossing the sorrowful ocean of the world, and both produce the same result—liberation.[16]

Depending upon individual disposition and nature, some find yoga more convenient and some gyana, but Vasishtha says that gyana is the easier of the two.[17] However, he adds, seekers should not talk in terms of options, and should not ask which is easier.[18] Rather, they should adopt the method that suits their natural disposition.

Having said this, it is repeatedly stressed throughout the Yogavasishtha that:

Knowledge alone is the supreme good, through it alone one becomes liberated;
Action (effort, karma, kriya) is advocated in passing, only for worldly pleasures.[19]

Knowledge alone is enough because we are liberated already. Bondage is impossible. It is only imagined by us because of ignorance of the self. The world is created out of ignorance, it is sustained by non-contemplation, but with knowledge of the self it disappears.[20]

If this fact is understood, how long does it take for us to be liberated? By clear understanding, liberation can be had in an instant because the matter is as simple as opening our eyes.

In the story titled Balyupakhyana, it is shown that the ultimate truth is so simple that it can be said in a few words, and if the seeker is receptive enough, liberation can be had in no time, and without recourse to meditation, rituals, reading of scriptures, or severe penance.

In reply to King Bali's questions regarding life, worldly indulgence, and selfhood, Sage Shukracharya, who is in a hurry to go elsewhere, gives a brief discourse on the subject, saying that it is enough if the disciple is mature enough. 'This world is consciousness alone, as its existence depends upon consciousness (chit). All that is visible is pure consciousness; you are consciousness (chit), I am consciousness. In short, everything is consciousness. Bondage is nothing but the result of the outward seeking tendency of the mind. Once that outward nature is given up, bondage turns into freedom. O King! If you are devoted and mature, knowing this much alone will gain you liberation, and if this is not enough, there is no point in elaborating further.'[21]

No teaching could be briefer than this, but if we are unable to grasp this simple truth, we have to go through a long process of yoga, meditation, devotion, *samadhi* and rituals.[22]

The question arises that if everything is a dream, what is the point of performing any worldly actions? To this, the sage adds emphatically, 'O King! Until this body exists, giving up necessary actions of the world is not right for the liberated, as it is against the laws of nature.[23] Incessant action is the intrinsic nature of the body, and this law cannot be violated.'

When Vedanta says that the world is a dream or an illusion, this does not mean that the world does not exist. All it means is that the world does not have an independent existence. We are seeing reality wrongly. This perception is called maya, illusion or ignorance. However, since this illusion has a profound effect on us, we cannot say it does not exist; at the same time, we cannot say that it does. It is indescribable in language, (*anirvachaneeya*); that is, we can neither categorically deny its existence nor assert it. Further, it is good that it is an illusion, otherwise how could it be dispelled by knowledge alone?

Self-knowledge and action are just methods or paths, and ultimately one has to be free of both, for only then can ultimate freedom be realised. As methods, both are valid, depending upon the psychological disposition (*svabhava*) of the seeker.

Having set the tone of the debate, we shall now examine the nature of knowledge and action in more detail.

SELF-KNOWLEDGE, THE EASIEST PATH TO LIBERATION

Although the Yogavasishtha strongly favours the path of self-knowledge, *gyana marga*, in a true sense it is not a path at all. It is an understanding of the truth.

Further, self-knowledge cannot be given as a gift by anyone else; we have to acquire it ourselves. It is generally said that a guru and scriptures can guide us, but the Yogavasishtha says even these are secondary, as self-knowledge can be had only through contemplation and first-hand experience.

Neither scriptures, words of a guru, charity, nor prayer to God;
Supreme understanding is beyond all these methods.[24]

The insistence is on direct knowledge (*tattva gyana*) and first-hand experience. Borrowed knowledge is of no use in this case. One has to acquire it through sheer contemplation. To see the world as it is without any kind of distortion is called tattva gyana.[25]

As long as we think we are nothing but a body, we are subjected to the cycle of birth, death, health, disease, happiness and sorrow. Once we realise we are not merely a body, we become free of it. This is called tattva gyana, the fundamental knowledge, the knowledge that frees us from worldly misery. When this kind of knowledge is gained, we realise that we are part of the body and yet not part of it, just as the wind is in space, and yet not in it.

Once we realise that we are nothing but pure consciousness, that we are complete, that our bliss is total, what can there be to gain from the world? Why would we do anything, if we are totally happy and satisfied? In this state, the phenomenal world begins to look like a dream. Is there any point in taking the achievements and failures of a dream seriously?

HOW DOES SELF-KNOWLEDGE QUIETEN THE MIND?

Since liberation can only be had by transcending the mind, Rama asks Vasishtha several times how the mind operates, how it pulsates and how it is controlled.

Citing the story of King Bali, Vasishtha tells Rama about a king and a minister.[26] The minister is ignorant but has managed to accumulate all the power into his hands because the king was not watching him. Taking advantage of this, the minister has made the king powerless.[27]

The king is a personification of universal consciousness (atman) in this story. The highly powerful minister is the mind. He has conquered even the gods and demons. Can this powerful and errant minister be brought under control?

Son! With proper contemplation, this minister can be controlled in an instant;
Without logical reasoning, he will kill you as a poisonous snake would.[28]

Vasishtha says that all talk of conquering or controlling the mind is for the sake of instruction because the mind is just a myth, and so the question of conquering it does not arise. That which does not exist, consider it conquered already.[29] The fool who is unable to conquer the non-existent mind is like someone who dies even without eating poison.[30] The wise man sees that breath, prana, moves the body, the senses see the world. What has the mind to do with this, asks Vasishtha.[31]

The mind becomes unruly only when it is not being watched. In order to conquer the mind, all that we have to do is watch its activities. In Vedanta, this is called witnessing (*sakshi*). Becoming a witness means to dissociate ourselves from the mind and just watch it. Nothing needs to be done because in order to do something, action (karma, kriya) is required. If we try to quieten the mind through actions, it means we accept that our true nature is not absolute, and something needs to be done to make it so. This means that the mind can be controlled in the future, but the future is nothing but desire (vasana), and desire is nothing but the mind. We once again fall into the trap of the mind. Since our nature is pure bliss, all we need to do is remember this fact.

Once the mind is transcended, all our failures turn into successes, and if the mind is not conquered, all our successes are failures. This is because everything in the world arises out of the mind so bondage and liberation are also in the domain of the mind.

The mind is a link between the phenomenal world and supreme consciousness. It makes us forget our true nature, which is pure consciousness and bliss, but the same mind could also be instrumental in waking us from forgetfulness. Although the enlightened talk about killing the mind, destroying the mind or conquering the mind, these are just metaphorical expressions. We have to disassociate ourselves from the pulsating and restless nature of the mind; that is all. After that, the mind quietens on its own. As it was mentioned earlier, the mind is not to be deadened; rather, it is to be made more alive, for only then can we use it optimally. Only after the mind is freed of all distortions can it begin to function efficiently.

The emphasis is on regulating the mind, not deadening the body and the senses. By regulating the mind, all senses come under control naturally and easily. Torturing or killing the body solves nothing. The mind is like a wild horse which we can train and use to our advantage. What use would a horse be if we flogged it so much that it became lifeless?

Torturing the body does not help because, apart from the physical body, we also have a subtle body.[32] It is the subtle body or mind that experiences joy or suffering, not the body that is made of flesh.[33] The physical body is nothing but matter, so it has no desires of its own. It is just an instrument of the mind, as it is created by the mind.

We must remember that with the dissolution of the mind, the body dissolves, but with the dissolution of the body, the mind does not.[34] There is no point in torturing the body or committing suicide because the subtle body is going to survive if there are still unfulfilled desires in us, and as long as there are unfulfilled desires, the mind will find a new body. This means that if we want liberation, we have to put an end to the mind, not the body.

Does this mean nothing needs to be done? If knowledge alone is enough, why do we not become liberated merely by reading or hearing the words, 'We are free and our bondage is only imagined' and 'We are Brahman itself'?

This is because, although these words may be true, they are not yet a part of our experience. We are hearing them in a state of deep sleep or forgetfulness. We are, for instance, hearing that the Sun is shining in all its glory, but our eyes are closed. The speaker is not lying, but until we open our eyes, we will never see the beauty of the Sun. The words of a guru and the scriptures are merely methods to awaken the memory. How is this done?

WAYS TO ATTAIN LIBERATION

Talking about methods, Vasishtha shows that there are several of them and the one to adopt depends upon the individual capabilities of the disciple. As if keeping a beginner in mind, Vasishtha says there are four guardians of moksha: self-control (shama); contemplation (*vichara*), contentment (*santosha*) and the company of the learned (*sajjana sangama*).[35]

'Shama' means restraint, self-control or patience. A seeker first needs to cultivate patience and restraint because if the seeker is impatient, nothing can be achieved. If we cannot focus on one thing, how can we contemplate? To contemplate, one ought to be content (santosha) with what the guru is teaching us. We must not rush him to impart knowledge. The guru knows when the time is ripe.

Man is known by the company he keeps because he normally gets affected by people he associates himself with. A seeker of knowledge should keep the company of learned gurus (sajjana sangama).[36]

The point of all these methods is to stop the ever-pulsating and restless mind. Vasishtha says:

Raghava, consider the mind to be the great navel of
the rotating wheel of the illusory world.[37]

Rama asks how one can stop this great wheel. Vasishtha replies that the navel of the illusory world can be stopped with effort and determination.

By controlling the mind with diligence and determined effort,
The navel of this fast rotating wheel can be stopped.[38]

By intelligence, Vasishtha does not mean intelligence of the brain, but the ability to know what the self is and what it is not. This is also called right knowledge, *samyak gyana*.

Elaborating further, Vasishtha says that perfect knowledge means to realise that everything in the world is nothing but universal consciousness.[39]

The universal self, which has no beginning or end, alone exists;
This realisation is called right knowledge by the learned.[40]

Knowledge: The Best Method   219

This kind of understanding comes only by finding out who the real self is. It should be pointed out that whatever we conclude depends a lot on the way we contemplate.

Thus, those who contemplate may reach four conclusions. A seeker might conclude, 'I am the physical body and mind that was born of my parents.' This kind of conclusion causes bondage, as the body is limited and subject to disease, old age and death. If we identify ourselves with the body, we automatically suffer the problems that are associated with the body.

Secondly, the seeker might conclude, 'I am beyond the body and the senses.' Thirdly, 'All the objects of the world are essentially not different from me,' and fourthly, 'I am as formless as space'. The first conclusion is the cause of our bondage and misery, and the other three lead us to liberation.[41]

'Contemplation' here does not mean mere theoretical knowledge, but experiential knowledge, which arises through the method of elimination, neti-neti (not this, not this). Neti-neti[42] is an analytical process of conceptualising something by showing what it is not. For example, to understand the self, we can begin by understanding that the external world, which is obviously separate and different from us, is not the self. The furniture in the room, the vehicles, trees, rocks and stars are not the self. In this way, the entire external world is eliminated, just as a detective eliminates people from a list of suspects.

The next step is to learn that the body is not the self, because if a limb is amputated, our sense of the self is not in any way diminished. The self also remains untouched by old age or disease. Next we might take emotions and feelings. They, too, go on changing. Thoughts never remain the same throughout our lives. In childhood, we have certain thoughts and in old age we might have the opposite thoughts. So the intellect also cannot be the self.

In this way, we go on negating things one by one until we hit rock bottom. We realise we can negate everything in the world but not our own self. This conscious self has remained the same from our birth to the present. Hence, the conscious self is the true self. Through this, we come to know that we are the conscious witness (*drishta, drik*) and not the objective world (*drishya*).

While discussing the ways we gain the knowledge of things (Chapter III), we spoke about the following: knowledge through direct cognition, indirect knowledge, knowledge by comparison, negation and verbal testimony. Since the self can neither be known through direct or indirect knowledge, we can never know it even by comparison, as there is nothing like it in the world we know.

This is because all our experiential knowledge is gained through the senses and the mind. All this knowledge is based on comparison with other things we know. For instance, we may never have tasted sugar, but if someone tells us that it tastes like honey, we get an idea of its taste.

We also gain knowledge by showing what a thing is not. When we say, 'this is a pen', the assertion means that it is not a pencil or a notebook. If we say, 'I am at home now', it means I was not at home earlier. If we say, 'this is a square', it means it is not a circle or a triangle.

All our knowledge is thus based on comparison, contrast, assertion or negation. This process is possible only when we know both things that are being compared or negated. All these things are within the domain of the mind and the intellect, so we can acquire some knowledge of them.

Supreme consciousness according to Vedanta is beyond the realm of the mind. It is that which gains knowledge. It is the one that sees; hence it is unlike anything else in the world. It is beyond all comparisons, assertions or negations, so all proofs of logic do not work in its case. Yet, the supreme self is the only thing about which we can be absolutely sure about. This is because, it is self-evident, as no proof is required about its existence.

In any kind of knowledge, there has to be a knower and an object that is to be known. The subject can never be known objectively because if you try that then the subject will also become an object. This is why the knower or the self, atman, will always remain beyond the scope of cognitive knowledge.

This should not dishearten us, for although no knowledge of the supreme self is possible, it is possible to realise that we are that supreme bliss itself.[43] The entire purpose of the Yogavasishtha is to lead us to supreme bliss or ananda by establishing the identity between the individual consciousness and supreme consciousness. Once we experientially arrive at this conclusion, our identity with the mind–body complex is broken and we become a witness of the activities of the mind. From being unruly, the mind becomes our obedient ally.

Whatever method we choose to understand this identity, it ought to be chosen wisely, according to our disposition, and most importantly, the method should not become another prison. Those who resort to methods usually apply them forcefully. Like a spoilt child, the mind becomes more defiant if force is employed. The Yogavasishtha says that those who forcibly try to control the mind are foolish.

Those who give up reason and resort to methods are called immature by the learned;
As they move from one fear to another fear, one conflict to another conflict.[44]

In fact, with such methods the mind becomes more wayward. By curbing our desires, we do not overcome them; all we manage to do is to suppress them. This is of no use, as they are seething within us, ready to explode at any time. Suppression only makes our minds sicker and deviant.

However, the vast majority of seekers can be helped only through methods, and the gurus have devised several of them. This is why, on rare occasions, the Yogavasishtha talks about methods other than self-knowledge (*gyanayukti*), such as determination (*sankalpa*), control of the senses (*indriya nigrha*), renouncing desires (*vasana tyaga*), and giving up the ego (ahamkara).

Gyanayukti means the method of knowledge in which the emphasis is on understanding and not on physical action to quieten the mind. People think that just as in order to achieve any result in the world we live in, we have to do something physical, so to quieten the mind we also have to do something physical. This argument is not without justification, but we forget that the mind does not fully belong to the physical world so what works in the physical realm will not work in the mental. Suppose we throw a stone into a silent lake, ripples are formed. If we wish the lake to become still again, all we need to do is nothing. Every effort on our part to quieten the lake only disturbs the surface of it even more.

The same law operates in the case of the mind. The more we try to quieten it, the more disturbed it becomes. But as it is difficult to break old habits, we believe that to quieten the mind, something has to be done.

Something does have to be done but not directly. All methods of yoga and meditation are nothing but preparation to quieten the mind. These methods only make us more capable of experiencing the silencing of the mind, and nothing more, as it is possible to quieten the mind even without them.

'Indriya nigrha' means to control the sense organs, as it is the sense organs that are the link between the mind and the external world. Since the sense organs are just instruments, they themselves have no preferences. It is the mind that likes or dislikes something. Whatever we offer the senses, they get used to, as they have the tendency to develop habits. If we engage them in external pleasures, they get used to them; if we engage them in intellectual activity, they get used to it, and if we engage them in vices, they hanker after them. This is why, among the first steps towards self-knowledge, withdrawal of the senses from external objects is recommended by the guru.

Just as the turtle hides its limbs under its shell of its own accord;
By withdrawing the senses from objects, one attains one's true nature.[45]

However, people have badly misunderstood the idea of the withdrawal of the senses. They think it means we have to deaden the senses.

Experience shows that deadening the senses makes matters worse. For instance, men who are troubled by sexual feelings usually give up the company of women, and withdraw themselves from society. Such measures do not help because in isolation the mind becomes even more active and begins to fantasise about the forbidden object. The root cause has to be eliminated, and the root cause is the mind, not the senses. This is why Vasishtha says that if you win the mind, the senses are won automatically.[46]

The body should be used to our benefit since we live in the world, but we need not be excessively attached to the body, as it is going to perish one day. The body is like a container (*adhara*), and the mind is that which is contained (*adheya*) within it. If the container is destroyed, what is contained in it does not get destroyed. If the body is tortured or destroyed, the mind will come back in a new body, creating a cycle of life and death. It is desire that creates this cycle, and until the mind is silenced, this cycle will continue.

We have seen that desires can never be fully satisfied. No matter how much we achieve, we always want more. 'Vasana tyaga' means to give up desire, because as long as desire exists, the mind can never be quietened. This does not mean we lose all interest in the world. It means we should live in the present and enjoy whatever

The Yogavasishtha of Valmiki

is at our disposal, without craving things we do not have. To enjoy what we have, is not 'desiring'. To crave about things we do not have is termed as 'desiring'.

Another important step is to cultivate equanimity (*samattava*). Equanimity does not mean to become stiff and wooden. It means to be in the world and rejoice in every moment, without getting swayed by joys and sorrows. One of the features of the mind is that it survives in the extremes and disappears in the middle. 'Extremes' here means 'imbalance', and 'middle' means 'balance' (samattava). 'Middle' does not mean 'aggregate', it means whatever is 'sufficient'. Most of us either love worldly attractions too much or become totally uninterested in them. These are two extremes, and it is in these extremes that the mind thrives. If you become a hedonist, the mind thrives, and if you become a mendicant, the mind thrives. In either case, the mind is happy because the ego is bolstered in both extremes. In the first, you care only for yourself, and in the latter, you feel you are doing something superior. On the other hand, when you live a balanced life, the ego cannot assert itself.

We either indulge ourselves or renounce every pleasure; we either eat too much or starve ourselves, either overwork or become lazy. Right living entails striking a balance in everything we do. Once this balance is achieved, our mind becomes calm, as we begin to see beyond duality. We realise that everything in the world is interrelated, as everything emerges from the same universal consciousness. All the conflicts and struggles are foolish. With struggle gone, the ego disappears and the mind becomes peaceful.

Here a natural question arises: How can we survive in this world without an ego or a sense of 'I'? Why would we do anything at all if there was no ego to motivate us? Similar thoughts occur to Rama when he says to Vasishtha, 'Your advice to renounce egoism and desire is too deep and grave. I wonder how I can follow your advice and yet survive in the world.'[47]

Vasishtha tells Rama that a person who is governed by the ego does not succeed as much as a person who is not, because the egoist is always greedy to acquire things, and once he acquires them, he is afraid of losing what he has. He is afraid of failure, afraid of death, so he never does anything with total dedication.

We have already mentioned that we must make a distinction between 'ego' (ahamkara) and 'the sense selfhood' (asmita). Ego means wrongly identifying ourselves with the body and the things we think we own, and 'selfhood' means the idea of being a person. Without the idea of selfhood, we cannot get by in the world. Even an enlightened person has an idea of selfhood. It is ego that must be given up, not selfhood.

The difference is illustrated in the story of Dama, Vyala and Kata[48] from the Yogavasishtha.

King Shambara of the underworld once waged a war on Indra, the king of the gods. Sometimes he won and sometimes Indra won, but the battles were never decisive. Shambara wanted a final victory over the gods, so he began to devise strategies. As he had secret occult powers, he created three giant demons named Dama, Vyala and Kata. These three were created in such a way that they had no ego. Without an ego, they had no desires and no fear either. They fought the battles with their full might without worrying about the outcome of the war or their own lives. As a result, they were unstoppable, and the gods suffered one defeat after another.

Indra, in desperation, begged Brahma, the creator of the world, to help the gods. Brahma told him that the reason the three giants were winning was that they were fighting without a sense of ego. Because of this, they were invincible. To defeat them, the battle must be fought in such a way that ego arises in them.

The gods followed this advice and managed to instil ego in the giants. Earlier, the three demons had just fought, but then they started fighting to win, to save their prestige and honour, and to save their lives. The result was that they became fearful of failure, lustful of victory and afraid of death. With such feelings, they were unable to fight with total dedication, and as a result, they lost the war.

The story shows that it is the ego that creates limits. If we transcend the ego, the entire energy of the universe becomes available to us.

One might ask if giving up the ego, and leaving everything to God or nature, is not a kind of fatalism.

A fatalist is one who is frustrated with life, and seeks consolation and justification of his failures and setbacks by blaming it on God or some supernatural agency. To surrender the ego is a totally different thing. It comes through understanding. It is not failure or helplessness but deep insight into reality. We realise we are part of the cosmic whole. With this realisation, the ego crumbles. Far from being a state of helplessness, it releases tremendous power within us because the burden of the ego is gone. Now we no longer fight with existence but just flow with it and merge in it, and exclaim, 'I am Brahman!'[49]

This is not fatalism. It is supreme understanding.

Such an enlightened person accepts both the good and the bad, success and failure, joy and sorrow, and transcends them both. Such a person truly understands reality and the result is absolute bliss.

Is the declaration, 'I am Brahman' not supreme egoism?

It would be supreme egoism if you declared, 'I alone am Brahman'. We forget that there is another declaration which says, 'You are that'. Here 'you' stands for everything other than the individual. Vedanta says once you realise that you are Brahman, you also realise that everything in the cosmos is Brahman. Each individual, each animal and plant, and even micro-organisms are Brahman. Far from being an egoistic declaration, this realisation makes us humble.

After studying Vedanta, if you come to the conclusion 'I alone am Brahman', then you can be sure that you have not understood Vedanta at all. Only when you realise that everything is Brahman including your enemies, you can say that you have truly understood Vedanta.

We have been talking about self-control, restraint, overcoming the senses, overcoming the ego, desires and so on. All this could be extremely daunting as there seem to be so many enemies to vanquish in order to be liberated.

As far as the Yogavasishtha is concerned, mind, ego, intellect and desires are different names for the same thing. They are pillars of one structure, and by pulling down any one of them, the entire infrastructure comes crashing down.

It would be wiser to catch the unifying factor behind these seemingly different mental states. We see that behind the ego, intellect or greed, the unifying factor is desire (vasana).

Vasishtha says that the desire for things of the ever-changing world is the root cause of all misery; all other distortions or palpitations of the mind, such as love, hate, anger, greed, avarice and jealousy are just by-products of desire.[50] Once desire is overcome, all other problems disappear, and so does the mind.

After all, why do we need to assert our ego, intellect or greed? It is mainly to achieve more and more from life. This is why desire is considered the root cause of misery. When desire is overcome, the mind becomes calm, as it is the race to fulfil our desires that makes the mind restless and miserable.

Why is desire so powerful in creating misery? First, no matter how hard we try, we can never obtain everything we desire; whatever little we manage to get, we will not like all of it, and the little that we like does not last, as the world is ever changing, and even our mind is ever changing. What we desired in our childhood, we do not desire now.

The Yogavasishtha of Valmiki

Furthermore, our mind is not a unified whole. There are schisms in it. We frequently desire contrary things at the same time. We all want a long life, yet how many of us have never thought of committing suicide? If our desires go on changing, and if there are so many conflicting voices in our mind, misery is inevitable. Further, there are others in the world besides us, and they, too, have desires and aspirations. We might wish that our enemy were dead, but our enemy might also wish for our death. How can both wishes be fulfilled?

It is desire that creates misery, and it is desire that exhausts our body, makes it old and leads to death. Vasishtha says it is desire that kills us, and if we could be totally free of desire, death could never kill us.

In the Yogavasishtha, there is a story about a brahmin named Akashaja who was born out of primal consciousness, and was thus free of any previous good or sinful deeds and desires. He went on living without any desires for such a long time that death began to wonder how to end his life. Death approached *Yama*, the Lord of Death and asked him how it could kill the brahmin. Yama said, 'O Death! You are just an instrument for ending life; it is not you that kills beings, but the results of their own deeds. Only those who perform acts with desire can be killed by you.[51] Akashaja was born from the space, and he is as pure as space. You will not find any karmas in him that will help you to kill him.'[52]

One whose heart is not adorned by the gems of desire;
Death cannot take away such a person.[53]

The secret of supreme bliss is to go on performing actions according to our capabilities, but without any desires. This is done by giving up the idea that we are the authors of our actions. As soon as the ego disappears, all our accumulated good deeds and sins disappear, as darkness disappears after the lights are turned on. This way, we give up our claim not only on bad deeds but also on good ones, as deeds, good or bad, are the main cause of bondage and misery. But giving up desires does not mean we become uninterested in life. In fact, once desires are given up, we do our work and enjoy life with more vigour. To crave for something lost, or to yearn for something that we do not have is termed as 'desire', but to accept what we have in the present is not.

We must find ways of extinguishing desire so that we can begin to live life. Desire arises when the mind looks for bliss outside. Mind which is oriented towards the external world becomes bound, whereas the mind that is oriented towards absolute consciousness is free and blissful.[54]

THREE SEEDS OF BONDAGE

Vasishtha says the body is the seed of the individual self, the mind is the seed of the body and desire is the seed of the mind. One might be the knower of what is right or wrong, a pundit of all knowledge, but if one is not free of desires, then one is caged like a pet bird.[55]

Rama asks which of the three seeds ought to be destroyed first. Vasishtha says that if desires are given up, the other two seeds will perish on their own. Giving up desire, however, is as difficult as moving the mighty Sumeru mountain.

Vasishtha says we must give up the desire for moksha, too, for any kind of desire strengthens the mind and creates bondage.[56] That I should be liberated, this thought alone makes the self limited.[57] One must give up thoughts of having moksha or not having it, as all thoughts create vibration (spanda), and this vibration creates the mind.

Until the mind is quietened, desires cannot be extinguished, and desires cannot be extinguished until absolute knowledge dawns.

230   The Yogavasishtha of Valmiki

SEVEN BASES OF KNOWLEDGE

Self-knowledge could be had in an instant, but since most are not ready for it, we have to make progress in stages. The Yogavasishtha calls these seven stages or bases of yoga or gyana (knowledge). The technical Sanskrit names of these seven bases of knowledge cannot be accurately translated into English, so the nearest meaning is given in brackets.[1]

Shubhechcha **(good intention)**: We realise that, in spite of all worldly success, we are unhappy; we may begin to get disenchanted with worldly objects and pleasures. We may begin to wonder why we are not happy in spite of all that we have acquired. Where have we gone wrong? We might begin to look for the cause of our suffering, and start looking for knowledge in the scriptures or we might begin the search for a guru. So the quest for knowledge begins with good intentions. Not all seekers of knowledge have the best of intentions. A person might want to learn the secrets of atomic energy, but his purpose behind it might not be to generate energy for the benefit of mankind, but to kill as many people as possible. This is why at the beginning of the Yogavasishtha, it is stated that knowledge should be given to a deserving person alone. This is why we must examine our intentions properly before we seek knowledge.[2] At this stage, the seeker begins to get disenchanted with worldly objects, and tries to serve others by doing good deeds.

Vicharana **(contemplation)**: We accept that there is something wrong with our attitude towards life, and we begin to contemplate it. In this, we might be guided by the scriptures, and we might interact with wise people. As a result, our character is ennobled. This stage is called Vicharana.[3] The seeker learns from the scriptures, and begins to practise the eight steps of yoga (yama, *niyama, asana,* pranayama, *pratyahara, dharana, dhyana* and samadhi). The yogi goes to a guru, learns various subjects and acquires the wisdom to know which deeds ought to be done and which are to be avoided.

Tanumanasa **(disinterestedness)**: As a result of good intentions and contemplation, we begin to have control over our senses. This stage is called Tanumanasa or Asangga.[4] Ignorance and the desires produced by it begin to abate. We begin to create a distance between ourselves and the world in order to contemplate. Here, we begin to interact with the wise and become austere. This stage is of two kinds: general aloofness (*samanya asangga*) and excellent aloofness (*shreshtha asangga*).[5]

In the first kind, we begin to think we are not the agents of actions and their results. Excellent aloofness is achieved when, after interacting with the wise, we gain supreme knowledge because of our own determination (purushartha). We realise that we are not the agents of our actions. With this knowledge, we become quiet and blissful.

Sattavapatti **(mental stability)**: With our senses coming under control, the mind begins to become stable. At this stage, we begin to be governed by sattva guna, and are called Brahmavit (the one who has understood the meaning of Brahman).[6] Here, ignorance begins to end.[7]

The first three stages come under the waking state (jagarat) because our behaviour in this state is outwardly no different from everyone else's. In the third state, we acquire a peaceful demeanour and become an inspiration to others to seek knowledge. We come to be known as Arya (cultured). We do what ought to be done and avoid what is not worth doing. In the first stage, the qualities of an Arya begin to sprout, in the second, they develop further, and in the third stage they flower. With the end of ignorance, we get a glimpse of the non-dual. Because of this, the world begins to look like a dream. However, as we are still not free of the cycle of birth and death, we return to the world.

Asamsakti **(unattachment)**: After the stability of the mind, we naturally stop hankering after worldly objects. We detach ourselves from the external world and its subjects.[8]

Padarthabhavana **(seeing objects as material)**: After strongly practising the first five stages, we no longer miss worldly material objects.[9]

Here we are neither attached nor detached from anything, neither egoistic, nor without an ego. We neither talk of duality nor non-duality. We are embodied as well as disembodied. We are silent and still within and without like the motionless flame of a lamp depicted in a painting.

Turyaga (**enlightened**): Progressing through the first six stages when our mind becomes peaceful, we attain what is called *samanya satta* (general existence). All worldly objects vanish within the self without any effort, just as the tortoise hides its body in its shell. When through constant practice this state becomes stable, it leads us to the seventh state. Ultimate bliss is experienced and persons in this stage are called *atmarama* (who live in their own self) or *jeevanmukta* (who are embodied but free). Beyond this stage there are yogis called *Videhamukta*. We cannot say much about this state as it is beyond the experience of the senses and the mind.[10]

These stages are classified slightly differently in different chapters of the Yogavasishtha. BL Atreya says, 'Upon thinking deeply readers might know that there is no significant difference between the second and third description. There is, however, some difference between the first and the last two descriptions. According to the first description, freedom (mukti, moksha) is beyond all the stages of knowledge, while according to the second and third classifications, mukti is also a stage. In fact, as the Yogavasishtha considers both bondage and freedom to be myths, it is right to consider mukti as the seventh stage.'[11]

One who progresses through these stages and sees everything as mere creations of the mind, and hence false, is a gyani. One who unites with the ultimate and yet keeps performing worldly acts with total detachment is a liberated person.[12] When a person becomes detached and joyful, he is called a supreme practitioner (*Uttamabhyasi* or *Brahmabhyasi*).[13]

ENDNOTES
1. II:118:1-30; These stages are again articulated in III: 122:1-16;
2. In VIA:120:1 this stage is simply called 'Prathma' (the first stage). Again in VIA:126:12 similar description is made;
3. III:118:5, VIA:120:2
4. III:118:5, it is called Asangga (aloofness) in VIA: 120:2;
5. VIA: 126:25;
6. III:118:11, this stage is called Vilapinee in VIA:120:2;
7. In VIA:126:60 this stage is called dream, Svapna;

8. III:118:12, this stage is called Anandaroopa in VIA: 120:3 as peace is experienced here, and in VIA:126: 62 it is called Sushupta because here the mind remains only in theory; for all practical purposes it ceases to exist;

9. III:118:13, Svasamvedanaroopa is the name given to this stage in VIA:120:4, and it is called Turiya in VIA:126:65

10. This stage is called Turyaga in III:118:15, and VIA:120, calls it Turiya, and Vasishtha says some call this indescribable state as Shiva, some call it Brahman, some call it Svarga, Vasudeva, Maheshwara and several other names based on choice (VIA:126:71-72);

11. Atreya, BL, Yogavasishtha aur Uske Sidhdhant, Shri Krishna–Janamsthan Seva Sansthan, Mathura, 1986, p 461;

12. VIB:22:1-2;

13. III:22:26-29

Since all these three are interrelated, what method should we employ in order to achieve our goal? All three seeds have to be attacked at the same time. To assist with this, breath regulation (pranayama) can also be helpful.[58] The most effective methods, however, are self-contemplation and the company of the learned.[59] Ignorance is stubborn and may take a long time to end, but some people do become liberated in an instant, as there was no bondage in the first place.

When the mind gains knowledge and begins to reflect on its own state;
The darkness of the heart disappears, like the darkness of the night at sunrise.[60]

The mind and the world are created because of pulsation. When pulsation is stopped, the world created by the mind also stops, leaving behind lasting bliss.

In this chapter, it has been shown that contemplation and understanding are enough to quieten the mind, but as most people do not like to contemplate deeply, they have to resort to methods such as yoga and meditation. We examine these in the next chapter.

ENDNOTES

1. Some commentators use the word 'karma' mainly for the Karmakanda section of the Vedas which deals with rituals and sacrifices to attain worldly gain.

It must be noted that 'karma' also means the accumulated good or bad actions of the past (see Chapter XVI). In this chapter, the word 'karma' refers to actions performed through free will, unless stated otherwise. The word 'action' is also used to mean actions carried out with free will.

2. I: 1:7
3. I:1:8
4. V:78:8
5. V:88:12
6. III:6:1
7. III:6:2
8. III:6:3
9. III:6:4
10. III:102:37, V:92:44
11. V:16:6
12. VIA:69:18
13. VIA:69:19
14. VIA:69:21; There is a verse in the Bhagavad Gita (V:5) using the exact words but with the order of lines interchanged. It is interesting to note that in a story from the Yogavasishtha called 'Arjunopakhyana', the verse quoted above is from a dialogue between Krishna and Arjuna which is reminiscent of the more famous Bhagavad Gita (700 verses). Arjunopakhyana is spread over seven chapters (237 verses depending upon the verse you consider the story begins from). One might wonder why this story is found in the Yogavasishtha, as Rama lived in Dvapara yuga and Krishna much later in Treta yuga. This story might have been added much later, but in one sense its inclusion is justified as in it we see Vasishtha making a prediction to Rama that a time is going to come when the earth will be full of sinners, and there will be injustice and violence all over. At that time, Vishnu will come as a twin-incarnation in the form of Krishna and Arjuna (VIA:52-58).
15. VIA:13:4
16. VIA:13:7
17. VIA:13:8
18. VIA:13:10
19. VIA:87:16
20. V:13:108-109
21. V:26: 9-14
22. In another story of Manki, the brahmin (VIB:23), Vasishtha shows Rama that self-knowledge can happen in an instant. One day as Vasishtha was going somewhere, he met a brahmin named Manki. Vasishtha found him quite worthy of self-knowledge, so as he walked with him he imparted some knowledge about the self to him, and in an instant Manki became liberated.

Knowledge: The Best Method

The Ashtavakra Gita also says that the wise can learn from very little instruction: The ones who are of pure intelligence can benefit from even scant instruction; Other seekers are involved in scholasticism all their lives; the Ashtavakra Gita, XV: 1

23. V:26: 16
24. VIB:197:18
25. V:43: 10-11
26. Story of King Bali, V:22-26
27. V:24:1-71; In another story, Shikhidvaja asks Kumbha how the mind can be controlled. In reply, Kumbha draws an analogy with a tree and says ignorance is the seed of the mind, which grows in the illusory world of maya. Ego is the flower of this tree. The unseen discriminatory power of the tree is called the intellect, and the entire complex is known by various names, such as mind, and chitta (VIA:94:12-16).
28. V:24:3
29. V:14:8
30. V:14:9
31. V:14:10
32. It is the mind that creates two bodies of every being, and it is the mind which creates the gross body like the potter makes a pot. The mind out of its own will makes a form out of the formless, just as a child creates a vetala (ghost) and then destroys it. Mind is one body, and the gross body is another (IV:11:18-22).
33. IV:13:8
34. V:53:66
35. II:11:59, II:13:50-84
36. II:11:59, II:13:50-84
37. V:50:6
38. V:50:7
39. V:79:3
40. V:79:2
41. V:17:13-18
42. We discussed the method of elimination in Chapter VIII but shall repeat it here briefly.
43. Although Brahman is beyond the scope of mind, the Anandabindu Upanishad says it is possible to know it through the eyes of wisdom or intuition (Mantra 11).
44. V:92:40; Ashtavakra tells King Janaka in the Ashtavakra Gita that all methods only create problems for the seeker:
You are unattached, action-free, self-effulgent, without any impurity;
Yet, you are bound because you are involved in meditation. (Ashtavakra Gita, I:15)
45. V:55:6
46. III:110:25

47. V:16:1-5
48. IV:25-31
49. I am Sachchidananda Brahman. I am formless Parabrahman, I am non-dual Brahman.
I am indivisible and complete Brahman. I am eternal, pure, perfect, all-knowing and ever-free Brahman (The Brahmanubhava Upanishad, Mantra 1).
50. V:21:5-8
51. III:2:10
52. III:2:19
53. VIA:23:5
54. III:96:57-59
55. VIA:55:44
56. V:74:8-9
57. VIA:59:39-40
58. V:92:25
59. V:92:2-34
60. V:5:29

CHAPTER XIV

THE METHOD OF YOGA

We shall now examine the method of 'prana yoga', or simply, 'yoga', although we shall not dwell on it at length as Vasishtha himself does not stress it. According to him, yoga is more difficult than self-knowledge. This is surprising, as the path of knowledge is generally considered to be the more difficult. This is because it involves analytical reasoning, logic, linguistics and other disciplines that are commonly considered 'intellectual'.

When people hear phrases such as 'self–world', 'cause–effect', 'space–time', 'subject–object', they are overwhelmed. They would rather learn mantras, yogic postures and methods of meditation which do not involve thinking. In fact, meditation and the chanting of mantras are a means to stop the mind from thinking.

Those who advocate the path of knowledge argue that the path of yoga is more difficult as it insists on action, and on doing something. What action is required to know the self? You are the self, Brahman. It is the only self-evident and self-accomplished thing in the world. The problem is we fail to make the connection between the self and Brahman. This happens because we erroneously take the body or the mind to be our true self. It is an error and an error can be corrected only by right knowledge. If a man is deluded by the belief that there is a cat in his stomach, do the doctors perform an operation to let the cat out?

Practitioners of yoga say, yes, an operation has to be performed because no matter how hard you try to convince the man, he will not believe you. A mock operation has to be performed to cure the patient of his delusion.

The advocates of self-knowledge counter this by saying that if the operation is a mock one, how can we prove it is the operation that has cured the patient? The patient is cured of his delusion with the knowledge that there is no cat in his stomach. The operation was just a ruse.

This is a very old debate and both sides have compelling arguments in favour of their views.

We shall briefly examine why Vasishtha says that the path of yoga is more difficult.

According to Patanjali, the author of *Yogasootram*, there are eight parts or limbs of yoga: yama, niyama, asana, pranayama, pratyahara, dharana, dhyana and samadhi. These have to be learnt in progressive order. Yama means to abstain from violence, to be truthful, not to steal from others and not to be self-indulgent and greedy.

Niyama can be translated as discipline. These are again five in number. We shall only mention the other stages without going into the details. Asana refers to various postures of yoga. Pranayama is breath control. To withdraw ourselves from a sense object is called pratyahara. Dharana is to cultivate the power of concentration. Dhyana means to meditate and samadhi is the stage where we attain the final blissful state.

Critics of yoga say that each of these steps can take years to master, as you have to practise these methods every day for hours. If one spent hours on yoga, when would there be time to perform the duties and functions of life? Even if you managed to do so, by the time you reached the eighth stage, you would be in your eighties. This is why Vasishtha does not advocate yoga. However, as yoga is very popular, we shall examine it briefly.

Vasishtha was the son of Brahma, the creator (Hiranyagarbha, the primal consciousness), who is considered the progenitor of yoga. Vasishtha learned yoga from his father and passed on the teachings to his son Parashara and the sage Narada, and they passed it on to other sages. Later, Patanjali systemised the secrets of yoga in his book, Yogasootram.

Yoga accepts the metaphysics of the Samkhya system, so it is traditionally considered to be its ally. While Samkhya is a philosophical system, yoga is its applied wing. However, yoga is not confined to Samkhya. It is accepted by all systems, not only of Hindu philosophy, but also Buddhism and Jainism. The influence of yoga is so strong that most people think it is the only way to attain moksha.

To put it briefly, yoga is a method of taking us from the gross to the subtle, from the external world to the knowledge of the self, step-by-step. All our miseries arise because of the nature of the mind to look outwards for happiness. Because of this, distortions arise in the mind. If these distortions could be corrected, we could reunite with our real self. This is why Patanjali defines yoga in the following way:

'Yoga is the regulation of the distortions of the mind.'[1]

Apart from self-knowledge, Vasishtha accepts yoga as a means to moksha, but only a preparatory means. He tells Rama how he met the enlightened crow, Bhashunda,[2] who was a great practitioner of yoga.

Vasishtha says that Bhashunda told him that contemplation is paramount in knowing the self,[3] as dispassionate self-contemplation ends all sorrows and desires that have accumulated. Although there are many methods of self-contemplation, he himself chose contemplation on the life force (*pranachinta*). Vasishtha asks him to elaborate on this.

Bhashunda begins by describing the human body and its external and internal organs. He says that the body comes to life because of breath, which is also called life force (prana). It is the life force that is responsible for all the functions and actions of the body.[4]

Breathing air in is called prana and breathing out is called *apana*.[5] Prana and apana are like two horses that run the great machine called the body.[6] Since the breath pervades the entire body, by understanding its mechanism, one becomes free of the shackles of death and is liberated.

How can we quieten the mind by controlling the breath? As we have already discussed, for the Yogavasishtha, not only are body and mind related, they are the same, and so affect each other.

We see that when our mood changes, the effect is felt in the body. For example, in anger we begin to breathe faster, clench our fists and gnash our teeth. From this we can imagine that the reverse may also be the case — if we can physically control the breath and make it slower, we can control anger.

The way we breathe has a profound effect on the internal organs and ultimately the mind, because breath and mind are intertwined and inseparable like the chariot and the charioteer.[7]

Yoga talks about three major veins (*nadis*) in the body: *ida, pingala* and *sushumna*, and says that the life force flows through them.

To make teaching easier to comprehend, ancient seers proposed that each element in the universe is presided over by a deity. In the yogic system, the moon is the deity of ida, the sun of pingala and fire of sushumna. The ida starts from the left nostril, the pingala from the right nostril and the sushumna starts where the nostrils meet. Hence, the sushumna is the central vein, or the *madhya* nadi.

Just as water flows through the earth, the life force flows through the numerous veins in the body.[8] Vasishtha says that just as fragrance is related to the flower, whiteness to snow, the mind (chitta) is related to the life force and depends upon it. Hence, prana is the essence (*rasa*) of the body.[9] The vibration of the life force makes the mind vibrate, and vice versa.[10] Since the life force and the mind are related, yoga says that if we can control the life force through yoga, the mind is controlled automatically.

Rama asks, 'If prana is the cause of mental distortion, should the end of it (death) not lead to liberation?' In other words, should not all the dead be considered liberated?[11] Vasishtha says that this is not the case because death is not the end. If it were, why would anyone bother with self-knowledge or yoga? One could do anything in life and wait for death if moksha were certain afterwards.

As long as we have unfulfilled desires, liberation is not possible. It is true that, sooner or later, the body is going to die, but if we die with unfulfilled desires, we are reborn in a new body to fulfil them.[12] With the death of the body, neither the life force nor the mind is destroyed.

We now come to the psychological function of the three veins. Ida is also called the vein of the moon. It is by nature cool, and its fundamental attribute (guna) is inertia (tamas). It is ida that regulates human thoughts.

The pingala, also called the vein of the sun, is warm, and its characteristic is dynamism (rajas). It regulates the energy in the human body.

The sushumna nadi, also known as the Brahma nadi, is the most important of the three. Some texts call it Saraswati nadi or shanti (bliss) nadi. This vein is neither warm nor cool; in other words, it is balanced. It is this vein that imparts wisdom and knowledge, and because of this it is the most useful for gaining self-knowledge.

Proper coordination of these three veins leads to good health, strength, vigour, long life and mental peace. This coordination can be achieved through breath regulation (pranayama).

Elaborating on breath control, Bhashunda says that it is

breath that vibrates the body; inhalation (prana) is situated in the upper part of the body, while exhalation (apana) is in the lower part.[13] The exhalation of the breath which happens naturally and without any effort is called *rechaka*,[14] and that which is as broad as the breadth of twelve fingers, enters the body from the outside and moves downward from the nostrils to the genitals is called *pooraka*.[15]

The breath that stays within the body until it is exhaled is called *kumbhaka*. Depending upon how the breath is inhaled, held within and exhaled, there are eight kinds of pranayamas, and one who does them with awareness surely attains liberation.[16] This is because when one does pranayama, the mind is diverted from the external world towards the inner.

The breath which creates the warmth of the sun in the external and internal space of the body also creates the blissful coolness of the moon.[17] However, if breath is not regulated properly, the same breath (*prana vayu*) can give up its coolness and become like an irksome heat in an instant.[18]

The result of breath exercises (pranayama) is that the darkness of ignorance ends, and the practitioner becomes liberated. When the mind disappears, the difference between the creator (Brahma), the individual self, the mind, the doer, action and the phenomenal world disappears.[19] At this point, one becomes united with absolute Brahman itself. That is what the word 'yoga' means. It is derived from the Sanskrit root *yuj*, which means 'to unite'.

With the regular practice of yoga, the mind and ego disappear and dormant psychic powers, (*siddhis*) arise in the yogi, such as the power to enter the body of someone else (*parakaya pravesha*), the power to levitate, the ability for astral travel (*akashagamana*), the power to cure the sick, and the power to perform miracles.[20]

Such powers are called *kundalini* in the yoga system. There are eight such powers: *anima, laghima, mahima, garima, prapti, prakamya, vashitva* and *ishitva*.

The Yogavasishtha of Valmiki

By developing the power of anima, the yogi can transform his gross body into the subtle body. With laghima, he can make his body so light that he becomes capable of astral travel. Mahima is the power which allows a yogi to make his body as large as he wishes. Garima allows the yogi to make his body as heavy as he desires. Prapti makes him capable to go to other worlds. The yogi who acquires the powers of prakamya can get whatever he desires. With vashitva, all the things in the world come within the power of the yogi. Ishitva is the power that allows the yogi to create or destroy anything.

However, Bhashunda cautions Vasishtha that as seekers, we should not try to acquire such powers, and if we acquire them, we should not make an exhibition of such powers because they can distract us from our real goal, self-knowledge.[21]

These powers, however, have their uses. For example, if we learn to enter someone else's body, we immediately break the identification with our own body. We realise that the present body is like a house, and as we have changed houses before, there is no point in being excessively attached to it. Astral travel makes us realise that we are not limited to the physical body.

There is another power called *shaktipata*. This is a method through which an enlightened person enters the bodies of his disciples and imparts teachings to them en masse, thus saving time and effort.

Advantages of these powers notwithstanding, there is a danger that we might get so enamoured by our own powers and their popular appeal that, instead of transcending the mind and ego, we end up becoming entangled in them. One must not seek such powers without the help of a guru who can guard us against misusing them.

Coming back to the discussion, controlling the mind and the senses does not mean one has to torture the body and deaden the senses by force. Yogavasishtha says that those who try to quieten the mind by hatha yoga are like the fools who try to kill the king of serpents, Nagendra, with a lotus stem.[22]

Yogavasishtha adds that rituals, prayers and the worship of idols are for those who have not attained self-knowledge. These are secondary means, and one must graduate to the primary means of pure contemplation as soon as possible because one who gives up primary means for secondary is like someone who gives up nectar in preference for a lower form of nourishment.[23]

However, those who are mature realise the formless absolute through mere contemplation because the supreme consciousness, atman, is neither far way nor illusive: it is our very self.

ENDNOTES

1. Patanjali Yogasootram, I:2, the same verse is also found in the Yogasootra Upanishad I:2 and the Yogasara Upanishad, Mantra 2.
2. While most Indian religions hold that to attain liberation, one has necessarily to be human, specifically, male, the Yogavasishtha says that any living being, even animals and birds, can attain moksha. This is because every creature is liberated already; self-ignorance makes them bound.
3. VIA:24:1
4. VIA:24:13-30
5. VIA:24:13-31
6. VIA:24:33
7. VIA:69:46
8. V:78:10
9. V:78:12
10. V:78:14
11. VIA:69:28
12. VIA:69:30-33
13. VIA:25:3-4
14. VIA:25:6
15. VIA:25:7-8
16. VIA:25:20
17. VIA:25:38
18. VIA:25:39
19. III:65:3
20. IV:20:5
21. VIA:80:27
22. V:92:38
23. V:43:28

CHAPTER XV

THE COMPLEXITIES
OF ACTION

In the last two chapters, we discussed the fact that teachers of self-knowledge have largely advocated two paths to obtain moksha: one of self-knowledge (atma gyana) and the other of yoga. Those who hold the first view argue that since moksha is our inherent nature, other than knowledge nothing is required to attain it. The emphasis is on 'knowing', not on 'doing'. On the other hand, those who hold the second view say that knowledge is not enough. Methods such as breath control and meditation are necessary. The emphasis is on 'doing' and not on 'knowing'. There are two other paths related to yoga called 'karma yoga' and 'bhakti yoga'. They hold that to know the self, something needs to be done. Contemplation is not enough.

Karma yoga says that incessant action is the law of nature, and since it cannot be avoided, we should perform all necessary actions without the sense of being their agent. This means giving up our ego. If ego is given up, liberation is gained automatically because it is ego which is the cause of bondage.

The path of devotion (bhakti yoga) advocates total surrender to God or a deity. Since total surrender can happen only by giving up the ego, one becomes liberated. We shall not discuss this method, as the Yogavasishtha does not recommend it. We shall examine the nature of 'action' (karma) and the path of 'action' (karma yoga).

The path of knowledge and the path of action both have associated problems. First of all, action presupposes an agent (karta), that is, a doer who performs the action, in other words, the individual (jeeva). We have shown in the previous chapters that the individual being is a product of ignorance or imagination of Brahman. If the individual beings are themselves a product of ignorance, how can actions performed by them lead to final liberation?

There is another problem with action. Actions produce results. The result of an action is called 'karmaphala' (*karma+phala*). In Sanskrit, *'phala'* means fruit and fruit is always limited and it also decays after a while. Hence, whatever we achieve through action will be limited and it will wither away sooner or later. Since we are limited to a body that has a limited lifespan, and since we have limited resources at our disposal, all our actions are necessarily limited. Whatever is achieved through limited action cannot be unlimited and eternal; it will certainly end one day. Thus, with limited actions how can we gain unlimited and unending freedom?

Bondage is caused by ignorance of the self, so it can be ended only by knowledge of the self, argue the advocates of self-knowledge.

But when we speak of 'knowing', we have the dilemma of knowing rightly or wrongly. If we are seeing things wrongly, the solution is to learn to see rightly. What is 'right' is not easy to determine. Everyone claims their method is the right one. On the other hand, when the question is of 'doing' or performing actions (karma) to achieve any kind of goal, we have to deal with a host of other issues, which we shall presently discuss.

Action involves choice. We may do a thing or not do it. This is why not everyone is interested in moksha. Secondly, a goal can be achieved through several means. Further, as 'actions' mean they were done of our free will, we become responsible for their outcome.

Although Vasishtha talks about the path of action, his emphasis is largely on the path of self-knowledge.

Those who have known the ultimate truth do not advocate action;
Just as those who live on a river bank care little about the well.[1]

The fools who are bound by desire advocate actions approved by the scriptures;
And they face the consequences of their actions as they lack right knowledge.[2]

If these lines are not read in context, they can lead to misunderstanding. Is Vasishtha saying we should not perform actions? Is he advocating that we should renounce an active life? Can we really give up all action? Even in a remote monastery, we would have to perform certain actions to keep ourselves alive. We cannot imagine a single moment in our lives when we are not engaged in some activity or the other. Sitting idle is an activity, as is sleep. If someone managed to become totally free of action, what would the difference be between that person and a dead body?

If Vasishtha were against human action, he would not have urged Rama to assert his free will, and he would not have denounced the idea of destiny so strongly (Chapter II). Vasishtha is not saying give up action; he is saying give up the claim that you are the doer of your actions.

According to Vedanta, we become responsible for our actions only when we do them with a sense of being their agent. When we give up this claim, our actions are not termed as actions at all.

One could be sitting idle and yet be involved in actions, and one could be involved in all sorts of activities and yet be free of actions. As this concept is difficult to grasp, we need to examine it further because it is different from the general idea about action.

It is a common experience that in order to achieve something, we have to perform some action or the other. The amount of action depends on the goal. Bigger the goal, bigger the action required to achieve it. By this logic, how can we ever gain final liberation, which is supposed to be the greatest goal of our lives, without action? Thus, to attain unlimited liberation, we would have to perform unlimited action.

This, however, is humanly impossible.

Many gurus, however, advocate the path of action and devotion to people who are not predisposed towards contemplation and logical reasoning. It is suggested for those who enjoy doing some kind of work or to those who are emotional.

The general view is that the path of action is easier than the path of self-knowledge. Contrary to this, Vasishtha considers the path of action more difficult than the path of self-knowledge. This is because the path of action is not as simple as it seems. It is so complicated that even great yogis often do not understand its mystery. As Krishna tells Arjuna in the Bhagavad Gita:

In making a distinction between action and non-action,
even the learned seers are confounded.[3]

THE NATURE OF ACTION

Action means to do something, and the biggest problem is to decide what right action is and what it is not. Often our actions bring about the opposite result of what we intended because the results of our actions can never be certain. Further, the path of action seems to be longer and more difficult. We could add or subtract using an abacus, pebbles or a mathematical formula. If we are asked to solve a rather simple mathematical problem such as 76883891 x 76598, which is the easier method: using pebbles or using the formula of multiplication? Using the formula is easier and quicker, but we can use the formula only if we understand mathematics.

If, however, we do not have the capability to learn the formula, we have to use pebbles. This is the reason the Yogavasishtha admits that for most of us action is the right path, although it is more difficult. Ultimately, the path that we take is of no importance. What really matters is whether we have understood the ultimate truth or not.

We shall now examine the complexities of action.

The actions we perform wilfully are called voluntary actions, but the vast majority of actions are not performed of our free will, as they happen naturally. Bodily functions, such as breathing and blood circulation, are called involuntary actions. We are not blamed for any outcome that might arise out of them, as these actions are not in our control. Vedanta would say that to call them 'involuntary actions' would be a contradiction, as anything that happens involuntarily cannot be called action at all. They are biological processes.

Then, there are many actions that we do not intend to do, but they happen nevertheless, as they are beyond our control. For instance, as we breathe, millions of germs are inhaled by us, and they might die in the process. We are not held responsible for them as we did not kill them intentionally.

Only actions that we perform wilfully are credited to us, and we suffer from or enjoy the results. This is because it is the mind that wills, and because we identify ourselves with the mind. If we break this identification with the mind, we become free of responsibility. However, this does not mean we are free to act irresponsibly.

Since our actions are judged as right or wrong, we ought to understand the nature of action. We are familiar with right action (*sukarma*) and wrong action (*vikarma*). There is a third category called non-action (*akarma*), and it is this that Vedanta advocates. It is this third category that is difficult to understand.

'Non-action' does not mean 'inaction'. The fundamental difference between the two is that non-action is done without a sense of authorship, while action is done with one. It is non-action that frees us from the bondage of misery, while action keeps us involved in the world.

First of all, why do we perform actions? We work because we feel there is something lacking in our lives, and we can achieve it if we do appropriate work. If we were totally satisfied with what we had, we would not be obliged to work. This is the image we have of people in heaven. However, when we think of achieving something, we set goals, and then find the means of achieving them.

Vasishtha points out that achievable things are of three kind: desirable (*upadeya*), undesirable (*heya*), and ignorable (*upekshya*). Whatever we consider beneficial to us is called desirable; what is not beneficial to us is called undesirable and that which is in between is ignorable.

An action that is considered desirable by one person might be seen as worth ignoring by another. Once the knowledge of the absolute is gained, we realise the worthlessness of all actions and opt for none of them.[4]

What does this mean? Does the liberated person (gyani) stop working? Does he become a recluse? Far from it, the gyani performs actions as before, but now his attitude is different. Now his actions are like the performance of an actor on the stage. He does them to the best of his ability, but remains detached, as it is, after all, just a stage play. He performs according to the role given to him, not out of his own desires.

The difference between the intentions of actions of the enlightened and the uninformed is that the enlightened do not perform actions out of desire.[5]

This is because desire creates bondage, and anything done out of desire only perpetuates bondage. In fact, the world came into existence only because of desire.

When the absolute consciousness desires, the world is created
But with the abatement of desire, it becomes quiet and liberation is realised.[6]

Although outwardly, the actions of the enlightened and the uninformed may appear to be similar, there is a world of difference between them. The worldly man (karta) performs actions because he has to achieve something; the enlightened man performs actions, not to achieve something, but because incessant action is the nature of the body. He gives up his personal desires, follows the natural law, and performs whatever is expedient at the time.

This is called '*akartabhava*', that is, doing necessary and appropriate actions but doing so by giving up the feeling of authorship of your actions. Akartabhava must not be confused with inaction, as there is a great difference between them.

Inaction is laziness, but we must remember that even sitting idle is action because we have chosen to sit idle. Choice means desire, and desire is nothing but bondage. The term gyani stands for someone whose ego is under his control, and who has left everything to the supreme law (rita). He does not choose to do anything, nor does he avoid doing anything. He just lets things happen.

This does not mean we are slaves to the inviolable supreme law. For example, it is true that we cannot violate the law of gravity, yet we walk and run. What we have to remember is that, even when we walk and run, we are obeying the laws of gravity, albeit unconsciously. We manage to do these activities only because we have mastered the law. Although we cannot violate the law of action, we need not feel helpless. If we understand the law of action, we can become free of the law.

An enlightened person gives up the idea of being the agent of his actions. If his inner feeling (antahkarana) is to do social work, he does; if it is to retire to the hills, he does; and if it is to fight in a war, he does so. Inaction is the cessation of action, while akartabhava means that actions continue, but without the idea of there being a doer.

A gyani acts out of sheer pleasure because, after self-knowledge dawns, the whole world appears like a dream or a stage play. Is there any point in worrying about the outcome of our actions in a dream or a play? We just perform our role according to the script and enjoy ourselves.

What do we mean by agent (karta)? We become the agents of our actions only when we perform actions out of ego, mind and desire. Because our efforts are influenced by our desires, our actions are termed either sinful or pious. What we do or not do is not important; it is the intent with which an action is done that is important, as it is the intention that leads to happiness or sorrow. This is why a gyani does everything as we do, but is neither happy nor unhappy, while we do things but are happy or unhappy, depending upon the result.

We perform actions out of desire, while a gyani performs actions without desire and without attachment to the results. This does not mean his actions are mindless or are without responsibility like those of a psychopath. All the so-called mindless actions are still actions, as they are urged by the mind, albeit a sick one. A gyani, on the other hand, is one who has purified his mind of all mental afflictions and distortions. He sees he is connected with the entire cosmos, and knows there is no difference between him and other beings. Such a person lives and acts according to the universal law (rita). The act, thus, is not important; what is important is whether it is urged by the mind or by the universal law.

Thus, it is the mind that is the doer of our actions, not the body. In other words, if our mind is not involved in our actions, they cannot be considered our actions, and there is no praise or blame attached to them. On the other hand, if our mind is involved, we become responsible for all our actions and reap the harvest accordingly. Whatever is done with the mind, whether good or bad, leads to bondage, and whatever is done without it is beyond good and bad.[7]

Bad actions, at worst, lead us to hell, and good ones, at best, to heaven, but in both places when the reward or punishment for our actions is exhausted, we come back to this world and become involved in actions again. This is because the stay in hell or heaven is not eternal according to Hinduism.

We might ask, 'If the world is just a dream, why should we do anything at all?' The Yogavasishtha says that the nature of the world is activity, and no one can remain without activity even for a moment. Once actions are performed out of desire, the vicious cycle of righteous and sinful deeds begins. These go on endlessly, and there seems to be no way out of it, as no action is free of sin. This is the nature of action.

Even when we try to do what we consider a virtuous deed, there is violence in it. For example, if we wish to give food to a hungry person, we make a bodily movement, and in this movement itself, millions of microscopic organisms are killed. The food that we give also means taking the life of a plant or an animal. Further, the person we feed might then have the strength to murder someone.

All opposites in this world are inseparably connected. Sin is an inseparable part of good, just as darkness is a part of light. Good is inseparable from sin, happiness from sorrow, and freedom from bondage. This is why no worldly action can ever satisfy us. How does one get out of this intractable situation?

Scriptures tell us that anything done by being the author of our actions is sin, and anything done by not being the author is good, moral and righteous. Even in a court of law, crimes performed accidentally or without knowledge are pardoned.

What the mind does alone is action, and what it does not is not action;
Hence, the mind alone is the doer, not the body.[8]

Since the body is never the doer of actions, the Yogavasishtha does not look down upon the body, rather considers it as a boon. It likens the body to a city. A liberated person rules this city but he is not caught in virtue or sin because virtue or sin is not in the action but in the intention. If we are the masters of the body, we make the best use of it; if not, we become slaves of it and suffer like slaves.

Vasishtha says that the body is a storehouse of misery for the uninformed, and a source of immense joy for those who know the self. Those who lack the knowledge of the self are always fearful of old age, disease and death, but as the gyani knows, with death only the gross perishes, not the absolute; he makes the best of his body as long as it lasts. He uses it like a chariot to go about in this world.[9]

In other words, what we do with the body is not important, but whether it is done under the directions of the mind is. This is because the world is the creation of the mind, and all our deeds are sinful or righteous only while the mind lasts.

When the ever-still self pulsates, it becomes the agent of its actions
After it gets involved in the results of its actions, it is called karma.[10]

Action, inaction, non-action, good and sin have meaning only in the domain of the mind. Although in reality:

In this world the idea of liberation is false, and so is the idea of bondage,
O Rama; Give up the mind, ego and actions; be valorous and perform your duties wisely.[11]

How does one perform actions wisely? By wisely, Vasishtha means to perform actions according to our individual disposition. This means doing our duty, according to our inherent nature, otherwise we will be unhappy. Our true nature is called *svadharma* (self-nature), although *svakarma* (dispositional-action) is a more accurate term here.

Children with a talent for abstract thinking and contemplation might not be very happy in life if they took up a profession that calls for a great deal of physical activity. Similarly, children who are very active physically might not be happy doing academic work. The vast majority of us are unhappy at work, as we did not choose our profession according to our natural disposition.

Another point is that, although we are free to act, we have to consider what effect our actions might have on the people around us as we live in a community. We are not free to act mindlessly.

We as individuals play several roles during our lifetime — father, mother, husband, wife, colleague, devotee, parent and so on, and each role has duties (dharma) that go with it. Duty means to do what is necessary in a given situation and circumstance. It must be noted that the suffix, 'dharma', in svadharma (sva+dharma) relates to the individual (sva) and not to the self (atman). Atman is not bound by these duties, only the mind is.

If we give up the idea of being the agent of our actions, there is a total transformation in our attitude towards these actions. Earlier, we performed actions out of desire or out of a sense of duty but not love. Because this child is ours, we have to take care of it; because this woman is our mother, we have to nurse her; because we belong to this country, we have to serve it. All our actions are conditional. There cannot be love and bliss where there are conditions. Any action that is done without love can hardly make us or others happy.

THERE IS NO 'OTHER' HERE

When the knowledge of the self dawns, we learn that there are not many selves. We realise that all of us have grown out of supreme self, and the dichotomy between 'you' and 'I' is false. If we accept that all are one, how can we hate anyone? We can only love.

The one who sees everything as the self, and
sees the self in everything cannot hate anyone.[12]

We, thus, become compassionate towards all humans, animals, and even objects, as there is nothing other than the self in this world. This makes us free of all compunctions and duties. Now life is nothing but love and enjoyment. We work for the sheer pleasure of it, and we perform our roles to the best of our ability. Now, we do not love someone because that person is related to us; we love because it is our nature to love. We love all that is there in the world, just as the sun shines on all that is.

Now that my mind is quiet, what is there for me to gain or lose?[13]

As we are liberated already, whether we become mendicants or indulge in worldly pleasures is of no consequence.

As my ignorance has ended, to me there is neither bondage nor liberation;
What have I got to gain by meditating or not meditating?[14]

By giving up the idea of both meditation and non-meditation;
I let things happen because the self neither grows nor abates.[15]

Although I have no duties, why should I not
perform actions expected of me wisely?[16]

Vasishtha tells Rama that the liberated are neither overjoyed by attaining success nor dejected by failure. They are balanced and unaffected in all the ups and downs of life like the sky that is pure and unsullied.[17]

As we are in a body, we should not give up what is necessary for the body, and at the same time not indulge ourselves too much. We should maintain a balance (*samata*).[18] There should be moderation because in moderation there is joy, whereas in the extreme there is misery.

Do not become sad and at the same time do not become happy;
Remain balanced because the supreme self is all-pervading.[19]

For those who become liberated, desire, greed, envy and pride become minimal. They are neither ecstatic nor sorrowful; they are neither attached to anything, nor do they accumulate material goods. They do not become perturbed by anyone, nor do they bother anyone. Outwardly, they perform all that is required of them, but deep inside they are untouched by the actions they perform.

'I wish to do this' and 'I do not wish to do this' is nothing but a sign of ignorance of the self. The enlightened do everything, and yet are totally liberated because their senses are unaffected by worldly objects, as there are no desires in their minds.[20]

Vasishtha urges Rama to give up the sense of being a doer of his actions, and keep doing all actions to the best of his ability. However, there is a danger to this. The fear is that now Rama might start considering himself a non-doer. This is also a kind of egoism. So Vasishtha cautions Rama:

You are not the doer, so why are you so eager to get involved in actions?
If there is nothing other than the self, how can there be action and for whom?[21]

At the same time do not say that you are a non-doer of your actions;
What is to be gained by saying so? Give up such thoughts and be blissful.[22]

ENDNOTES

1. VIB:22:18
2. VIB:22:19
3. The Bhagavad Gita, IV:16
4. VIA:80:19-28
5. VIB:22:53
6. VIB:22:54
7. IV:38:1-23; This is also elaborated in IV:46:16-18, IV:56:5, V:18:1-65
8. IV:38:7
9. IV:23:1-61
10. III:96:21
11. IV:38:23
12. Eshavasya Upanishad 6
13. V:29:9
14. V:29:11
15. V:29:12
16. V:29:18
17. V:29:37-38
18. VIA:55:1
19. V:18:42
20. VIA:56:5-7
21. III:113:6
22. III:113:7

CHAPTER XVI

THE KARMA IMBROGLIO

Having discussed the nature of voluntary action, it is time to discuss karma or destiny as, in the general conception, it is an integral part of Hinduism. In Chapter II, we saw how Rama begins to feel helpless at the hands of destiny, and how Vasishtha gets him out of this by stressing upon human free will. He debunks the idea of karma and says that humans can achieve whatever they wish if they will it strongly enough and work hard towards achieving it.

If, after listening to Vasishtha's motivational discourse in favour of human action, Rama had been convinced, he might have thanked him and left, but he does not because every answer gives rise to hundreds of new questions. We often find ourselves more confused than before in such situations. This is because life is extremely complex, and our intellect is not equipped to grasp it fully. Until the whole is grasped, questions will continue to crop up.

Although Vasishtha's discourse on human effort is very motivating, we know that there are many things over which we have no control. For instance, we have no say regarding the time and place of our birth, the kind of body we possess and the kind of family we are born into. Even in our daily lives, there are few things we seem to have control over – the majority of things are beyond our control. This naturally makes us wonder if we are really masters of our own lives or guided by some unseen hand.

Rama asks Vasishtha in the beginning of Yogavasishtha:

O wise one! You know everything, please tell me
What it is that is known all over the world as destiny?[1]

Vasishtha knows that Rama is currently going through a crisis, and is perhaps trying to withdraw from the affairs of the world. At this stage, if he were told that our lives were governed by destiny, he would lose interest in life and become a mendicant. However, Vasishtha cannot dismiss the question. He proceeds by first defining destiny.

The good or bad consequences that follow our actions
Have always been known by the name, destiny.[2]

All actions are done by the individual, and he alone suffers or enjoys their consequences, destiny has nothing to do with it.[3]

To think things are done by an unseen hand is called destiny; the assertion that you do them is called effort;
Destiny is unable to produce any result, while human effort is always successful.[4]

Vasishtha is stating a universal law: Every action we perform will necessarily bring about unpredictable results. There are no exceptions to this law. However, the result of a human action is always unpredictable; it is rarely commensurate with the amount of labour entailed. Sometimes, with little action we get huge rewards, and sometimes we get nothing, in spite of putting all our energy into the act. Often the outcome is contrary to what we expected. This is why Krishna says to Arjuna in the Bhagavad Gita:

You only have the right to perform actions, never over their results.[5]

The Yogavasishtha of Valmiki

In the realm of human action, only one thing is certain: every action has an effect, albeit unpredictable.

There is no mountain, no sky and no ocean
and no place where actions do not bear fruit.[6]

Once the arrow leaves the bow, it will strike somewhere. Sometimes it strikes where we intended it to, but quite often it does not. There are also times, when the arrow returns and strikes us.

What we call destiny is nothing but the result of our own actions, most of which we have forgotten. We might have forgotten the actions we did but the law never forgets. These actions are the ones that we performed long ago in our lives, or even in past lives. This is why karma perplexes us, and makes most of us feel helpless, but Vasishtha says if our present condition is unfavourable because of our past actions, we can change this condition as the present action is always stronger than the past. There is no need to despair.

Destiny and human effort (karma) are synonyms, according to Vasishtha. When the world comes into existence, it comes to be governed by laws that did not exist earlier. These laws are created by the absolute consciousness itself, so we can call them destiny or self-willed action (purushartha).

Laws are formulated in such a way that certain things will have certain characteristics, and other things will have another kind of characteristics. That fire burns, that ice is cold, and that life is followed by death—these are the laws of nature. Without these laws the world would be impossible. When we become part of creation, we become subject to its inviolable laws. However, after the dissolution of the phenomenal world (as whatever is created has to end one day), these laws cease to exist, and if another world were created, it might be built on a different set of laws. It is the conscious self that makes these laws, and if it wishes it can change them. In the ultimate sense, however, we are not subject to these laws.[7]

The matter is complex and needs further elaboration.

All the actions that we perform bear fruit or bring about consequences, but not all the consequences are apparent to us. The result is always hidden and unpredictable, for if it were apparent and predictable, none of us would do anything wrong. Whatever we do, we do with a belief that our action will bring about the result that we have in mind. We perform actions according to our best judgement. We term the result of an action successful or unsuccessful, and right or wrong only in hindsight.

According to Hinduism, actions produce a two-fold result (phala): seen (drishta) and unseen (*adrishta*) — known and unknown. Sometimes, the result is immediate, as in the case of your deciding to buy a gun to protect your family. You go to a shop and buy a gun and feel you are safe now. This is the 'seen result' of your action of buying a gun. Months later, when you are out, your child might accidentally fire the gun and hurt someone. This is an 'unseen and unintended result' of your action. This is because every action sets in motion a chain of multi-pronged intended as well as unintended events which are beyond our control.[8] Most of the results, however, manifest much later in life or perhaps in future births, leaving us baffled, as we are unable to connect the present result to our past actions. These are the unseen results of past actions that have come to fruition. They are generally called 'karma'.

Do we not often wonder what we did to deserve such misery? Do we not ask why the wicked prosper and the innocent suffer, why some are born healthy while others are born blind or deaf, why some are very intelligent from childhood and others not? These inexplicable situations are the unseen results (adrishta phala), of past actions.

How is this unseen or remote result possible? Unseen result is brought about by the mental impressions that are left behind by actions. Any action done with desire or motive leaves in our mind

264   The Yogavasishtha of Valmiki

subtle impressions called 'samskaras', and these bring about good or bad consequences in due course. The cumulative effect of such impressions determines the course of our present and future lives.

There are three kinds of karma: *sanchita karma, prarabdha karma,* and *agami karma.* Sanchita karmas are the accumulated karmas of this and past lives. Prarabdha karmas are actions that have begun to bear good or bad fruit. Agami karmas are actions that we are going to do in the future.

Imagine you are an archer. The arrows that are in the quiver are your accumulated karmas (sanchita karma). The arrow that you have shot is your karma that is going to bring about some result (prarabdha karma), and the arrow in your hand is the karma that you are going to perform (agami karma). You can do nothing about the arrow that has left the bow, but you certainly can do something about the arrow that you have in hand now.

Coming back to human action, by action we normally mean physical action. Hinduism says there is more to action than mere physical activity. Human actions are of three kind: bodily actions (*kayika karma*), verbal actions (*vachika karma*) and mental actions (*manasika karma*). Kaya means body, so all bodily actions are called kayika karmas, but Hinduism does not stop here.

We also perform verbal actions, vachika karmas. We could make someone's day or ruin it with our words. Verbal actions are more potent than physical actions. Most revolutions were sparked off by the words of thinkers or writers. Then there are mental actions, manasika karmas. Bodily actions and verbal actions can be cognised, but mental actions cannot. I may be thinking of harming you, but never harm you physically. Societal law cannot punish me for mental actions. Hinduism says that mental actions are even more potent than physical and verbal actions. They are the seeds of karmas.

Thus, actions are performed, and strong desire itself is karma;
Desires are none other than the mind, and mind is the performer.[9]

The Karma Imbroglio

Here, the mind is equated with the self (purusha) because the mind ultimately is the self. It is the self which imagines and gives birth to the myth called mind. Thus, governed by mind, desires and mental impressions we perform actions, and face the consequences sooner or later.

In modern parlance, samskaras could be termed 'programming'. We are conditioned by the culture and the family we are born into, the kind of people we grow up with, and the kind of education we are exposed to. This conditioning leaves lasting impressions upon our mind. Conditioning can be either good or bad. Thus, we ought to keep good company so that we cultivate good samskaras, but ultimately, we have to become free of all conditioning.

How is samskara related to karma? We normally act according to a belief system, which is why actions that are normal to us might be unthinkable for someone from an alien culture. Most Indians, for instance, touch the feet of their elders out of reverence, but others might find this ridiculous. Meat is the staple diet in many cultures but even the thought of eating it is disgusting to many people. They would rather die of starvation. Samskaras thus have a vice-like grip on our conscience, but conscience is not our true self, because it can be changed by changing our samskaras. There are people who grow up in a religious family, but after going to university, they may become atheists, or vice versa.

Regarding the general idea of karma, according to Hinduism, samskaras do not end with this life because they are carried over from one birth to another. How is this information carried over from one birth to another? Hinduism, Buddhism and Jainism believe that, besides our physical bodies, there are subtle bodies, and samskaras survive through these. This is why some people are born with a certain talent that is not present in the family. Some are child prodigies, and some people are born with certain traits, and some with deformities.

Any kind of action (karma) presupposes an agent. You cannot be held responsible for the karmas of someone else. The doer and the one who faces the consequences have to be the same person. Similarly, regarding the karmas of our past lives, the agent who enjoys or suffers the fruits of previous birth has to be the same.

Hinduism says that after we die, we are reborn in a new body but the old samskaras continue as this is the law of karma. In the present birth, we enjoy ourselves or suffer for the actions we did in our past lives, although we have no memory of our past life actions. These karmas are not destiny, argues Vasishtha. He says that what we call destiny is nothing but actions we did of our own free will in our past lives. If we have done bad actions and are suffering for them, we can undo those bad actions with good actions. Where does destiny come into this?

Karma also is part of causality, otherwise the idea has no leg to stand on. However, causality, examined carefully, negates the idea of free will. We have already discussed this in Chapter VII, but shall go through it briefly.

If the present is determined by the past, and the future by the present and the past, what about free will? If the present is not determined by the past, why do we see causal relations? Further, we trace back the cause of an event only up to a certain point that is convenient, and call it the cause. This is like reading a page of a huge novel and passing judgement on the hero or heroine of the novel. Until the first cause is known, and until the last effect is seen, all judgements and theories as to cause and effect are interim, and only posited for practical purposes. They cannot be the entire truth.

If every action necessarily has a result, we seem to be caught in a bind, because the chain of action and result is endless. If this is the case, there can be no possibility of becoming free of misery, or of attaining moksha.

As mentioned earlier, Vedanta says that karma operates only as long we consider ourselves the agents of our actions, and as long as we take the world to be real.

The important thing to remember is that only if you identify yourself with the body–mind–sense complex are you bound to perform according to your station and situation in life. If you give up the ego and detach yourself from the body–mind complex, you are not duty-bound to do anything, just as you are bound by the rules of a sport only as long as you are part of the team. If you opt out of the team, you are no longer bound by the rules. Similarly, if you consider yourself to be a worldly person and the agent of your actions, karma holds. If you give up the claim of being the agent of your actions, all the karmas of all your past lives and the present are annulled in an instant. How is this possible?

Although the supreme reality is one and absolute, it can be viewed and experienced on several levels. This is the freedom we have. Karma, causality and reincarnation doctrines come into effect only at the phenomenal level (*vyavaharika bhoomi*). At the transcendental level (*paramarthika bhoomi*), they have no meaning. The conscious self never gets involved in any kind of action. It is the mind–body complex that does things and reaps the harvest accordingly. Karma comes into effect only on the phenomenal plane.

Since most of us are not interested in going beyond the phenomenal level, some explanation or doctrine has to be given to people, otherwise there would be chaos. Such doctrines were devised by the wise, knowing full well they are false and irresolvable.

Is the destiny versus free will debate irresolvable?

If this question still arises, it means we are overlooking a point that Vasishtha made throughout this discourse. He kept reminding Rama throughout that the individual self and the absolute self (Brahman) are one. All the logic and other devices he used were only to prove the equivalence between the individual and Brahman.

If at the end of this long debate we are convinced of the equivalence between individual consciousness and universal consciousness, the question whether we have a free will or not should dissolve.

If the individual and the universal are the same, where is the question of two wills? There is only one will.

There is just one consciousness (atman), which through its own will (sankalpa) creates imaginary duality. It is this duality that gives rise to all questions and misery.

In the Yogavasishtha, Rama asks many questions, and Vasishtha answers them through reason and logic, all the time reminding Rama that the ultimate truth cannot be expressed in language. Language, logic and reason should be used to make us understand absolute truth, but we must remember that none of the arguments and reasons is the exact truth.

For example, in school they teach us the structure of the atom using the planetary model, although this model is not an accurate picture of the structure of the atom. Inaccurate it might be, but it helps us to understand atomic structure. One can use any model to drive home a point. The same is true of absolute truth. Nothing can be said about it, but discourse can give us some idea about it. The fact is that we are bound by neither action nor destiny, as everything is just a game or stage play. It is the imagination of absolute reality, Brahman.

We might now deal with a question that occurs to most of us. Why is life so difficult? Why is it not smooth and easy?

It is difficult because it is just a game or stage play. The more difficult a game, the more enjoyable it is both for the player as well as the spectator. Computer games, for example, have various levels. You may choose to play at the beginner level, advanced level or expert level. The beginner level is fairly easy and at the expert level, the game gets very difficult. Very few manage to reach there.

Those who play such games are not satisfied until they reach the expert level. It is only at the expert level that your ability shows. Similarly, actors enjoy playing challenging roles.

The same is true of life. The more difficult it is, the more our ability to deal with it is tested. Our aim should be to play the difficult game of life well and emerge winners. Nothing can be more satisfying than this. This cannot be done by running away or escaping from life, as we see in the next chapter.

ENDNOTES

1. II:9:1
2. II:9:5
3. II:9:2
4. III:62:28
5. The Bhagavad Gita, II:47
6. III:95:33
7. III:62:8-33
8. In the sixties, a new theory called 'Chaos' began to take shape. It was realised that simple mathematical equations could model systems of astounding proportions. Those who predict weather jokingly call it the Butterfly Effect. They say a butterfly flapping its wings today in Peking can transform storm systems next month in New York.
9. II:9:17

CHAPTER XVII

THE RETURN OF
THE RENUNCIATE

We have seen that supreme bliss is gained by giving up likes and dislikes (raga–dvesha), by maintaining the right balance in everything we do, by cultivating detachment from the world and by being totally aware of our actions and thoughts. This makes many conclude that an enlightened person is totally unemotional and dry.

If moksha makes us an unemotional person, it is not moksha. Liberated persons are full of vigour and enthusiasm. They are warm and loving, not unfeeling machines. There is only one proof of liberation: absolute bliss and joy. If this has not happened, it means all that Vasishtha has taught so far has just escaped us.

Rama asks Vasishtha how the enlightened behave in society, and what their characteristics are.[1] The sage says that the way a person will behave after liberation cannot be predicted. Some perform worldly duties like everyone else, some withdraw from the world, while others enjoy sensuous pleasures. Such people are neither too eager to do a thing nor do they avoid it.

The enlightened is neither eager to perform actions, nor uninterested in them,
Owing to the knowledge of absolute truth, he is anchored in his own self.[2]

To be 'anchored' in oneself means to be in samadhi. Contrary to the
popular view, to be in samadhi does not mean to be in a meditative
trance.

Vasishtha says that performing actions while seeing the world
as different from the self is called meditation (samadhi), and to see it
as otherwise is to be worldly. If the mind is thinking about the world
during meditation, it is not meditation. It is like any other worldly
activity. On the other hand, if we are active in the world, but our
mind is unperturbed, our state is comparable to a meditative trance.

It is not a question of performing actions or not performing
them. What really matters is our state of mind. Anything done with
the mind is action, and anything that happens after the mind is
quietened is samadhi, moksha or *kaivalibhava*. Samadhi is the state
where we are the masters of our own mind. Enlightened people do
everything, but just as the reflection in a mirror has no effect on the
mirror, they are not affected by anything they do or anything that
happens around them.

Vasishtha tells Rama that understanding (*bodha*) is real
renunciation (tyaga), not the giving up of action (*karma tyaga*).[3] The
yogi who performs actions without being attached to the results
(*karmaphala tyaga*) does not suffer or enjoy the consequences of his
actions.[4]

THE NATURE OF LIBERATED PERSONS
Although truth is one, the ways to realise it are different, and because
of this, not only is it expressed differently by different enlightened
people, but the behaviour of these people is also different. The
Yogavasishtha says that some gyanis live in mountain caves, some
are family men, some travel, some become silent, some meditate
all the time, some become great scholars, some rule as kings, some

become craftsmen, some give up all action, some rejoice in worldly pleasures and some renounce the world.[5] As Shankaracharya says:

At times, he appears to be uninformed, at times a wise man, at times with all the majesty of a king, at times like a misguided person, at times blissful, at times quiet like a motionless python;
At times honoured, at times disgraced, often wandering unknown,
Thus, lives an enlightened person in everlasting supreme bliss.[6]

Since enlightened persons perform actions as we all do, it is difficult to differentiate them from other people. Just as the Sun reflected in a pond appears to be unstable, the enlightened person who keeps performing worldly duties looks like an ordinary person.[7]

It is our state of our mind that makes us liberated or bound. If we are detached internally, even if we are engaged in worldly activities, we are in a state of liberation. On the other hand, if we are attached to the world internally but are not engaged in worldly activities, we are essentially bound. Without allowing our inner self to be disturbed, we should do all worldly activities and duties, because incessant activity is a fundamental characteristic of the body.[8]

Vasishtha says that when a person reaches this balanced mental state, even stones, trees and animals are friendly to him. He is in samadhi even when he is engaged in worldly activities. He may be speaking externally for the benefit of others, but deep inside he is silent. He performs actions that he feels are necessary, yet he is not their agent.[9]

As he begins to love everything, he seems very kind and merciful, but there is a difference between his kindness and ours. Most of us are merciful because we cannot see the suffering of others. The concern is not for the other person but for our own self. We are kind and charitable because the suffering of others makes us miserable. We may do kind deeds because they are approved by society or God, and will lead us to heaven. There is always a reason behind being kind.

A liberated person is also kind, but his reasons are different. He is not moved by our suffering because he knows it is nothing but a bad dream of ours. He is kind not because he cannot see us suffer, because one has to be kind to others, or because kindness is a pious act. He is kind to others because being compassionate has become his very nature. His compassion is not directed towards anyone in particular, and it is not conditional. It is like the light of the Sun, which is not directed towards any particular thing or person.

Before showering kindness on someone, most of us see if the other person is a friend or a foe, a good person or a sinner. An enlightened person showers kindness on anyone who comes near him. On the gross level he appears to be kind, but on the absolute level he is not. He just is what he is.

The Yogavasishtha says that an enlightened person (gyani) does not intimidate anyone, or get intimidated by anyone. He is neither overjoyed by acquiring something, nor miserable after failing to acquire something. He may appear to be happy or sad, but is neither because he has become like a character in a stage play.

BECOMING SILENT WITHIN

Once a yogi becomes like a character on stage, he performs his role to the best of his ability. An actor may be playing the role of a jealous and violent character like Othello, and might look really angry, but deep down he is not affected by his emotions. He is untouched by what is happening on the stage.

The Yogavasishtha says that whether they are actively involved in the world or not, the enlightened (gyanis) become silent from within. These gyanis are of two types: *kashthatapasvi* and *jeevanmukta*. The former quieten their external senses by sheer force and determination, and the latter become contented without any self-imposed austerities. Their silence manifests itself in four ways: *vangamauna, indriyamauna, kashthamauna,* and *sushuptamauna.*

Vangamauna means giving up speech; indriyamauna is forcefully controlling the senses; kashthamauna is giving up all effort, and to be untouched by all actions, thoughts and intentions is sushuptamauna.

Vasishtha says that the first three kinds of silence are nothing but mind game, so not worth adopting. The fourth, sushuptamauna, is the one that leads to liberation.[10] There is a fifth kind of silence, *turiyamauna,* but Vasishtha does not mention it, as it is beyond the grasp of the intellect.[11]

Vasishtha says that when the mind, which is the treasure house of all desire, is quietened, we become free of bondage and suffering. The question arises, what state does such a liberated person live in?

We have mentioned the three states of the mind: wakeful, dream and deep sleep. There is another which is called 'the fourth' (turiya). It is not even called a 'state' because it is beyond the domain of the mind. If we call it a 'state' it means it will change, it means it is limited. Turiya never undergoes any change as it is our very nature. It is the self.

In the wakeful state, the ego is fully active; in the dream state it is weakened, and in deep sleep, the ego nearly disappears. This is why we do not remember anything and feel fresh and relaxed upon waking. What happens to the ego in turiya? In turiya, the ego disappears. This is why bliss is experienced.

If this is the case, what is the difference between deep sleep and turiya? The difference is that in deep sleep the ego almost disappears. We are not aware of it as we are in deep slumber. It is also temporary; this is why we return to our misery upon waking. In turiya, on the other hand, we are full of awareness. It is as restful as deep sleep and we are as awake as in the wakeful state. In deep sleep, the ego only becomes temporarily dormant. In turiya, it does not become dormant, but is transcended. The ego is still there, but we have become its masters.

Those who experience turiya cannot speak about it afterwards because the duality between the experiencing subject and the experienced is dissolved. This is called *nirvikalpa samadhi*; that is, consciousness without subject–object duality. In wakeful state, we do not see things as they are because we are under the influence of illusion (maya). In the nirvikalpa state, we 'see' things as they are because we gain knowledge of ultimate reality directly, as the difference between the knower and the known dissolves.

All the joys of life end sooner or later, but turiya is true bliss, and it never ends. In our case, even when we are happy, we are not truly happy because we know deep inside that it is not going to last, as our happiness depends on external objects or people. Vasishtha reiterates that in this world only a gyani is happy, only a gyani lives and only a gyani is strong because his happiness does not depend on external objects. His happiness is unconditional. It is his nature.[12]

The general belief is that an enlightened person does not take any interest in the activities and pleasures of life. Paradoxically, only after giving up the claim on our actions, and only after giving up all desire and becoming a witness (sakshi) can we actually begin to enjoy worldly attractions. Earlier, we were just doers (karta), but after liberation we become super-doers (*mahakarta*), super-enjoyers (*mahabhokta*) and super-renouncers (*mahatyagi*).

According to the Yogavasishtha, the one who is in company of the learned, has conquered his ego, is without afflictions, envy, and who performs worldly actions without any mental anxiety is called 'super-doer'. One who does not hate anything and does not hanker after anything, relishes all sensual pleasures without getting involved in them and enjoys whatever comes their way is called super-enjoyer. Finally, the one who has given up all physical and mental desires is called super-renouncer.[13]

The Yogavasishtha of Valmiki

The purpose of the mammoth Yogavasishtha discourse was not to turn Rama into an ordinary mendicant but a super mendicant. An ordinary mendicant is nothing but an escapist, whereas a super-mendicant remains in the world, does everything, enjoys everything, but is unaffected by it because he realises that the dichotomy between the phenomenal world and the supreme self is a false one. Just as there is an unintentional relationship between the mirror and what is reflected in it, the same is true of the self and the world. If we look at it falsely there is a difference; if we look at it rightly there is no difference at all because ultimately:

There is neither bondage nor liberation, nor any cause of bondage
Ignorance of the self causes misery, and self-knowledge ends it.[14]

This realisation comes after the knowledge of the self becomes part of our being, not just theoretical understanding. It should be as real as the feeling of being alive.

Vasishtha, however, cautions Rama that after gaining self-knowledge, one must not impose it on others. You must not be too eager to impart it to unwilling listeners (*anadhikari*) or try to convert them. This creates misery in the world. You may have woken from a bad dream, but you must let others sleep as long as they wish.

The liberated must not disturb the equilibrium of others who are involved in the world. Only those who come to you willingly and sincerely should be given the supreme knowledge called Brahmavidya.

ENDNOTES

1. VIB:102:1-53
2. V:56:62
3. VIB:4:1-4
4. VIA:122: 5
5. VIB:102:57-58
6. Shankaracharya, Vivekachoodamani (543)

7. The Ashtavakra Gita also says that it is often difficult to differentiate between the enlightened and unenlightened.

'Those whose inner self has become free of modifications do all out-worldly actions freely,

Such people can be understood only by those who are of their kind.' (XIV:4)

8. IV:15:41-45; see also IV:23:33-41; VIB:1-56
9. VIB:102:1-62
10. VIA:68:1-31
11. VIA:69:16
12. V:92:49
13. VIA:115:9-40
14. IV:38:22

AFTERWORD

A guru sends ten disciples on an errand to a village across a river. After finishing the work, when the disciples are on their way back, it begins to rain heavily. The river they crossed earlier is in full spate now but they manage to cross it and reach the hermitage of their guru.

Before meeting their guru, they decide to do a headcount to be sure no one has drowned. When they finish counting, they realise one of them is missing. What has happened to the tenth man? Has he drowned? They count several times, but find that there is still one man missing.

Finally, they go to the guru and tell him they have lost a friend. The guru counts them and finds that no one is missing. He says, 'Count in my presence.' They all take turns and count and say only nine are there. The guru realises the mistake they are making. Whoever is counting, forgets to count himself.

The guru then makes them stand in a row and counts them one by one, showing no one is missing. 'You are the missing tenth man,' he says to each one of them. The disciples are overjoyed and thank the guru for creating a miracle.

The guru has performed no miracle. He has just corrected a mistake.

We count everything in this world but forget to count ourselves. We know everything in the world but forget to know ourselves. This is why our life is full of misery.

This story has a deeper allegoric meaning, and there is a reason for the number of disciples being ten.

The whole cosmos exists at the individual (*vyashti*) level and cosmic (*samashti*) level and both these levels have three dimensions: gross, subtle and causal. In addition to these six levels, we have three states of consciousness: waking, dream and deep sleep. All these make nine dimensions.

Beyond these nine, there is the tenth dimension. It is the dimension of the self. It is the one because of which all the other dimensions exist, and the irony is we count all the nine dimensions but forget to count the tenth. Until the tenth is counted, we can never be happy.

This is the purpose of the long dialogue between Vasishtha and Rama, and the main purpose of Vedantic literature: to remind the seeker that the missing tenth man is you—*Dashamotvam asi*—You are the tenth one.

After we rediscover the tenth man, all doubts and questions just dissolve and we become blissful. Once blissful, we begin to spread happiness around us without making any effort on our part.

सदाशिवसमारम्भां शङ्कराचार्यमध्यमाम्।
अस्मदाचार्यपर्यन्तां वन्दे गुरुपरम्पराम्।।

My obeisance to the tradition of gurus from
Shiva, Shankaracharya down to my own guru.

APPENDIX: SHLOKAS

INTRODUCTION

मा निषाद प्रतिष्ठां त्वमगमः शाश्वतीः समाः।
यत् क्रौञ्चमिथुनादेकमवधीः काममोहितम्।।

आदावन्ते च यन्नास्ति वर्तमानेऽपि तस्य च।
कश्चित्काललवं दृष्टा सत्ताऽसौ संविदो भ्रमः।।

संकल्पनं मनो विद्धि संकल्पात्तन्न भिद्यते ।
यथा द्रवत्वात्सलिलं तथा स्पन्दो यथाऽनिलात् ।।

ज्ञानेनाकाशकल्पेन धर्मान्यो गगनोपमान्।
ज्ञेयाभिन्नेन संबुद्धस्तं वन्दे द्विपदां वरम्।।

उपदेशादयं वादो ज्ञाते द्वैतं न विद्यते।।

न बन्धोऽस्ति न मोक्षोऽस्ति देहिनः परमार्थतः।
मिथ्येयमिन्द्रजालश्रीः संसारपरिवर्तिनी।।

पूर्णात्पूर्णं विसरति पूर्णे पूर्णं विराजते।
पूर्णमेवोदितं पूर्णे पूर्णमेव व्यवस्थितम्।।

यदिहास्ति तदन्यत्र यन्नेहास्ति न तत् क्वचित्।
इमं समस्तविज्ञानशास्त्रकोशं विदुर्बुधा:।।

स्वपौरुषप्रयत्नेन विवेकेन विकासिना।
स देवो ज्ञायते राम न तप:स्नानकर्मभि:।।

शुद्धं बुद्धं प्रियं पूर्णं निष्प्रपञ्चं निरामयम्।
आत्मानं तं न जानन्ति तत्राभ्यासपरा जना:।।

एकं सत् विप्रा: बहुदा वदन्ति

CHAPTER I

किं नामेदं बत सुखं येयं संसारसन्तति:।
जायते मृतये लोको म्रियते जननाय च।।

असतैव वयं कष्टं विकृष्टा मूढबुद्धय:।
मृगतृष्णाम्भसा दूरे वने मुग्धमृगा इव।।

किं मे राज्येन किं भोगै: कोऽहं किमिदमागतम्।
यन्मिथ्यैवास्तु तन्मिथ्या कस्य नाम किमागतम्।।

संसारदु:खपाषाणनीरन्ध्रहृदयोऽप्यहम्।
निजलोकभयादेव गलद्वाष्पं न रोदिमि।।

यदि विज्ञानविश्रान्तिर्न भवेद्भव्यचेतस:।
तदस्यां संसृतौ साधुश्चिन्तामौद्यं सहेत क:।।

अहो बत कुमारेण कल्याणगुणशालिनी।
वागुक्ता परमोदारा वैराग्यरसगर्भिणी।।

बीभत्सं विषयं दृष्ट्वा को नाम न विरज्यते।
सतामुत्तमवैराग्यं विवेकादेव जायते।।

ते महान्तो महाप्राज्ञा निमित्तेन विनैव हि।
वैराग्यं जायते येषां तेषां ह्यमलमानसम्।।

The Yogavasishtha of Valmiki

निर्दय: कठिन: क्रूर: कर्कश: कृपणोऽधम:।
न तदस्ति यदद्याऽपि न कालो निगिरत्ययम्।।

अत्रैव दुर्विलासानां चूडामणिरिहापर:।
करोत्यत्तीति लोकेऽस्मिन्नैवं कालश्च कथ्यते।।

यदिदं दृश्यते किञ्चिज्जगदाभोगि मण्डलम्।
तत्तस्य नर्तनागारमिहासावतिनृत्यति।।

CHAPTER II

उद्यमेन हि सिध्यन्ति कार्याणि न मनोरथै:।
न हि सुप्तस्य सिंहस्य प्रविशन्ति मुखे मृगा:।।

मुक्ताभिमानी मुक्तो हि बद्धो बद्धाभिमान्यपि।
किंवदन्तीह सत्येयं या मति: सा गतिर्भवेत्।।

पौरुषं स्पन्दफलवद् दृष्टं प्रत्यक्षतो नयत्।
कल्पितं मोहितैर्मन्दैर्दैवं किञ्चिन्न विद्यते।।

यो यमर्थं प्रार्थयते तदर्थं चेहते क्रमात्।
अवश्यं स तमाप्नोति न चेदर्धान्निवर्त्तते।।

यदेव जीवनं जीवे चेत्योन्मुखचिदात्मकम्।
तदेव पौरुषं तस्मिन्सारं कर्म तदेव च।।

द्वौहूडाविव युध्येते पुरुषार्थौ समासमौ।
प्राक्तनश्रैहिकश्चैव शाम्पत्यत्राल्पवीर्यवान्।।

ह्यास्तनी दुष्क्रियाभ्येति शोभां सत्क्रियया यथा।
अद्यैवं प्राक्तनी तस्माद्यत्नात्सत्कार्यवान्भवेत्।।

आबालमेतत्संसिद्धं यत्र यत्र यथा यथा।
दैवं तु न क्वचिद्दृष्टमतो जगति पौरुषम्।।

प्राज्ञश्चेतनमात्रस्त्वं न देहस्त्वं जडात्मक:।
अन्येन चेतसा तत्ते चेत्यत्वं क्वेव विद्यते।।

अन्यस्त्वां चेतयति चेत्तं चेतयति कोऽपरः।
क इमं चेतयेत्तस्मादनवस्था न वास्तवी।।

यथा संवेदनं चेतस्थता तत्स्पन्दमृच्छति।
तथैव कायश्चलति तथैव फलभोक्तृता।।

राम राम महाबाहो महापुरुष चिन्मय।
नायं विश्रान्तिकालो हि लोकानन्दकरो भव।।

यावल्लोकपरामर्शो निरूढो नास्ति योगिनः।
तावद्रूढसमाधित्वं न भवत्येव निर्मलम्।।

CHAPTER III

त्रिवर्गमात्रसिद्ध्यै यन्न मोक्षाय च तच्छ्रुतम्।
विपुलश्रुतचर्चासु तुच्छमश्रुतमेव तत्।।

श्रद्धावीर्यस्मृतिसमाधिप्रज्ञापूर्वक इतरेषाम्।

न हि श्रुतिशतम् अपि शीतः अग्निः अप्रकाशो वा इति ब्रुवत् प्रामाण्यम् उपैति।

युक्त्यैव बोधयित्वैष जीव आत्मनि योज्यते।
यद्युक्त्यासाद्यते कार्यं न तद्यत्नशतैरपि।।

यन्नाम युक्तिभिरिह प्रवदन्ति तज्ज्ञास्तत्रावहेलनमयुक्तमुदारबुद्धेः।
यो युक्तियुक्तमवमत्य विमूढबुद्धिः कष्टाग्रहो भवति तं विदुरज्ञमेव।।

बालानां सुखबोधाय क्रियते तर्कसंग्रहः।।

नास्ति चेत्तद्विचारेण दोषः को भवतां भवेत्।
अस्ति चेत्तत्समुत्तीर्णा भविष्यथ भवार्णवात्।।

CHAPTER IV

आत्मज्ञानप्रधानानामिदमेव महामते।
शास्त्राणां परमं शास्त्रं महारामायणं शुभम्।।

यथाभूतार्थवाक्यार्थाः सर्वा एव ममोक्तयः।
नासमर्था विरूपार्था पूर्वापरविरोधदाः।।

The Yogavasishtha of Valmiki

परं रूपमनाद्यन्तं यन्ममैकमनामयम्।
ब्रह्मात्मपरमात्मादिशब्देनैतदुदीर्यते।।

यथाभूतार्थवाक्यार्था: सर्वा एव ममोक्तय:।
नासमर्था विरूपार्था: पूर्वापरविरोधदा:।।

यावदप्रतिबुद्धस्त्वमनात्मज्ञतया स्थित:।
तावच्चतुर्भुजाकारदेवपूजापरो भव।।

तत्क्रमात्संप्रबुद्धस्त्वं ततो ज्ञास्यसि तत्परम्।
मम रूपमनाद्यन्तं येन भूयो न जायते।।

कयैतज्ज्ञायते युक्त्या कथमेतत्प्रसिध्यति।
न्यायानुभूत एतस्मिन्न ज्ञेयमवशिष्यते।।

युक्त्या प्रबोध्यते मूढ: प्राज्ञस्तत्त्वेन बोध्यते।
मूढ: प्राज्ञत्वमायाति न युक्त्या बोधनं विना।।

एतावन्तमबुद्धस्त्वं कालं युक्त्या प्रबोधित:।
इदानीं संप्रबुद्धस्त्वं मया येनावबोध्यसे।।

अनुभूतिं विना तत्त्वं खण्डादेर्नानुभूयते।
अनुभूतिं विना रूपं नात्मनश्चानुभूयते।।

CHAPTER V

गुरुशास्त्रादिविज्ञाने कारणं वास्त्यकारणम्।

ज्ञप्तेस्तु कारणं शुद्धा शिष्यप्रज्ञैव राघव।।

अपुनर्जन्मने य: स्याद्बोध: स ज्ञानशब्दभाक्।
वसनाशनदा शेषा व्यवस्था शिल्पजीविका।।

गुरुर्हीन्द्रियवृत्तात्मा ब्रह्म सर्वेन्द्रियक्षयात्।

श्रवणायापि बहुभिर्यो न लभ्य:शृण्वन्तोऽपि बहवो यं न विदु:।
आश्चर्यो वक्ता कुशलोऽस्य लब्धाऽऽश्चर्यो ज्ञाता कुशलानुशिष्ट:।।

बहुकालमियं रूढा मिथ्याज्ञानविषूचिका।
जगन्नाम्न्यविचाराख्या विना ज्ञानं न शाम्यति।।

वदाम्याख्यायिका राम या इमा बोधसिद्धये।
ताश्रेच्छृणोषि तत्साधो मुक्त एवासि बुद्धिमान्।।

नो चेदुद्वेगशीलत्वादर्धादुत्थाय गच्छसि।
तत्तिर्यग्धर्मिणस्तेऽद्य न किञ्चिदपि सेत्स्यति।।

ब्रह्म सर्वेन्द्रियातीतं श्रुतादीन्द्रियसंविद:।
तेनोपदेशादनघनात्मतत्त्वमवाप्यते।।

गुरूपदेशं च विना नात्मतत्त्वागमो भवेत्।
केन चिन्तामणिर्लब्ध: कर्पदन्वेषणं विना।।

क्रमे गुरूपदेशानां प्रवृत्ते शिष्यबोधत:।
अनिर्देश्योऽप्यदृश्योऽपि स्वयमात्मा प्रसीदति।।

उपदेश्योपदेशार्थं शास्त्रार्थप्रतिपत्तये।
शब्दार्थवाक्यरचनाभ्रमो मा तन्मयो भव।।

ज्ञानिनैव सदा भाव्यं राम न ज्ञानबन्धुना।
अज्ञातारं वरं मन्ये न पुनर्ज्ञानबन्धुताम्।।

CHAPTER VI

को अद्धा वेद क इह प्र वोचत्कुत अजाता कुत इयं विसृष्टि:।
अर्वाग्देवा अस्य विसर्जनेनाथा को वेद यत आबभूव।।

इयं विसृष्टिर्यत आबभूव यदि वा दधे यदि वा न।
यो अस्याध्यक्ष: परमे व्योमन्सो अंग वेद यदि वा न वेद।।

रूपमीदृशमेवास्य चिन्मात्रस्यास्त्यकृत्रिमम्।
सर्वगस्य यदेतद्यद्यत्र वेत्यस्ति तत्र तत्।।

मन एव विरिञ्चित्वं तद्धि संकल्पनात्मकम्।
स्ववपु: स्फारतां नीत्वा मनसेदं वितन्यते।।

चित्स्वभावात्समायातं ब्रह्मत्वं सर्वकारणम्।
संसृतौ कारणं पश्चात्कर्म निर्माय संस्थितम्।।

संकल्पयति यन्नाम प्रथमोऽसौ प्रजापतिः।
तत्तदेवाशु भवति तस्येदं कल्पनं जगत्।।

स्वयमक्षुब्धविमले यथा स्पन्दो महाम्भसि।
संसारकारणं जीवस्तथायं परमात्मनि।।

तेष्वप्यन्तस्थसगौंघाः कदलीदलपीठवत्।
सर्वसर्गान्तराद्दूरं पत्रपीवरवृत्तिमत्।।

स्वभावशीतलं ब्रह्म कदलीदलमण्डपः।
कदल्यामन्यता नास्ति यथा पत्रशतेष्वपि।।

अणोरणीयान् महतो महीयानात्मा गुहायां निहितोऽस्य जन्तोः।

यान्तः स्वप्नादिविभ्रान्तिः सैवेयं बाह्यतोदिता।
मनागप्यन्यता नात्र द्विभाण्डपयसोरिव।।

स्वप्नवत्पश्यति जगच्चिन्नभोदेहवित्स्वयम्।
स्वप्नसंसारदृष्टान्त एवाहंत्वंसमन्वितम्।।

संवित्स्वप्नार्थयोर्द्वित्वं न कदाचन लभ्यते।
यथा द्रवत्वपयसोर्यथा वा स्पन्दवातयोः।।

स्वप्नद्रष्टा स्वप्नमृतः प्रबुद्ध इह कथ्यते।
इह जाग्रन्मृतो जन्तुः प्रबुद्धोऽन्यत्र कथ्यते।।

इतिहासमयावेव जाग्रत्स्वप्नावुभावपि।
परस्परं गतावेतावुपमानोपमेयताम्।।

आकाशविशदो द्रष्टा सर्वाङ्गःगोऽपि न पश्यति।
नेत्रं निजमिवात्मानं दृशीभूतमहो भ्रमः।।

पूर्णात्पूर्णं प्रसरति संस्थितं पूर्णमेव तत्।
अतो विश्वमनुत्पन्नं यच्चोत्पन्नं तदेव तत्।।

नाधेयं तत्र नाधारो न दृश्यं न च द्रष्टृता।
ब्रह्माण्डं नास्ति न ब्रह्मा न च वैतण्डिका: क्वचित्।।

CHAPTER VII

काणादं पाणिनीयं च सर्वशास्त्रोपकारकम्।

अशक्तिरपरिज्ञानं क्रमकोपोऽथ वा पुन:।
एवं हि सर्वथा बुद्धैरजाति: परिदीपिता।।

पूर्वापरापरिज्ञानमजाते: परिदीपकम्।
जायमानाद्धि वै धर्मात्कथं पूर्वं न गृह्यते।।

हेतुर्न जायतेऽनादे: फलं चापि स्वभावत:।
आदिर्न विद्यते यस्य तस्य ह्यादिर्न विद्यते।।

यदि नास्ति विकारादि ब्रह्मन्ब्रह्मणि बृंहिते।
तदिदं कथमाभाति भावाभावमयं जगत्।।

अपुन:प्रागवस्थानं यत्स्वरूपविपर्ययः।
तद्विकारादिकं तात यत्क्षीरादिषु वर्तते।।

इदमादावनुत्पन्नं कारणाभावत: किल।
कारणेन विना कार्यं न हि नामोपपद्यते।।

एवं चेत्तद्भद ब्रह्मन्द्रष्टृदृश्यावभासनम्।

सहकारिकारणानामभावे कार्यकारणम्।
एकमेतदतो नान्य: परस्मात्सर्गविभ्रम:।।

अस्मादेकप्रतिस्पन्दाज्जीवा: संप्रसरन्ति ये।
सहकारिकारणानामभावाच्च स एव ते।।

सति बीजे प्रवर्तन्ते कार्यकारणदृष्टय:।
निराकारस्य किं बीजं क्व जन्यजनकक्रम:।।

न बीजांकुरयोर्भेदो विद्यतेऽग्न्यौष्ण्ययोरिव।
बीजमेवांकुरं विद्धि विद्धि कर्मैव मानवम्।।

The Yogavasishtha of Valmiki

भात्यकारणकं ब्रह्म सर्गात्माऽप्यबुधं प्रति।
तं प्रत्येव च भात्येष कार्यकारणदृग्भ्रमः।।

एवं सकारणं सर्वं सर्वदा दृश्यमण्डलम्।
यस्य सर्गे यतः कालात्ततः प्रभृति तं प्रति।।

मनोनिर्मलसत्त्वात्म यद्भावयति यादृशम्।
तत्तथाशु भवत्येव यथावर्तो भवेत्पयः।।

अबुद्धिपूर्वं चानिच्छमेवमेव प्रवर्तते।
काकतालीयवत्स्पन्दादावर्ता इव वारिणि।।

काकतालीययोगेन संजातोऽस्ति मुधैव हि।
मृगतृष्णाद्विचन्द्रत्वमिवासत्यं च वर्धते।।

अकारणं प्रवर्तन्त इव भावा अकारणात्।
अविद्यमाना अप्येतेऽविद्यमाना इव स्थिताः।।

असतः शशशृंगादेर्मृगतृष्णाम्भसो यथा।
आलोकनादलभ्यस्य कीदृक् स्यात्किल कारणम्।।

असतः शशशृंगादेः कारणं मार्गयन्ति ये।
वन्ध्यापुत्रस्य पौत्रस्य स्कन्धमासादयन्ति ते।।

चित्तं न संस्पृशत्यर्थं नार्थाभासं तथैव च।
अभूतो किं यतश्चार्थो नार्थाभासस्ततः पृथक्।।

तस्मान्न जायते चित्तं चित्तदृश्यं न जायते।
तस्य पश्यन्ति ये जातिं खे वै पश्यन्ति ते पदम्।।

अन्तःस्थानात्तु भेदानां तस्माज्जागरिते स्मृतम्।
यथा तत्र तथा स्वप्ने संवृतत्वेन भिद्यते।।

जाग्रत्स्वप्नदशाभेदो न स्थिरास्थिरते विना।
समः सदैव सर्वत्र समस्तोऽनुभवोऽनयोः।।

स्पन्दे समुदेतीव निःस्पन्दान्तर्गते न च।
इयं यस्मिञ्जगल्लक्ष्मीरलात इव चक्रता।।

ऋजुवक्रादिकाभासमलातस्पन्दितं यथा।
ग्रहणग्राहकाभासं विज्ञानस्पन्दितं तथा।।

अस्पन्दमानमलातमनाभासमजं यथा।
अस्पन्दमानं विज्ञानमनाभासमजं तथा।।

न स्वतो नापि परतो न द्वाभ्यां नाप्यहेतुत:।
उत्पन्ना: जातु विद्यन्ते भावा: क्वचन केचन।।

CHAPTER VIII

संप्रबुद्धजनाचारे वक्तुमेतन्न शोभनम्।
यद् ब्रह्मण इदं जातं न जातं चेति राघव।।

शून्यं शून्ये समुच्छूनं ब्रह्म ब्रह्मणि बृंहितम्।
सत्यं विजृम्भते सत्ये पूर्णे पूर्णमिव स्थितम्।।

न कदाचिदुदेतीदं परस्मान्न च शाम्यति।
इत्थं स्थितं केवलं सद्ब्रह्म स्वात्मनि संस्थितम्।।

अहं हि हेमकटके विचार्यापि न दृष्टवान्।
कटकत्वं क्वचिन्नाम ऋते निर्मलहाटकात्।।

जलादृते पयोवीचौ नाहं पश्यामि किञ्चन।
वीचित्वं तादृशं दृष्टं यत्र नास्त्येव तत्र हि।।

CHAPTER IX

पर्वताग्रपरिभ्रष्टो ह्याधोध उपलो यथा।
परमात्मपरिभ्रष्टो जीव: स्वप्नमिमं दृढम्।।

घटे कपालतां याते घटाकाशो न नश्यति।
यथा तथा शरीरेऽस्मिन्नष्टेऽपि न विनश्यति।।

विस्तार: कर्मणां देह: सोऽहन्तात्मा ससंसृति:।
अचेतनानहंत्वेन शाम्यत्यस्पन्दवातवत्।।

स्वयं कल्पितसंगल्पमात्मरूपं यदाविलम्।
तदेव वासनाकारं जीवं विद्धि महामते।।

रथः स्थाणुर्देहस्तुरगरचना चेन्द्रियगतिः
परिस्पन्दो वातो वहनकलितानन्दविषयः।
परोऽणुर्वा देही जगति विहरामीत्यनघया
धिया दृष्टे तत्त्वे रमणमटनं जागतमिदम्।।

द्वा सुपर्णा सयुजा सखाया समानं वृक्षं परिषस्वजाते।
तयोरन्यः पिप्पलं स्वाद्वत्त्यनश्नन्नन्यो अभिचाकशीति।।

यथा पयोदमरुतोर्यथा षट्पदपद्मयोः।
तथा राघव सम्बन्धस्त्वच्छरीरत्वदात्मनोः।।

न कश्चिद्विद्यते भेदो द्वैतैक्यकलनात्मकः।
ब्रह्मजीवमनोमायाकर्तृकर्मजगद्दृशाम्।।

पञ्चीकृतानि भूतानि स्थूलानीत्युच्यते बुद्धैः।7।
पृथिव्यादीनि भूतानी प्रत्येकं विभजेद्द्विधा।
एकैकं भागमादाय चतुर्धा विभजेत्पुनः।8।
एकैकं भागमेकस्मिन् भूते संवेशयेत् क्रमात्।
ततश्चाकाशभूतस्य भागाः पञ्च भवन्ति हि।।9।।
वाच्यवादिभागाश्चत्वारो वाच्यवादिष्वेवमादिशेत्।
पञ्चीकरणमेतत्स्यादित्याहुस्तत्त्ववेदिनः।।10।।

असावन्नमयः कोशः पञ्चभूतात्मकः स्मृतः। आद्यन्तवान् जडश्चायं भूतोत्पाद्योऽथ खण्डवान्।।11।।
मलसान्द्रोऽप्यतो न त्वं कोशोऽयं पार्थिवाङ्ग.भृत्। त्वमस्य वर्ष्मणः साक्षी तद्ब्रह्मास्यमिदं शृणु।। नाहं शरीरमेवास्मि ब्रह्माहं केवलं त्विति।।2।।

अथ प्राणमयः कोशो रजोगुणसमुद्भवः।आद्यन्तवान् जडः कार्यस्तत्त्वं न प्राणकोशकः।।3।।
अस्य कोशस्य साक्षी त्वं तद्ब्रह्मास्यमिदं शृणु। नाहं प्राणमयः कोशो ब्रह्माहं केवलं त्विति।।4।।

योऽयं मनोमयः कोशः स च सत्त्वगुणोद्भवः।आद्यन्तवान् जडः कार्यस्तत्त्वं नैव मनोमयः।।5।।
अस्य कोशस्य साक्षी त्वं तद्ब्रह्मास्यमिदं शृणु। नाहं मनोमयः कोशो ब्रह्माहं केवलं त्विति।।6।।

यो विज्ञानमयः कोशः सोऽपि सत्त्वगुणोद्भवः।
आद्यन्तवान् जडः कार्यत्वं विज्ञानमयो न तत्॥7॥
अस्य कोशस्य साक्षी त्वं तद्ब्रह्मस्यमिदं शृणु।
नाहं विज्ञानकोशो हि ब्रह्माहं केवलं त्विति॥8॥

यो आनन्दमयः कोशः स च प्रकृतिसंभवः।अविद्याकर्मजन्योऽपि व्यभिचारिगुणान्वितः ॥9॥
जडश्रायं त्वमानन्दकोशो नैव भवस्यतः।अस्य कोशस्य साक्षी त्वं तद्ब्रह्मस्यमिदं शृणु॥
नाहमानन्दकोशोऽपि ब्रह्माहं केवलं त्विति॥10॥

CHAPTER X

मनोमात्रं जगत्कृत्स्नं मनः पर्यन्तमण्डलम्।
मनो व्योम मनो भूमिर्मनो वायुर्मनो महान्॥

मनो यदि पदार्थे तु तद्भावेन न योजयेत्।
ततः सूर्योदयेऽप्येते न प्रकाशाः कदाचन॥

सूर्यसन्निधिमात्रेण यथोदेति जगत्क्रिया।
चित्सत्तामात्रकेणेदं जगन्निष्पद्यते तथा॥

इदमस्मात्समुत्पन्नं मृगतृष्णाम्बुसन्निभम्।
रूपं तु क्षणसंकल्पाद्द्वितीयेन्दुभ्रमोपमम्॥

लघु दीर्घं करोत्येव सत्येऽसत्तां प्रयच्छति।
कटुतां नयति स्वादु रिपुं नयति मित्रताम्॥

यदर्थप्रतिभानं तन्मन इत्यभिधीयते।
अन्यन्न किञ्चिदप्यस्ति मनो नाम कदाचन॥

चित्तमेतदुपायातं ब्रह्मणः परमात्पदात्।
अतन्मयं तन्मयं च तरंगः सागरादिव॥

प्रबुद्धानां मनो राम ब्रह्मैवेह हि नेतरत्।
जलसामान्यबुद्धीनामब्धेर्नाऽन्यस्तरंगकः॥

मनो हि भावनामात्रं भावना स्पन्दधर्मिणी।
क्रिया तद्भावितारूपं फलं सर्वोऽनुधावति॥

The Yogavasishtha of Valmiki

यत्र संकल्पनं तत्र तन्मनोऽङ्ग. तथा स्थितम्।
संकल्पमनसी भिन्ने न कदाचन केचन।।

एतावच्चेतसो जन्म बीजं संसारभूतये ।
संकल्पोन्मुखतां यातः संविदो वा किलात्मनः ।।

जगद्दीर्घमहास्वप्नः सोऽयमन्तः समुत्थितः।
स्वप्नात्स्वप्नान्तरं यान्ति काश्चिद्भूतपरम्पराः।।

तेनोपलम्भः कुड्यादावसौ दृढतरः स्थितः।
यद्यत्र चिद्भावयति तत्तत्राशु भवत्यलम्।।

यदाधिभौतिकं भावं चेतोऽनुभवति स्वयम्।
चेत्यं सन्मयमेवात आतिवाहिककल्पनम्।।

चित्तायत्तमिदं सर्वं जगत्स्थिरचरात्मकम्।
चित्ताधीनवतो राम बन्धमोक्षावपि स्फुटम्।।

शीतता तुहिनस्येव कज्जलस्येव कृष्णता।
लोलता मनसो रूपं तीव्रातीव्रैकरूपिणी।।

चिच्छक्तेः स्पन्दशक्तेश्च संबन्धः कल्प्यते मनः।
मिथ्यैव तत्समुत्पन्नं मिथ्या ज्ञानं तदुच्यते।।

एषा ह्याविद्या कथिता मायैषा सा निगद्यते।
परमेतत्तदज्ञानं संसारादिविषप्रदम्।।

विश्वबीजमहंत्वं त्वं विद्धि तस्माद्धि जायते।
साद्रयब्ध्युर्वीनदीशादिजगज्जरठपादपः।।

एवं जीवाश्रितो भावा भवभावनयोहिताः।
ब्रह्मणः कल्पिताकाराल्लक्षशोऽप्यथ कोटिशः।।

असंख्याताः पुरा जाता जायन्ते चापि वाद्य भोः।
उत्पत्स्यन्ति चैवाम्बुकणौघा इव निर्झरात्।।

येन येन यथा यद्यद्यदा संवेद्यतेऽनघ।
तेन तेन तथा तत्तत्तदा समनुभूयते।।

अमृतत्वं विषं याति सदैवामृतवेदनात्।
शत्रुर्मित्रत्वमायाति मित्रसंवित्तिवेदनात्।।

सर्वेषु सुखदुःखेषु सर्वासु कलनासु च।
मनः कर्तृ मनो भोक्तृ मानसं विद्धि मानवम्।।

न निम्बेक्षू कटुस्वादू शीतोष्णौ नेन्दुपावकौ।
यदयथा परमाभ्यस्तमुपलब्धं तथैव तत्।।

शुक्लं कृष्णीकरोत्येव कृष्णं नयति शुक्लताम्।
विनैव देशकालाभ्यां शक्तिं पश्यास्य चेतसः।।

मनस्यन्यत्र संसक्ते चर्वितस्यापि जिह्वया।
भोजनस्याऽपि मृष्टस्य न स्वादोऽस्याऽनुभूयते।।

यच्चित्तदृष्टं तद् दृष्टं न दृष्टं तदलोकितम्।
अन्धकारे यथा रूपमिन्द्रियं निर्मितं तथा।।

CHAPTER XI

सतोऽसत्ता स्थिता मूर्ध्नि मूर्ध्नि रम्येश्वरम्यता।
सुखेषु मूर्ध्नि दुःखानि किमेकं संश्रयाम्यहम्।।

यत्कृतं मनसा तात तत्कृतं विद्धि राघव।
यत्त्यक्तं मनसा तावत्तत्त्यक्तं विद्धि चानघ।।

CHAPTER XII

जीवनाच्चेतनाज्जीवो जीव इत्येव कथ्यते।
चेत्योन्मुखतया चित्तं चिदित्येव निगद्यते।।

इदमित्थमिति स्पष्टबोधाद्बुद्धिरिहोच्यते।
कल्पनान्मननज्ञत्वान्मन इत्यभिधीयते।।

अस्मीति प्रत्ययादन्तरहंकारश्च कथ्यते।
चेतनाढ्यमृतं चित्तमिति शास्त्रविचारिभिः।।

यत्किञ्चिदिदमायाति सुखदुःखमलं भवे।
तदहंकारचक्रस्य प्रविकारो विजृम्भते।।

यदा मिथ्याभिमानेन सत्तां कल्पयति स्वयम्।
अहंकाराभिमानेन प्रोच्यते भवबन्धनी।।

CHAPTER XIII

उभाभ्यामेव पक्षाभ्यां यथा खे पक्षिणां गति:।
तथैव ज्ञानकर्मभ्यां जायते परमं पदम्।।

केवलात्कर्मणो ज्ञानान्नहि मोक्षोऽभिजायते।
किन्तूभाभ्यां भवेन्मोक्ष: साधनं तूभयं विदु:।।

द्वौ क्रमौ चित्तनाशस्य योगो ज्ञानं च राघव।
योगस्तद्वृत्तिरोधो हि ज्ञानं सम्यगवेक्षणम्।।

ज्ञानान्निर्दु:खतामेति ज्ञानादज्ञानसंक्षय:।
ज्ञानादेव परा सिद्धिर्नान्यस्माद्राम वस्तुत:।।

एकं सांख्यं च योगं च य: पश्यति स पश्यति।
यत्सांख्यै: प्राप्यते स्थानं परं योगैस्तदेव हि।।

ज्ञानं हि परमं श्रेय: कैवल्यं तेन वेत्यलम्।
कालातिवाहनायैव विनोदायोदिता क्रिया।।

न शास्त्रान्न गुरोर्वाक्यान्न दानान्नेश्वरार्चनात्।
एष सर्वपदातीतो बोध: संप्राप्यते पर:।।

पुत्र युक्त्या गृहीतोऽसौ क्षणादायाति वश्यताम्।
युक्तिं विना दहत्येष आशीविष इवोद्धत:।।

अस्य संसाररूपस्य मायाचक्रस्य राघव।
चित्तं विद्धि महानाभिं भ्रमतो भ्रमदायिन:।।

तस्मिन्दुतमवष्टब्धे धिया पुरुषयत्नत:।
गृहीतनाभिवहनान्मायाचक्रं निरुध्यते।।

अनाद्यन्तावभासात्मा परमात्मेह विद्यते।
इत्येको निश्चय: स्फार: सम्यग्ज्ञानं विदुर्बुधा:।।

साधयन्ति समुत्सृज्य युक्तिं ये तान्हठान्विदु:।
भयाद्भयमुपायान्ति क्लेशात्क्लेशं व्रजन्ति ते।।

कूर्मोऽङ्गानीव दृश्यानि लीयन्ते स्वात्मनात्मनि।
अभावितान्येव यदा सत्तासामान्यता तदा।।

दोषमुक्ताफलप्रोता वासनातन्तुसन्तति:।
हृदि न ग्रथिता यस्य मृत्युस्तं न जिघांसति।।

संप्रबुद्धे हि मनसि स्वां विवेचयति स्थितिम् ।
नैशमर्कोदय इव तमो हार्दं पलायते ।।

CHAPTER XIV
योगश्चित्तवृत्तिनिरोध:।

CHAPTER XV
ये परां दृष्टिमायाता: संसृते: पारदर्शिन:।
न ते कर्म प्रशंसन्ति कूपं नद्यां वसन्निव।।

ये बद्धवासना मूढा: कर्म शंसन्ति तेऽनघ।
श्रुतिस्मृत्युचितं तेन विनाबोधं प्रयान्ति ते।।

किं कर्म किमकर्मेति कवयोऽप्यत्र मोहिता:।

तज्ज्ञाज्ञयोरशेषेषुभावाभावेषु कर्मसु।
ऋते निर्वासनत्वात्तु न विशेषोऽस्ति कश्चन।।

सत्तैवैषा विदो यत्सा भवत्युन्मिषिता जगत्।
परं तत्त्वं निमिषिता दृगिवानामकं ततम्।।

मनो यत्करोति तत्कृतं भवति यन्न करोति तन्न कृतं भवति अतो मन एव कर्तृ न देह:।

यदा स्पन्दैकधर्मत्वात्कर्तुर्या शून्यशासिनि।
आधावति स्पन्दफलं तदा कर्मेत्युदाहृता।।

संकल्पिता जगति मोक्षमतिर्मुधैव संकल्पिता जगति बंधमतिर्मुधैव।
संत्यज्य सर्वमनहंकृतिरात्मनिष्ठो धीरो धिया व्यवहरन्भुवि राम तिष्ठ।।

The Yogavasishtha of Valmiki

यस्तु सर्वाणि भूतान्यात्मन्येवानुपश्यति।
सर्वभूतेषु चात्मानं ततो न विजुगुप्सते।।

चित: क्षीणविकल्पस्य किमुपादेयमस्ति मे।

न बंधोऽस्ति न मोक्षोऽस्ति मौर्ख्ये मे क्षयमागतम्।
किं मे ध्यानविलासेन किं वा ध्यानेन मे भवेत्।।

ध्यानाध्यानभ्रमौ त्यक्त्वा पुंस्त्वं स्वमवलोकयत्।
यदायाति तदायातु न मे बृद्धिर्न वा क्षय:।।

न किंचिदपि कर्त्तव्यं यदि नाम मयाधुना।
तत्कस्मान्न करोमीदं किंचित्प्रकृतकर्म वै।।

मा गच्छ दु:खितां राम सुखितामपि मा व्रज।
समतामेहि सर्वत्र परमात्मा हि सर्वग:।।

नासि कर्ता किमेतासु क्रियासु ममता तव।
एकस्मिन्विद्यमाने हि किं केन क्रियते कथम्।

मा वाऽकर्ता भव प्राज्ञ किमकर्तृतयेहिते।
साध्यं साध्यमुपादेयं तस्मात्स्वस्थो भवानघ।।

CHAPTER XVI

भगवन्सर्वधर्मज्ञ प्रतिष्ठामलमागतम्।
यल्लोके तद्वद ब्रह्मान्दैवं नाम किमुच्यते।।

पौरुषोपनता नित्यमिष्टानिष्टस्य वस्तुन:।
प्राप्तिरिष्टाप्यनिष्टा वा दैवशब्देन कथ्यते।।

पौरुषं सर्वकार्याणां कर्तृ राघव नेतरत्।
फलभोक्तृ च सर्वत्र न दैवं तत्र कारणम्।।

अपौरुषं हि नियति: पौरुषं सैव सर्गगा।
निष्फलाऽपौरुषाकारा सफला पौरुषात्मिका।।

कर्मण्येवाधिकारस्ते मा फलेषु कदाचन।

न स शैलो न तद्व्योम न सोऽब्धिश्च न विष्टपम्।
अस्ति यत्र फलं नास्ति कृतानामात्मकर्मणाम्।।

एवं कर्मस्थकर्माणि कर्मप्रौढा स्ववासना।
वासना मनसो नान्या मनो हि पुरुष: स्मृत:।।

CHAPTER XVII

कर्मणास्ति न तस्यार्थो नार्थस्तस्यास्त्यकर्मणा।
यथास्वभावावगमात्स आत्मन्येव संस्थित:।।

क्वचिन्मूढो विद्वान्क्वचिदपि महाराजविभव:
क्वचिद्भ्रान्त: सौम्य: क्वचिदजगराचारकलित:।
क्वचित्पात्रीभूत: क्वचिदवमत: क्वाप्यविदित:
इचरत्येवं प्राज्ञ: सततपरमानन्दसुखित:।।

न बंधोऽस्ति न मोक्षोऽस्ति नाबंधोऽस्ति न बंधनम्।
अप्रबोधादिदं दु:खं प्रबोधात्प्रविलीयते।।

BIBLIOGRAPHY

Yogavasishtha (Sanskrit, Hindi, and English)

Atreya BL, *Yogavasishtha aur Uske Sidhdhant*, Shri Krishna–Janamsthan Seva Sansthan, Mathura, 1986

Atreya BL, *The Philosophy of the Yogavasistha*, Second Edition, Darshana Printers, Moradabad, 1981

Atreya BL, *Yogavasistha and Its Philosophy Lectures*, The Indian Bookshop, The Theosophical Society, Varanasi, 1932

Atreya, BL, (Samvid Tr.), *The Vision and the Way of Vasistha*, Samata Books, Chennai, 2005

Arya, Ravi Prakash (Ed.); *Yogavasishtha of Valmiki*, (Vol. I-IV), Parimal Publications, Delhi, 2005

Goswami, Mahaprabhulal, *Yogavasishtha of Mahakavi Valmiki*, Vol. I-V, First Edition, Tara Book Agency, Varanasi, 1994

Gupta, Kanta, *Yogavasishtha*, Nag Publishers, Delhi, 1998

Maharshi Valmiki, *Sri Yogavasishtam Maharamayanam*, Vol. I-VI, Bharatiya Vidya Bhavan, Mumbai, 2000

Saraswati, Prakhar Pragyanand Swami, *Yogavasishtha Saar*, Chaukhamba Sanskrit Sansthan, Varanasi, 2009

Dwivedi, Thakurprasad, *Yogavasishtha Maharamayanam*, Chaukhamba Sanskrit Pratishthan, Delhi, 1977

Gupta, Kanta, *The Yogavasishtha of Valmiki*, Vol. I-IV, Nag Publishers, New Delhi, 1998

Jnananda Bharati, *The Essence of Yogavasishtha* (The Great Book of Vedanta), Samta Books, Madras, 1985

Shastri, Mulshankar, *Yogavasishtha*, Vol. I-V, Achyutgranthmala Karyalaya, Kashir

Panasikara, Vasudeva Sharma, *Laghuyogavasistha*, Motilal Banarsidass, Delhi, 1985

Pansikar, Vasudeva Laxmana Sharma (Ed.), *Shrimadvalmikimaharshpranitah Yogavasishtha*, Vol. I& II, Motilal Banarsidass, Delhi, 2008

Venkatesananda, Swami, *The Supreme Yoga: A New Translation of the Yogavasishtha*, The Chiltern Yoga Trust, PO Elgin, Cape Province, SA, 1975

Venkatesananda, Swami, *The Supreme Yoga*, Motilal Banarsidass, Delhi, 2010

Venkatesananda, Swami, *The Means to Liberation: Selected Verses from Valmiki's Yoga Vasistha*, from a Translation by Swami Venkateshananda, Edited by Dennis B. Hill, The Divine Life Society, Tehri-Garhwal, India.

Bhoomananda Tirtha, Swami, *Quietitude of the Mind: Its Science and Practice*, Narayanasrama Thapovanam, Trichur, 1985, 2010

Sahdev, Manjula, *Yogavasistha Maharamayana*, Maharshi Valmiki Chair, Panjabi University, Patiala, 2004

Saraswati, Prakhar Pragyanand Swami, *Yogavasistha Sara*, Chaukhamba Sanskrit Sansthan, Varanasi, 2009

Saxena, Bhaskar Raj, *Yoga Vasistha: Vedanta Wisdom through Miniature Paintings*, Rupa and Co., New Delhi, 2008

Other Literature (Sanskrit and Hindi)

Brahmsutra Bhashyam, Shri Shri Jagadguru Shankaracharya Mahasansthanam, Shringeri

Brihadaranyaka Upanishad, Gita Press, Gorakhpur

Chhandogaya Upanisad, Gita Press, Gorakhpur

Dwarikadas Shastri, Swami, *Vigrahavyavartini*, Bauddha Bharati, 1994

Jha, Harimohan, *Bharatiya Darshan Parichaya—Nyaya Darshan*, Pustak Bhandar, Laheriasarai

Mandukyopanisad, Gaudapada Karika tatha Shankarabhashya, Gita Press, Gorakhpur

Goyandka, Harikrishandas, *Ishadi Nau Upanishad*, Gita Press, Gorakhpur

Goyandka, Harikrishandas, *Yoga-Darshan*, Gita Press, Gorakhpur

Goyandka, Harikrishandas, *Shrimad Bhagavadgita Shankarbhashyam*, Gita Press, Gorakhpur

Goyandka, Jayadayal, *Shrimad Bhagavadgita*, Gita Press, Gorakhpur

Hari Om, Kaka, *Ashtavakra Mahagita*, Manoj Publications, 2008

Haridas Tyagi, Swami, *Shri Rama Gita*, Randhir Prakshan, 2002

Jha, Acharya Anand, *Charvaka Darshan*, Hindi Smiti, Lakhnow, 1969

Jha, Shriharimohan, *Bharatiya Darshan Parichay*, Nyaya Darshan, Pustak Bhandar, Laheriyasaray

Maheshananda Giri, Swami, *Shri Krishna Sandesh*, Shri Dakshinamurti Math Prakashan, Varanasi, 2009

Mandukyopanishad Gaudapada Karika, Gita Press, Gorakhpur

Ramsukhdas, Swami, *Shrimad Bhagavadgita*, Sadhaka Sanjivini, Gita Press, Gorakhpur

Shukla, Badrinarayan, *Tarka Bhasha*, Motilal Banarasidass, Delhi, 2010

Omananda Tirtha, Swami, *Patanjalayogapradip*, Gita Press, Gorakhpur

Pandeya, SK, *Shankargita*, Sahitya Bhandar, Allahabad, 2007

Pagycikaranam and Shri Sureshvaracharya's Varttikam with commentary

Rajneesh Osho, *Ashtavakra Gita*, Vol. I-IX, Fusion Books, 2006

Rajneesh Osho, *Gita Darshan*, Vol. I-VIII, Rebel Publishing, Pune, 2005

Ramswarup, Swami, *Shrimad Bhagvadgita*, Vol. I-IV, Ved Mandir Prakashan, 2012

Sharma, Dharmanand, *Sankhyapravachanbhashya* of Vigyanabhikshu, Amargranth
    Publication, 1999

Shrimad Bhagvat Mahapurana, Vol. I-II, Gita Press, Gorakhpur

Tattva Prakashika by Swami Tattvavidananda Saraswati, Ed. Krishnakumar S. Davey
    and Jayshree Ramakrishnan, Brahma Vidya Kuteer, Secunderabad

Vaidyonamkomusalganwkar, Gajanan Shastri, *Sankhyadarshnam*, Chaukhamba Sanskrit
    Sansthan

Vedant Tirtha, Acharya, *Atharva Veda*, Manoj Publications, 2012

Vedant Tirtha, Acharya, *Rig Veda*, Manoj Publications, 2012

Vedant Tirtha, Acharya, *Sama Veda*, Manoj Publications, 2012

Vedant Tirtha, Acharya, *Yajur Veda*, Manoj Publications, 2012

Vidyanand Giri, Swami, *Brahmsutram*, I-II, Shri Kailash Vidya Prakashnam, Rishikesh,
    1997

Vidyanand Giri, Swami, *Shrimad Bhagavadgita Ashtadashah Pravachan*, Brahma Vidya
    Kutir Kailas Ashram, Rishikesh, 1992

Vidyanand Giri, Swami, *Mandukyopanishad*, Kailas Vidya Prakashan, Rishikesh

Yogindra, Sadanand, *Vedanta Sara*, Ramakrishna Math, Nagpur, 2009

Yoga-Darshan, Gita Press, Gorakhpur

English

Abhedananda, Swami, *True Psychology*, Ramakrishna Vedanta Math, Kolkata, 2000

Abhedananda, Swami, *Yoga Psychology*, Ramakrishna Vedanta Math, Kolkata, 2002

Akhilananda, Swami, *Hindu Psychology*, Georg Routledge & Sons Ltd, 1947

Ashtavakragita, translated by Radhakamal Mukerjee, Motilal Banarsidass, Delhi, 2009

Atmaprajnananda Saraswati, Swamini, *Nomenclature of the Vedas*, DK Printworld (P)
    Ltd, 2012

Atreya, BL, *The Vision and the Way of Vasishtha*, Samata Books, Chennai, 2005

Atreya, BL, *Elements of Indian Logic*, Hindu University, Benares, 1934

Aurobindo, Sri, *The Bhagvad Gita*, Sri Aurobindo Divine Life Trust, Pondicherry,
    2008

Aurobindo, Sri, *The Life Divine*, Sri Aurobindo Ashram, Pondicherry, 2001

Bernard, Theos; *Indian Philosophy*, Motilal Banarsidass, Delhi, 2005

Bhaktivedanta, AC, Swami Prabhupada, *Sri Isopanisad*, Bhaktivedanta Book Trust, 1997

Bhoomananda Tirtha, Swami, *Brahmavidya Abhyasa*, Narayanashrama Tapovanam, 2007

Bhoomananda Tirtha, Swami, *Essentials Concepts in Bhagbavadgita*, Narayanashrama Tapovanam, 2010

Bhoomananda Tirtha, Swami, *Quietitude of the Mind*, Narayanashrama Tapovanam, 2010

Chennakesavan, Sarasvati, *The Concept of Mind in Indian Philosophy*, Asia Publishing House, 1960

Chidbhavananda, Swami, *The Bhagavad Gita*, Sri Ramakrishna Tapovanam, 1972

Chinmayananda, Swami, *Aitareya Upanisad*, Central Chinmayananda Mission Trust, 2010

Chinmayananda, Swami, *Aparokshanubhuti*, Central Chinmayananda Mission Trust, 2009

Chinmayananda, Swami, *Ashtavakra Gita*, Central Chinmayananda Mission Trust, 2010

Chinmayananda, Swami, *Atmabodha*, Central Chinmayananda Mission Trust, 2011

Chinmayananda, Swami, *Kathopanishad*, Central Chinmayananda Mission Trust

Chinmayananda, Swami, *Sri Rama Gita*, Central Chinmayananda Mission Trust, 1986

Dalal, AS (Ed), *A Greater Psychology: An Introduction to the Psychological Thought of Sri Aurobindo*; Sri Aurobindo International Centre of Education, Pondicherry, 2001

Dalmia Vasudha and von Stietencron, Heinrich, *The Oxford India Hinduism Reader*, OUP, 2007

Dayananda, Swami, *Action and Reaction*, Arsha Vidya Centre, Chennai, 2011

Dayananda, Swami, *Bhagavad Gita*, Arsha Vidya Centre, Chennai, 2007

Dayananda, Swami, *Exploring Vedanta*, Arsha Vidya Centre, Chennai, 2009

Dayananda, Swami, *Introduction to Vedanta*, Vision Books, 1998

Dayananda, Swami, *Mundakopanishad*, I & II, Arsha Vidya Research and Publication Trust, Chennai, 2000

Dayananda, Swami, *Tattvabodhah*, Arsha Vidya Research and Publication Trust, Chennai, 2013

Dayananda, Swami, *Teaching Tradition of Advaita Vedanta*, Arsha Vidya Centre, Chennai, 2011

Gambhirananda, Swami, *Aitareya Upanishad*, Advaita Ashrama, 2006

Gambhirananda, Swami, *Brahma Sootra Bhashya*, Advaita Ashrama, 1965

Gambhirananda, Swami, *Eight Upanishads*, Advaita Ashrama, 2012

Gambhirananda, Swami, *Isha* Upanishad, Advaita Ashrama, 2010

Gambhirananda, Swami, *Kena Upanishad*, Advaita Ashrama, 2009

Gambhirananda, Swami, *Shrutigita*, Advaita Ashrama, 1998

Gambhirananda, Swami, *Taittiriya Upanishad*, Advaita Ashrama, 2009

Ghose, Sisirkumar, *Mysticism: Views and Reviews*, Clarion Books, 1987 (34 lib 149.3 17745)

Hiriyanna M, *Outlines of Indian Philosophy*, Motilal Banarsidass, Delhi, 2005

Jnanananda Bharati, *The Essence of Yogavaasistha*, Samata Books, Madras, 1987

Karmarkar, Raghunath Damodar, *Gaudapada-Karika*, Bhandarkar Oriental Research Institute, Poona, 1953

Krishnanda, Swami, *A Short History of Religious and Philosophic Thought in India*, The Divine Life Society, 1973

Krishnanda, Swami, *The Chhandogya Upanishad*, The Divine Life Society, 1984

Life, Mind and Consciousness, The Ramakrishna Mission Institute of Culture, Kolkata, 2004

Lokeswarananda, Swami, *Prasna Upanisad*, Ramakrishna Mission Institute of Culture, 2007

Lokeswarananda, Swami, *Taittiriya Upanisad*, Ramakrishna Mission Institute of Culture, 2005

Madhavananda, Swami (Tr.), *Bhasha Pariccheda*, with Siddhanta-Muktavali, Advaita Ashrama, Kolkata, 2004

Madhavananda, Swami, *Viragya Satakam*, Advaita Ashrama, Kolkata, 2004

Madhavananda, Swami, *Vedanta Paribhasha of Dharmaraja Adhvarindra*, Advaita Ashrama, Kolkata, 2008

Mahadevan, TMP, *Invitation to Indian Philosophy*, Arnold-Heinemann Publishers, New Delhi, 1974

Mohanty, JN, *Classical Indian Philosophy*; Oxford University Press, 2000

Muni Narayana Prasad, Swami, *Karma and Reincarnation*, DK Printworld, New Delhi, 2006

Muni Narayana Prasad, Swami, *Vedanta Sutras of Narayana Guru*, DK Printworld, New Delhi, 1997

Nikhilananda, Swami, *Drig-Dṛshya-Viveka*, Advaita Ashrama, Kolkata, 2011

Nikhilananda, Swami, *The Upanishads: A New Translation*, I-IV, Advaita Ashrama, Kolkata, 2008

Nityaswarupananda, Swami, *Astavakra Samhita*, Advaita Ashrama, Kolkata, 2006

OUP 2007

Pañcikaranam of Shri Shaṅkaracarya, Advaita Ashrama, 2009

Pandeya, Ramchandra, *Indian Studies in Philosophy*, Motilal Banarsidass, Delhi, 1977

Pandurangi, KT, *The Principal Upanisads*, Dvaita Vedanta Studies and Research Foundation, Bangalore, 1999

Parthasarathy, A, Swami, *The Complete Works of Swami Parthasarathy*, A Parthasarathy, 2011

Philosophy and Science: An Exploratory Approach to Consciousness, The Ramakrishna Mission Institute of Culture, Kolkata, 2003

Prabhavananda, Swami & Christopher Isherwood, *Patanjali Yoga Sutras*, Sri Ramakrishna Math

Radhakrishnan, S, *Indian Philosophy*, Vol. I, George Allen & Unwin Ltd., 1958

Radhakrishnan, S, *The Principal Upanishads*, Harper Collins Publishers, Delhi, 2012

Rama Gita, translated by Swami Vijnanananda; Advaita Ashrama, Calcutta, 1990

Ramachandra Rao, SK, *Bhavanopanishad*, Divine Books, 2012

Ramachandra Rao, SK, *Sankara Bhashya*, Abhijnana, 2002

Ramamurty A, *Vedanta and Its Philosophical Development*, DK Printworld (P) Ltd, New Delhi, 2006

Rao, Venkoba A, 'Mind' in Indian Philosophy, *Indian Journal of Psychiatry*, 2002, 44(4), 315-325

Ravishankar, Sri Sri, *Ashtavakra Gita*, Sri Sri Publications, 2010

Samvid (Translator), *Tripurarahasyam*, Ramana Maharshi Centre for Leaning, 2000

Shankaracarya, 2006, *Chandogya Upanisad*, With the commentary of Shankaracarya (Gambhirananda, Swami, Tr.), Advaita Ashrama

Shankaracarya, Laghu Vakya-Vṛitti, Advaita Ashrama, 2010

Shankracaraya, Samvid (Tr); *Prabodhasudhakara: The Nectar-Ocean of Enlightenment*, Samata Books, Madras, 1987

Shankaracarya, *Upadesa Sahasri*, Ramkrishna Math, 2009

Sarvananda, Swami, *Aitrayeopanishad*, Sri Ramakrishna Math, Madras, 2005

Sarvananda, Swami, *Prasna Upanishad*, Sri Ramakrishna Math, Madras, 2009

Sastri, PS, *Jaimini Sutram of Maharshi Jaimini*, Ranjan Publications, Delhi, 1996

Satprakashananda, Swami, *Mind According to Vedanta*, Sri Ramakrishna Math, Madras, 2007

Satprakashananda, Swami, 2007, *Vedanta for All*, Sri Ramakrishna Math, Chennai, 2009

Sharma, Arvind, *Classical Indian Thought*, Oxford University Press, New Delhi, 2000

Sharma, Chandradhar, *A Critical Study of Indian Philosophy*; Motilal Banarsidass, Delhi, 2000

Sinha, Jadunath; *Indian Psychology*, Vol. I, Cognition, Motilal Banarsidass, Delhi, 2008

Sinha, Jadunath; *Indian Psychology*, Vol. II, Emotion and Will, Motilal Banarsidass, Delhi, 2008

Sinha, Jadunath; *Indian Psychology*, Vol. III, Epistemology of Perception, Motilal Banarsidass, Delhi, 2008

Shivananda, Swami, *Brahma Sutras*, The Divine Life Society, 1999

Shivananda, Swami, *Ten Upanishads*, The Divine Life Society, 2007

Suddhabodhananda Saraswati, Swami, *Vedantic Ways to Samadhi*, Drik-Drishya-Vivekah, Sri Visweswar Trust, Mumbai, 1996

Sunirmalananda, Swami, *Insights into Vedanta*, Tattvabodha, Sri Ramakrishna Math, Chennai, 2005

Tattvavidananda Saraswati, Swami, *Ganapati Upanisad*, DK Printworld, 2009

Tejomayananda, Swami, *Amrtabindu Upanisad*, Central Chinmaya Mission Trust, 2012

Tejomayananda, Swami, *An Introduction to Advaita Vedanta Philosophy*, The Divine Life Society, 1999

Tejomayananda, Swami, *Tattvabodha*, Central Chinmaya Mission Trust, 2011

Tejomayananda, Swami, *Upadesa Sara*, Central Chinmaya Mission Trust, 2011

The Brihadaranyaka Upanisad, translated by Madhavananda, Swami, with the commentary of Sankracarya, Advaita Ashrama, 1965

Tripurari Rahasya, translated by Swami Ramananda Saraswathi, Sri Ramanasramam, 2011

Uddhava Gita: The Last Message of Sri Krishna, translated by Swami, Madhavananda, Advaita Ashrama, 2005

Venkateshananda, Swami & Hill, Dennis B; *The Means to Liberation: Selected verses from Valmiki's Yoga Vasishtha*

Vijnanananda, Swami, *Rama Gita*, Advaita Ashrama, Kolkata 1997

Vimalananda, Swami, *Mahanarayaṇa Upanishad*, Sri Ramakrishna Math, Madras, 2008

Vireswarananda, Swami, *Brahma Sutras According to Sri Sankara*, Advaita Ashrama, 2005

Virupakshananda, Swami (Tr.), *Tarka Samgraha*, Sri Ramakrishna Math, Madras, 2010

Vivekananda, Swami, *Vedanta: Voice of Freedom*, Advaita Ashrama, Kolkata, 2011

Woodroffe, Sir John, *Sakti and Sakta: Essays and Addresses*, Ganesh & Company, 2010

Yogananda, Paramahansa, *The Bhagavad Gita*, Yogoda Satsanga Society of India, 2007

INDEX

ego 68, 75, 93, 97, 124, 125, 148, 151, 152,
    158, 159, 161, 162, 166, 170, 176, 177,
    182, 183, 186, 197, 198, 199, 203, 204,
    205, 206, 207, 208, 223, 225, 226, 227,
    228, 229, 232, 244, 245, 247, 248, 253,
    254, 256, 268, 275, 276
elements 41, 87, 88, 89, 91, 132, 139, 152,
    153, 155, 156, 160, 161, 190
enlightened 2, 4, 5, 61, 64, 74, 75, 126, 130,
    150, 173, 189, 199, 208, 217, 226, 227,
    233, 241, 245, 252, 253, 259, 271, 272,
    273, 274, 276, 278
eternal non-existence 35, 36
equanimity 225
experience 8, 12, 30, 32, 37, 40, 41, 59, 62,
    63, 68, 70, 82, 83, 85, 86, 89, 93, 94, 95,
    96, 97, 99, 123, 124, 130, 135, 148, 155,
    167, 169, 188, 194, 202, 204, 206, 215,
    218, 233, 249, 276

F

fatalism 13, 227
fatalist 227
fire 6, 13, 40, 50, 51, 80, 87, 102, 118, 121,
    123, 125, 155, 166, 188, 211, 242,
    263, 264
freedom 4, 9, 11, 17, 18, 20, 42, 52, 65, 68,
    72, 74, 80, 143, 163, 165, 184, 185,
    187, 205, 209, 210, 211, 214, 215, 233,
    248, 255, 268
free will 13, 17, 18, 20, 25, 65, 177, 184,
    186, 235, 249, 251, 261, 267, 268, 269
Freud 17, 95

G

Gaudapada 109, 110, 111, 112, 113, 114,
    118, 122, 125, 126, 127
Gaudapada Karika 109, 112, 113, 126, 127
God 6, 11, 16, 56, 66, 77, 78, 101, 108, 182,
    215, 227, 248, 274
grammar 46, 59, 65, 140
grammarians 59, 61, 137
greed 198, 206, 228, 258
guna 80, 160, 232, 243

guru 2, 4, 5, 6, 13, 23, 26, 31, 34, 39, 40, 46,
    48, 49, 50, 51, 54, 55, 56, 63, 64, 65, 67,
    68, 69, 70, 71, 72, 73, 75, 108, 130, 134,
    135, 136, 137, 138, 164, 210, 215, 218,
    219, 224, 231, 245
gyana 58, 61, 69, 208, 209, 210, 211, 212,
    213, 215, 216, 219, 231, 247
Gyanakanda 46, 210

H

hate 184, 228, 257, 276
heaven 39, 176, 183, 211, 252, 254, 255, 274
Hinduism 8, 38, 46, 53, 54, 81, 143, 155,
    161, 255, 261, 264, 265, 266, 267
Hiranyagarbha 154, 157, 241

I

ida 242, 243
ignorance 5, 14, 30, 31, 34, 35, 49, 68, 69,
    72, 81, 85, 89, 90, 98, 100, 104, 111,
    134, 143, 145, 152, 153, 156, 160, 164,
    165, 166, 171, 179, 180, 182, 185, 186,
    205, 210, 211, 212, 213, 215, 232, 236,
    244, 246, 248, 258, 259
illusion 2, 81, 85, 89, 95, 98, 100, 107,
    109, 113, 117, 121, 125, 145, 167, 171,
    177, 178, 179, 181, 185, 186, 212, 214,
    215, 276
imagination 19, 83, 85, 86, 92, 100, 111,
    119, 122, 123, 144, 152, 161, 165, 166,
    170, 171, 177, 180, 182, 184, 248, 269
individual 20, 24, 30, 38, 39, 42, 43, 47, 52,
    63, 72, 80, 83, 84, 94, 95, 100, 102, 116,
    133, 134, 138, 140, 141, 147, 148, 149,
    150, 151, 158, 159, 160, 161, 162, 163,
    164, 165, 166, 167, 169, 170, 171, 177,
    178, 179, 182, 183, 184, 203, 207, 210,
    212, 213, 218, 222, 227, 230, 244, 248,
    256, 257, 262, 268, 269
individuation 170, 182, 212
indriya 178, 223
inference 33, 35, 37, 38, 40
infinite 24, 77, 90, 91, 98, 119, 120, 138,
    143, 150, 183

infinity 120
instinct 18
intellect 6, 32, 41, 42, 49, 57, 58, 61, 67, 68,
    70, 73, 78, 93, 121, 131, 133, 138, 145,
    152, 155, 156, 160, 161, 162, 163, 176,
    177, 182, 203, 206, 207, 220, 221, 228,
    236, 261, 275

J

jagarat 94, 166, 168, 203, 232
Jainism 241, 266
jala 87
Janaka 195, 197, 236
jealousy 228
jeeva 52, 83, 148, 150, 151, 152, 159, 160,
    161, 162, 164, 165, 166, 167, 168, 170,
    178, 184, 207, 248
jeevanmukta 233, 274

K

kaivalibhava 272
kalpana 84, 86, 177
kama 8, 9, 20, 143
Kant 97
karana 104, 155, 156, 158, 163
karma 20, 82, 118, 125, 171, 177, 183, 210,
    213, 217, 234, 235, 247, 248, 256, 261,
    263, 264, 265, 266, 267, 268, 272
Karmakanda 46, 210, 234
karmaphala 248, 272
karta 152, 248, 253, 254, 276
karya 104
knowledge 3, 4, 12, 13, 26, 27, 29, 30, 31,
    32, 33, 34, 35, 37, 38, 39, 40, 41, 42, 43,
    46, 48, 49, 51, 52, 53, 54, 55, 56, 57, 58,
    61, 63, 64, 65, 66, 67, 68, 69, 70, 71, 72,
    73, 75, 85, 90, 95, 97, 98, 99, 100, 102,
    121, 134, 137, 145, 157, 158, 164, 168,
    171, 179, 181, 182, 184, 185, 186, 196,
    199, 208, 209, 210, 211, 212, 213, 215,
    216, 218, 219, 220, 221, 222, 223, 224,
    230, 231, 232, 233, 234, 235, 239, 240,
    241, 243, 245, 246, 247, 248, 249, 250,
    252, 253, 255, 256, 257, 272, 276, 277

kosha 155, 156, 157, 160, 163
kreeda 120
Krishna 12, 19, 54, 65, 154, 234, 235,
    250, 262
kriya 61, 152, 178, 213, 217
kumbhaka 244

L

lakshana 29, 59, 136, 137, 138, 139, 140, 145
lakshana vakya 29
language 32, 42, 46, 52, 53, 55, 57, 58, 59,
    60, 61, 62, 63, 67, 70, 73, 74, 75, 78, 96,
    104, 139, 157, 182, 215, 269
leela 120
liberation 9, 13, 21, 24, 31, 34, 48, 49, 50,
    51, 58, 64, 70, 80, 116, 125, 148, 149,
    150, 158, 164, 165, 168, 169, 180, 209,
    210, 211, 212, 213, 214, 215, 216, 217,
    218, 220, 243, 244, 246, 247, 248, 250,
    252, 256, 258, 271, 273, 275, 276, 277
life 1, 2, 3, 4, 5, 6, 7, 8, 9, 10, 11, 12, 13, 14,
    16, 20, 21, 23, 24, 27, 28, 31, 38, 42, 50,
    51, 52, 62, 67, 68, 69, 80, 81, 87, 92, 96,
    103, 104, 106, 130, 143, 148, 152, 156,
    162, 165, 176, 177, 181, 183, 187, 193,
    195, 198, 210, 211, 214, 224, 225, 227,
    228, 229, 230, 231, 240, 242, 243, 249,
    255, 256, 257, 258, 261, 262, 263, 264,
    266, 267, 268, 269, 270, 276
logic 32, 42, 43, 46, 52, 57, 58, 60, 65, 73, 74,
    100, 104, 110, 117, 120, 122, 143, 144,
    198, 221, 239, 250, 268, 269
love 7, 8, 142, 184, 225, 228, 257, 258, 273

M

mahavakya 30, 144
manana 23, 24
manas 152, 177, 178
Mandookya Karika 109
Materialism 16
matter 6, 7, 10, 16, 29, 31, 32, 40, 47, 52,
    68, 78, 80, 82, 85, 88, 89, 91, 92, 93, 95,
    99, 102, 108, 122, 123, 125, 130, 131,
    136, 144, 150, 152, 153, 176, 177, 181,

space 11, 30, 38, 78, 87, 88, 89, 91, 92, 93,
    95, 97, 98, 119, 124, 132, 133, 141,
    144, 150, 151, 153, 155, 156, 159, 176,
    178, 188, 190, 197, 199, 207, 216, 220,
    229, 239, 244
spanda 152, 181, 230
srishti 79, 80
state 3, 4, 11, 12, 13, 30, 47, 50, 58, 59, 61,
    63, 83, 86, 87, 93, 94, 95, 96, 99, 110,
    115, 116, 118, 123, 124, 138, 144, 153,
    154, 155, 156, 166, 167, 169, 173, 180,
    193, 195, 203, 211, 213, 216, 218, 227,
    232, 233, 234, 240, 272, 273, 275, 276
subject 10, 29, 32, 42, 47, 49, 52, 83, 91, 93,
    100, 105, 117, 119, 124, 125, 135, 137,
    148, 150, 156, 183, 194, 198, 202, 203,
    214, 220, 222, 239, 263, 276
subsequent non-existence 35, 36
sushumna 242, 243
sushupti 94, 166, 168
svabhava 215
Svabhavavada 107
svadharma 256, 257
svapna 94, 154, 166, 168

T
taijasa 154
tamas 80, 86, 87, 89, 101, 168, 243
Tarkabhasha 43, 44
Tarkasangrha 43, 104, 126
tat tvam asi 56, 138
The Fourth' 154
time 10, 11, 12, 13, 15, 16, 17, 19, 22, 26, 27,
    30, 34, 38, 41, 42, 62, 71, 78, 79, 83, 84,
    86, 87, 89, 90, 91, 92, 95, 97, 98, 108,
    109, 112, 113, 117, 120, 123, 124, 126,
    131, 132, 135, 136, 141, 152, 165, 167,
    176, 188, 189, 193, 194, 197, 198, 203,
    211, 212, 214, 215, 219, 222, 229, 234,
    235, 239, 240, 241, 245, 253, 258, 259,
    261, 269, 272
trigunas 89
truth 17, 43, 48, 51, 52, 53, 55, 56, 60, 63,
    64, 72, 73, 74, 78, 79, 81, 84, 104, 129,

130, 132, 134, 137, 147, 148, 153, 158,
    164, 171, 178, 185, 187, 193, 195, 205,
    213, 214, 215, 249, 251, 267, 269, 272
turiya 99, 158, 168, 173, 275, 276
tyaga 138, 223, 224, 272

U
universe 6, 19, 37, 56, 60, 77, 79, 83, 84,
    87, 91, 102, 103, 119, 122, 131, 132,
    133, 135, 141, 150, 161, 169, 182, 199,
    227, 242
untruth 158, 164, 178, 195
upadesha vakya 30
upadhi 206
Upanishad 14, 43, 72, 76, 80, 81, 101, 102,
    109, 134, 145, 157, 159, 172, 173, 190,
    191, 236, 237, 246, 259
upmana 33, 35
Uttarameemamsa, 211

V
vairagya 5, 12, 14
Vaisheshika 104, 106
Vaishvanara 154, 157
Valmiki 4, 46, 47, 52, 64, 70
vasana 80, 162, 177, 196, 217, 223, 228
Vasishtha 4, 13, 18, 19, 20, 21, 22, 23, 24,
    26, 27, 31, 33, 42, 43, 46, 48, 49, 51, 52,
    53, 55, 57, 64, 65, 68, 69, 70, 72, 73,
    74, 75, 79, 81, 85, 94, 95, 96, 98, 115,
    117, 118, 119, 122, 123, 125, 130, 131,
    132, 144, 145, 150, 151, 152, 158, 159,
    160, 161, 162, 164, 169, 170, 171, 175,
    176, 177, 178, 179, 180, 181, 183, 185,
    186, 188, 189, 210, 211, 212, 213, 216,
    217, 218, 219, 224, 225, 226, 228, 229,
    230, 234, 235, 239, 240, 241, 242, 243,
    245, 249, 250, 252, 256, 258, 259, 261,
    262, 263, 267, 268, 269, 271, 272, 273,
    275, 276, 277
vayu 87, 244
Veda 46, 78, 101, 172
Vedanta 6, 11, 12, 20, 27, 29, 31, 33, 37, 38,
    40, 41, 42, 43, 45, 46, 48, 49, 52, 63, 64,

The Yogavasishtha of Valmiki